TEACHING AND LEARNING IN DIGITAL WORLDS.
STRATEGIES AND ISSUES IN HIGHER EDUCATION

(Ed.: Gisbert & Bullen)

[publicacions]
urv

Tarragona, 2015

Published by
Publicacions Universitat Rovira i Virgili
Av. Catalunya, 35 • 43002 Tarragona
publicacions@urv.cat
http://www.publicacionsurv.cat

1st edition: June 2015
Legal deposit: T-785/2015
ISBN: 978-84-8424-376-2

Photocomposed: Gráficas Alcoy
Printed: Gráficas Alcoy

   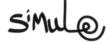

TABLE OF CONTENTS

PROLOGUE _____

Tony Bates

One of the main lessons from history is that new technology results in new ways of working, in order for the benefits of the technology to be fully exploited. This lesson applies as much to teaching in higher education as it does elsewhere, although it is taking some time for this lesson to be fully appreciated. Thus we have had technology added to classroom teaching without changing the fundamental methods of teaching, such as Powerpoint slides to support lectures, and this has merely added costs without noticeable benefits in terms of learning.

Even when technology has been applied to distance learning, the same structures and pedagogical approaches found in the classroom have been applied to the online learning environment, whether through the use of learning management systems or lecture capture, as in MOOCs. Even with hybrid or blended 'flipped' classrooms, where the lecture is recorded and studied in advance, followed by discussion in the classroom, the pedagogy has not changed, only the delivery method.

However, there is a growing recognition among faculty, instructors and learning technology support staff that technology will not be fully exploited unless our methods of teaching also change. There are several reasons for doing this:

- to achieve existing academic goals in a more productive way. This could mean using technology to facilitate better learning outcomes, such as higher quality student work or higher completion rates within existing academic goals, or, by enabling greater efficiency in the use of an instructor's time, through enabling the instructor to handle more students without losing quality in the learning
- to achieve new academic goals that are required in a digital society, such as knowledge management, independent learning, collaborative learning, and IT skills embedded within a subject domain. Digital technologies lend themselves particularly well to supporting such outcomes
- to use the technology to make learning more engaging and motivating for students, who are immersed themselves in digital technologies
- to help students develop more general digital literacy, an essential skill in a digital world.

However, changing teaching methods to accommodate the potential of new technologies presents a major challenge to most faculty and instructors, simply because most have not received any form of training in teaching. A Ph.D. is a training in research, and any support post-graduates receive as teaching assistants is focused on managing traditional teaching such as large lectures. Mid-career professional development can help, but this is mainly on an optional basis.

Thus the value of this book is that it offers pragmatic cases or case studies of new methods of teaching that fully exploit new, emerging technologies. You may not always agree with the approaches taken. Good. These developments are so new that we are all learning how best to exploit them. I hope this book will challenge you to not only critique what others have done, as illustrated by the cases in this book, but also to think creatively about how you can apply lessons from this book, or your own unique approach to the use of new technologies, within your own teaching.

AUTHORS

Tony Bates, *Tony Bates Associates Ltd, Vancouver, Canada, and Research Associate, Contact North, Ontario*

Introduction

Many reports over the last few years have analysed the potential use of games, video-games, 3D environments and virtual reality for educational purposes. Numerous emerging technological devices have also appeared that will play important roles in the development of teaching and learning processes. In the context of these developments, learning rather than teaching becomes the main axis in the organisation of the educational process. This process has now gone beyond the analogue world and face-to-face education to enter the digital world, where new learning environments are being produced with ever greater doses of realism.

Virtual worlds, metaverses and 3D virtual environments are now demonstrating huge potential for educational purposes because they enable analogical environments and processes to be recreated with a high degree of realism and where "physical" and communicative interactions closely approximate the effects of interactions that occur in our real world. Avatars bearing the identities of the users in these worlds take on important roles for the development of training strategies in environments where simulation is fundamental, where all agents of education must always assume the roles to which they are assigned, and where teachers (mainly) are obliged to redefine their professional role while also becoming a learner like their students in the same learning environment. Are users of this virtual world prepared for this challenge?

Clearly, it is not enough for the users of these 3D learning environments to be digitally literate: they must also improve their digital competence to a high level. Digital competence has been defined in the principal reports of international organisations such as the OECD and UNESCO as one of the key competences of the 21st century. It is not a competence that is always displayed by students entering higher education, or even by their teachers, but it is one we need to work hard to develop and consolidate. We must accept that students can be characterised as digital learners while bearing in mind, as we have already mentioned, that the strategies needed to develop their education and update their training cannot be formulated from separate perspectives. Moreover, when we talk about teachers and students we are referring to learners in both cases. What we need is therefore to plan the training and development of these learners from the perspective of citizens who are living and developing personally and professionally in a constantly changing digital society in which it is difficult —if not impossible— to predict how quickly the technologies we currently recognise as emerging will continue to grow and how quickly they will be introduced.

To meet the challenges posed by these constant changes, we need to appreciate that digital learners do not always begin their university studies having already acquired this competence. We must also recognise that we now need to speak simultaneously of digital and analogue learning environments, not just of analogue ones. These digital learning environments oblige us to speak in terms of "environments" or "spaces" rather than "classrooms". They remind us that flexibility, change and innovation are necessary conditions for developing a technology whose latest generation is represented by 3D virtual environments, most of which can be accessed from personal computers and even from mobile devices.

One of the main didactic and pedagogical challenges educational professionals face is to integrate all these elements into an educational process that takes into account the points of view of both educators and learners. At the same time, our main responsibility is to harness the educational process to develop the cross-disciplinary competences of university students.

This book comprises our experiences and main conclusions from the SIMUL@ project [Ref. EDU2008-01479]. It also draws conclusions from the International Seminar on Virtual Environments for the Acquisition of Cross-Disciplinary Competences at University, held as part of that project and partly financed by the Spanish Ministry of Economy and Competitiveness [Ref. EDU2011-15624-E].

Teaching and Learning in Digital Worlds examines the teaching and learning process in 3D virtual environments from both the theoretical and practical points of view. It is divided into four sections.

The first section discusses education in the 21st century from the perspective of learners in a digital society and examines the basic competences students need to respond to the personal and professional challenges they are likely to face. It also explores the issue of quality. This essential feature of any e-learning programme should be considered at the planning stage, during the programme, and on completion of the programme when conclusions are drawn from the students' learning experiences.

The second section focuses on the educational and teaching strategies higher education professionals must take into account when developing educational processes in technological environments. Through gamification these environments must enable us to teach cross-disciplinary competences to university students. In such environments, simulation will be our best teaching strategy and evaluation our greatest challenge.

The third section explores the use of 3D virtual environments in education in general and in higher education in particular. It analyses the educational potential of immersive environments, the design and development of 3D objects for training environments, and the process for designing and developing training programmes in 3D environments.

The fourth section examines the range of experiences we consider to be good practice when applying 3D technological environments to the teaching of competences at secondary and tertiary levels of education both nationally and internationally.

CHAPTER 1:

21st CENTURY EDUCATION: GENERIC COMPETENCES AND DIGITAL LEARNERS.

Mark Bullen
Tannis Morgan

1.1
DIGITAL LEARNERS IN HIGHER EDUCATION: IMPLICATIONS FOR TEACHING, LEARNING & TECHNOLOGY

1. BACKGROUND

Central to the "digital natives" discourse is the notion that the generation born between 1980 and 2000 has been profoundly influenced by its immersion in the world of networked, digital technology and, because of this, we need to make radical changes to our educational systems. These "digital natives", it is argued, are fundamentally different than young people of previous generations and, more specifically, have different approaches to learning and different ways of using and making sense of information, all due to their exposure to digital technology. (Howe & Strauss, 2000; Oblinger & Oblinger, 2005; Palfrey & Gasser, 2008; Prensky, 2001a, b, 2005; Tapscott, 1998, 2009). However, there is no empirical support for these sweeping claims and, furthermore, there is a growing body of evidence that suggests a generational frame of reference obscures deeper issues and that the implications for learning are more complex and nuanced (Bullen et al, 2011; Bennett et al., 2008; Cameron et al., 2011; Corrin, et al., 2011; Smith, 2012). In this chapter we provide a critical review of the digital natives discourse and report on the results of an international research project that is attempting to gain a deeper understanding of digital learners and their use of information and communication technologies (ICTs).

2. THE DIGITAL NATIVES DISCOURSE

The key claims in the digital natives discourse emerge primarily from non-scholarly literature. Some appear in the popular or lay press; others are found in proprietary research funded by and conducted for private business. Still others can be found in quasi-academic publications that have the appearance of academic or scholarly quality but turn out not be informed by empirical research. These claims can be sorted into three categories: claims about the widespread use ICTs, claims about the impact of digital immersion (particularly on learning) and claims about the distinctive personal and behavioral characteristics of this generation. The latter two categories have particular relevance for open and flexible distance learning.

3. THE WIDESPREAD USE OF ICTS

There is little doubt that the use of ICTs is growing and that younger people tend to use digital technologies more than older people, although digital technology use by older people is growing faster. Numerous surveys have been conducted over the past 10 years that confirm this and, in the developed world at least, we can observe the pervasive of digital technology use in all facets of life (Jones and Fox, 2009).

4. THE IMPACT OF DIGITAL IMMERSION

The impact of being immersed in a digital world is at the heart of the digital natives discourse and it is claims related to this that provoke controversy both because they are more bold and because the evidence to support them is often absent or of dubious quality. Prensky (2001a, 2001b, 2005), Tapscott (1998, 2009) and, to a lesser extent, Palfrey & Gasser (2008) have all claimed that the ubiquity of digital technologies and digital natives' intensive use of these technologies is affecting how digital natives think, interact, and makes sense of the world. The following assertions are typical of the claims in popular literature about the impact on this generation of being immersed in digital technology:

> Digital Natives accustomed to the twitch-speed, multitasking, random-access, graphics-first, active, connected, fun, fantasy, quick-payoff world of their video games, MTV, and Internet are bored by most of today's education, well meaning as it may be. But worse, the many skills that new technologies have actually enhanced (e.g., parallel processing, graphics awareness, and random access) −which have profound implications for their learning− are almost totally ignored by educators... The cognitive differences of the Digital Natives cry out for new approaches to education with a better −fit. (Prensky, 2001b)

5. PERSONAL AND BEHAVIOURAL CHARACTERISTICS OF DIGITAL NATIVES

The personal and behavioural characteristics of digital natives have been the subject of numerous books and articles. These claims are often difficult to separate from the claims about digital immersion and it is not always clear if an argument is being made that the characteristics attributed to this generation are due to their intensive use of digital technology or to other social and environmental factors unique to this generation.

One of the more widely-cited references in support of the claims about the distinct characteristics of digital natives is Howe & Strauss' Millennials Rising: The Next Great Generation (2000). They state: "Over the next decade, the Millennial Generation will entirely recast the image of youth from downbeat and alienated to upbeat and engaged - with potentially seismic consequences for America" (p. 4).

Tapscott (2009) also makes some sweeping statements about digital natives and coined the term the "net generation". He proposes what he calls his eight net generation norms: freedom, customization, integrity, scrutiny, collaboration, entertainment, innovation and speed. Oblinger & Oblinger (2005) echo much of what Howe & Strauss (2000) say about this generation but they tend to conflate claims about the impact of digital immersion and personal and behavioural characterstics. Drawing on the work of Prensky (2001a, b), Tapscott (1998), Seely-Brown (2002) and Howe & Strauss (2000), they argue that the net generation is digitally literate, connected, social, and has a preference for experiential learning and immediate feedback.

6. THE DIGITAL NATIVES DISCOURSE AND IMPLICATIONS FOR TEACHING, LEARNING & TECHNOLOGY

If one accepts these claims, there are clear implications for higher education. In fact, there is a distinctly prescriptive thread to the digital natives discourse. Tapscott (2009), for example, argues that we need to move away from what he claims is the dominant broadcast mode of education and incorporate more interactive, collaborative and constructivist pedagogies and instructional designs. Prensky (2001a, 2001b) makes similar recommendations but also argues for greater use of gaming and game-based designs. Palfrey & Gasser (2008) are more cautious in their recommendations, arguing that "learning will always have certain enduring qualities that have little or nothing to do with technologies" (p. 246). They urge educators to resist the temptation to implement radical changes but they also suggest we need to respond to the changing nature of learners by using more team-based, collaborative learning, and game-based learning. In addition to more team-based and collaborative approaches, Oblinger & Oblinger (2005) also recommend structured learning experiences that are socially meaningful and use visual and kinesethic approaches.

Fuelled by the sudden popularity of massively open online courses (MOOCs), higher education institutions are increasingly turning to eLearning which is more often than not viewed from a technological perspective and thus seen as something that today's "digital natives" will not only be comfortable with but will demand. A deterministic "digital native" rationale, for example, is evident in institutional strategic plans for eLearning (see, for example, the East Tennessee State University eLearning strategic plan, 2009).

There is an intuitive appeal to the idea that using digital technologies intensively should have some impact, and that if today's students are indeed learning differently then we should consider new instructional designs, incorporate more technology-based approaches and make greater use of technology-based open and flexible distance learning. However, to date there is no convincing evidence to support these claims (Bekebrede et al 2011, Bennett et al, 2008; Bullen et al., 2011; Guo, Dobson & Petrina, 2008; Jones & Cross, 2009; Kennedy et al, 2007, 2009; Margaryan et al, 2011; Pedro, 2009; Reeves & Oh, 2007; Selwyn, 2009, van den Beemt et al, 2010). Furthermore, there is an increasing body of empirical research that contradicts the main arguments of the digital natives discourse. As well, surveys have shown that most students prefer a more traditional, face-to-face learning experience and, at most, want only moderate amounts of eLearning (Kaznowska et. al., 2011).

Until recently, there has been a largely uncritical acceptance of the digital natives discourse. The claims have been repeated by other researchers, writers and commentators, which has helped to give the discourse a sense of legitimacy. This phenomenon has been called the "snark syndrome", the idea (taken from the Lewis Carroll poem, The Hunting of the Snark) that if you repeat something frequently enough it eventually becomes accepted as fact (Byrne, 1993). Even researchers who acknowledge the lack of empirical support for the generational argument continue to either frame the issue in generational terms or give prominence to the unfounded generational claims, which further entrenches the digital natives discourse (Bates & Sangrà, 2011; Corrin et al, 2011; Gilewicz, 2011).

7. DIGGING DEEPER

However, the lack of empirical support for the key claims of the digital natives discourse does not imply that the educational landscape has been unaffected by the growth in the use of digital technology. While today's students may not fit digital natives stereotype, there is no question that digital technologies are an important part of their social and educational lives, as it is for most students in the developed world. Educators need to understand the rapidly changing technological landscape and determine how, or if, their teaching should change to accommodate emerging technologies. And while we can now say with certainty that generation is not relevant, the question of how post secondary education should respond to the growth in digital, networked technology use remains to be explored.

Our discussions with international researchers investigating this topic have underlined the importance of investigating these questions on a global scale, given the penetration of ICTs in the developed world, and the increased mobility of students internationally. Our goal is to build on the completed and active research in this area to try to develop a comprehensive understanding of the issues that take into account the diversity of cultural and institutional contexts.

8. RESEARCH QUESTIONS

There are three research questions driving our research:
1. Do postsecondary students distinguish their social and educational use of ICTs?
2. What impact do students' social use of ICTs have on postsecondary learning environments?
3. What is the relationship between social and educational uses of ICTs at in postsecondary education?

9. THEORETICAL FRAMEWORK & RESEARCH DESIGN

The question of social versus educational use implies a sociocultural orientation to our study, and requires the use of theories or frameworks that help to understand use-in-context. We used a third generation activity theory (AT) (Engestrom, 1987) as a framework to examine more closely the nature of social and educational use, and the implications for teaching and learning. AT provides a means of looking at both social and educational contexts and a way of examining how these two contexts intersect or collide. AT is also valuable when examining larger units of analysis (e.g. institutions) in understanding the phenomenon being investigated.

We used a multi-case study embedded research design of three cases of social and educational use of digital technology. Data was collected through in-depth individual and focus group interviews with students at each institution.

Case Contexts

BC Institute of Technology: BCIT is a Canadian campus-based polytechnic teaching institution with a large online and distance education program. It offers career-oriented programs in trades, professional and technical fields that are driven by employer-identified needs.

Open University of Catalonia: OUC is a fully online European university that offers undergraduate and graduate programs. It tends to attract older learners who have delayed their postsecondary education or are returning because of career changes or the need for new skills. They offer programs in Spanish, Catalan and English. Students come from Spain, Latin America and, increasingly, other European countries.

University of Regina: The University of Regina is relatively small Canadian research-intensive university. Students are primarily from Saskatchewan but it has international students and number of international programs.

10. FINDINGS

Our analysis of the data from one institution (BC Institute of Technology) provides further confirmation of the lack of empirical support for the digital native stereotype but also provides a more nuanced understanding of how students are using and thinking about digital technologies. Initially we found that there were clear resistors to technology, cautious users, specific or limited users, and integrators (Morgan & Bullen, 2011). However, as we continued our analysis of the data, we refined these profiles and the associated characteristics further, while noting that participants do not always fit neatly into a profile and at times made statements that were characteristic of another profile (Morgan & Bullen, 2013). Given our critical stance towards the generational profiling of technology and learners (Bullen, Morgan & Qayyum, 2011) we have been cautious about how we classified the students in our study and have been extraordinarily careful not to force a classification scheme on the data. However, assigning students to a profile provides some conceptual order to the data to discuss the extent to which the question of whether students distinguish, or even how they perceive their social and educational use of ICTs.

Profiles of Use

The following are the profiles of use that emerged from the data from one of the three institutions in the study (BCIT). These profiles were constructed based on how we understood students to be mediating their social and academic use of technology.

Instrumental users (or tool limited, tool specific users) generally used only one or two technology tools, or only one or two functions of a tool. In other words, instrumental users mediated their activity using limited technology resources (tools), or used a technology towards a specific activity or more narrowly defined object (eg., Gaming vs. connecting with others). In our study, students in this profile typically:

- Made use of largely one tool for many purposes, e.g., email for communication
- Were highly task-oriented in their use, e.g., they only go online or use a technology for a specific purpose such as gaming
- Did not have a broad understanding of affordances or constraints of technology or generally seemed less knowledgeable about technology

Importantly, instrumental users did not necessarily report less Internet activity than the other profiles even though they were more limited or specific in the technologies they used.

Separators consciously or unconsciously separated their academic and social practices. In activity theory terms, the social and academic lives remain as separate activity systems, where boundary crossing is avoided. While the same tools may be part of both systems, for the most part the community and rules mediate the activities differently and therefore these shared tools do not function as boundary objects.

This is a broad category that includes separators who express caution or reluctance with technology, as well as separators who desire more integration. Generally separators:

- separate their lives/worlds/identities
- feel there is a need (either individually or collectively) to separate social use from academic use, either/both in terms of tools used and practices. This occurs even when more integration is desired
- some separators consciously and deliberately manage this separation

It is important to point out that some separators who are cautious or resistant are increasingly aware and concerned about their privacy and online activity and have begun resisting certain technologies such as Facebook. Specifically, they could be integrators as articulated below but separate their use as a result of an increased concern for privacy and security or are abandoning or resisting certain technologies such as Facebook as they evolve towards a more cautious or reluctant attitude. In some respects, they are integrators who are consciously tightening the boundaries of their social use.

We also note a category of separators who, because of the academic environment of the institution, have for various reasons begun separating their tools and practices as a result of academic practices. These separators:

- experience tensions because their social practices do not have a place in academic practices because of the nature of the program in which they are enrolled
- perceive this tension as unnecessary or
- perceive this tension as justified because it helps to eliminate distraction or
- perceive this tension as justified because there is no need for technology in their program

Integrators have overlapping social and academic practices both in the types of tools they use and their practices. In other words, there is evidence of boundary objects and boundary crossing that have been negotiated by the subject. Integrators:

- see overlapping lives/worlds/identities
- do not feel the need to separate social use from academic use, and
- can speak to the affordances of social use for academic use, as well as the affordances of a range of technologies

11. LIMITED CHALLENGE TO THE CURRENT ACADEMIC PARADIGM

One of the most surprising findings to emerge out of the data from BCIT is that none of the students challenged the dominant academic paradigm. In fact, several students talked about the importance of paying attention in lectures, of limiting distractions, and of the value of notetaking by hand. One student told us how she used Facebook during her lectures to keep her awake so she could pay attention. When asked if she thought the technology might be used more directly to support her learning, she was uncertain. Furthermore, when students were asked if they could recommend any changes to their programs or how technology might be used more effectively, they had little to say and generally expressed satisfaction with the status quo. This conservative perspective is in direct contradiction to the digital natives discourse, which argues that today's students are bored with conventional teaching methods and are demanding more interactive, collaborative, and technology-based approaches. We hasten to emphasize that this apparent support for the status quo by our students does not absolve us from our responsibility to innovate. If students have not been exposed to innovative teaching and have not seen how digital technology can be used to enhance learning, it should not be surprising that they are unable to offer suggestions for change.

Our results further confirm the fallacy of the digital native stereotype but go further by uncovering how students can have quite different approaches to the use of digital technologies and different use profiles. The aggregation of these profiles provides a starting point for understanding the nuances of digital learners in higher education but more research, in particular ethnographic research, is needed to better refine our understanding of digital learners.

12. RECOMMENDATIONS FOR TEACHING, LEARNING & TECHNOLOGY

Based on our research to date, we can make some preliminary observations about the implications for higher education:

1. It is essential that we design instruction based on the needs of the students that we are actually serving, not a mythical "net generation" student. This does not mean we make design decisions solely based on what our students want. Sometimes what students want is not necessarily the best approach to teaching. However, good instructional design begins by analyzing the audience and taking that into consideration as one of the many factors that influence our design.

2. Use technologies that are program-relevant. There is a tendency to jump on technology bandwagons. MOOCs and social media are the current rage and we are being urged to use tools like Twitter and Facebook in our teaching and to consider converting our courses to online delivery. We believe there may be a place for these tools in some programs but are they the most useful and relevant for the programs you are teaching? As an example, we found that in one of the steel fabrication programs at BCIT, the students' ability to see the instructor demonstrations of how to use particular steel fabrication tools was limited by the large number of students in the class. The technology solution for this problem was to make simple video demonstrations available online so that students could view them at a time and place that was convenient.

3. Do not assume that all your students have access to the latest technologies or are proficient in their use. Our research is showing clearly that there is a continuum of access, use and comfort with digital technologies. This will vary from institution to institution but also within institutions. It will also vary from one country to another and is clearly a much more salient issue for developing countries where students may lack Internet access or access to the devices that are needed to use eLearning.

13. CONCLUSION

Our research as well as research conducted in six different countries and at a range of different institutions suggest we need to resist the technological imperative of the digital natives discourse. While the use of digital, networked technology is growing, it is a social not generational issue and the implications for education are far from clear. Our research suggests today's learners, regardless of age, are on a continuum of technology access, skill, use and comfort. They have differing views about the integration of social and academic uses and are not generally challenging the dominant academic paradigm. This is not a rationale for maintaining the status quo but it does suggest a need for caution and for ensuring that the use of ICTs in higher education is driven by instructional design that is clearly grounded in the context, i.e., that it takes into account the specific student, program and technology variables. It is time to put the digital natives discourse to rest and focus on digital learners.

REFERENCES

Bates, A.W., & Sangrà, A. (2011). *Managing Technologies in Higher Education: Strategies for Transformation.* Jossey Bass: San Francisco.

Bekebrede, G., Warmelink, H.J.G., Mayer, I.S. (2011). Reviewing the need for gaming in education to accommodate the net generation. *Computers & Education.* doi: 10.1016/j.compedu.2011.02.010

Bennett, S., Maton, K. & Kervin, L. (2008). The `digital natives' debate: A critical review of the evidence. *British Journal of Educational Technology 39* (5), 775-786.

Bullen, M., Morgan, T. & Qayyum, A. (2011). Digital Learners in Higher Education: Generation is Not the Issue. *Canadian Journal of Learning Technology,37*(1).

Byrne, E. (1993). *Women in Science: The Snark Syndrome.* Bristol, PA: Falmer Press.

Cameron, T., Bennett, S., & Agostinho, S. (2011). *ICT Literacy and the Second Digital Divide: Understanding Students' Experiences with Technology.* Proceedings of the ED MEDIA 2011 conference, Lisbon.

Corrin, L., Lockyer, L., & Bennett, S. (2011). *The Life of a Digital Native.* Proceedings of the ED MEDIA 2011 conference, Lisbon.

East Tennessee State University (2009). *E-Learning and Information Technology Services Strategic Plan, Fall 2009.* Unpublished document.

Engeström, Y. (1987). *Learning by expanding: an activity-theoretical approach to developmental research.* Helsinki: Orienta-Konsultit.

Gilewicz, N. (2011). *Teaching the Net Generation: Exploring Networked Learning and Digital Collaboration Methods.* Proceedings of the ED MEDIA 2011 conference, Lisbon.

Guo, R.X., Dobson, T., & Petrina, S. (2008). Digital Natives, Digital Immigrants: An Analysis of ICT Competence in Teacher Education. *Journal of Educational Computing Research, 38*(3), 235-254.

Hargitttai, E., Fullerton, L., Menchen-Trevino, E., & Yates Thomas, K. (2010) Trust Online: Young Adults' Evaluation of Web Content. *International Journal of Communication 4,* 468–494

Howe, N. & Strauss, W. (2000). *Millenials Rising: The Next Great Generation.* New York: Random House.

Jones, S & Fox, S. (2009). *Generations Online in 2009.* Pew Internet and American Life Project. Available online at: http://www.pewinternet.org/Reports/2009/Generations-Online-in-2009.aspx

Jones, C. & Healing, G. (2010). Net generation students: agency and choice and the new technologies. *Journal of Computer-Assisted Learning, 26,* 344-356.

Jones, C. & Cross, S. (2009). Is There a net generation Coming to University? In *ALT-C 2009 "In dreams begins responsibility": Choice, evidence and change,* 8-10 September 2009, Manchester, UK.

Kennedy, G., Dalgarno, B., Gray, K., Judd, T., Waycott, J., Bennett, S., Maton, K., Krause, K., Bishop, A. , Chang, R. & Churchward, R. (2007). *The net generation are not big users of Web 2.0 technologies: Preliminary findings.* Paper presented at the ASCILITE conference, Singapore.

Margaryan, A., Littlejohn, A. & Vojt, G. (2011). Are digital natives a myth or reality?: Universtiy students' use of digital technologies. *Computers & Education, 56* (2), 429-440

Morgan, T. & Bullen, M. (2013). *Crossing Boundaries: Digital Learners and the Social and Academic Use of Technology in Higher Education.* Unpublished paper.

Oblinger, D.G. & Oblinger, J.L. (Eds) (2005). Educating the Net Generation. Boulder, CO: EDUCAUSE.

Palfrey, J. & Gasser, U. (2008). *Born Digital: Understanding the First Generation of Digital Natives.* Philadelphia, PA: Basic Books.

Pedró, F. (2009). *New Millennium Learners in Higher Education: Evidence and Policy Implications.* Paris: OECD-CERI.

Prensky, M. (2001a). Digital Natives, Digital Immigrants. *On the Horizon, 9*(5)

Prensky, M. (2001b). Digital Natives, Digital Immigrants, Part II; Do They Really Think Differently? *On the Horizon, 9*(6).

Prensky, M. (2005). Listen to the Natives. *Educational Leadership, 63*(4), 8-13

Reeves, T. & Oh, E. (2007). Generational Differences. In J.M. Spector, M.D. Merrill, J. van Merrienboer, & M.P. Driscoll (Eds.) *Handbook of Research on Educational Communications and Technology*, 295-303.

Seely-Brown, J. (2002). Growing Up Digital. *USDLA Journal, 16*(2).

Selwyn, N. (2009). The Digital Native: Myth and Reality. *Aslib Proceedings: New Information Perspectives, 61*(4), 364-379.

Smith, E. (2012). The Digital Native Debate in Higher Education: A Comparative Analysis of Recent Literature, *Canadian Journal of Learning & Technology, 38*(3)

Tapscott, D. (1998). *Growing Up Digital: The Rise of the Net Generation*. Toronto: McGraw-Hill.

Tapscott, D. (2009). *Grown Up Digital: How The Net Generation is Changing Your World*. Toronto: McGraw-Hill.

University College, London, British Library, & Joint Information Systems Committee. (2008). *Information behaviour of the researcher of the future*. [London]: UCL.

Kaznowska, E., Rogers, J., and Usher, A. (2011). *The State of E-Learning in Canadian Universities, 2011: If Students Are Digital Natives, Why Don't They Like E-Learning?* Toronto: Higher Education Strategy Associates.

van den Beemt, A., Akkerman, S, & Simons, P.R.J. (2010). Patterns in interactive media use among contemporary youth. *Journal of Computer Assisted Learning*, no. doi: 10.1111/j.1365-2729.2010.00384.x

AUTHORS

Mark Bullen. *The University of British Columbia, Canada. Email: mbullen54@gmail.com*

Tannis Morgan. *Justice Institute of British Columbia. Vancouver, Canada. Email: tmorgan@jibc.ca*

1.2

DESIGN, DEVELOPMENT AND EVALUATION OF GENERAL COMPETENCIES

1. INTRODUCTION

It is practically impossible nowadays to discuss educational issues without making some reference to the term competence. And, likewise, it is also practically impossible to reach agreement on the meaning of this term (an agreement that is made more difficult by its various meanings), which has prompted authors such as Garagorri (2007) to refer to it as a hotchpotch concept.

Accepting the fact that the concept of competence can depend on context is an interesting point of departure because, from the educational point of view, it forces us to focus on a particular educational stage and define as explicitly as possible the function that these competencies are assigned. As Otero and Luengo point out (2011: 16), "The meaning that is ultimately given to the term competence has consequences on both the shaping of curricular designs and the shaping of the real curricula of individual schools."

In a structured and systematic fashion, competencies were first included on curricula after the reform of Vocational Training at the beginning of the 1990s in the framework of LOGSE (Organic Law for the General Regulation of the Education System). Initially, the world of work was used as a source for identifying and selecting competencies so that the provision of courses and educational opportunities was better adapted to the (dynamic, emerging and changing) needs of the system of production. The competencies on which this model[1] was based were

---

1. The work carried out by the Spanish Ministry of Education and Science (MEC), coordinated by the teacher Antonio Rueda, was wide ranging, systematic and applicable to more than twenty families of professions, for which the Vocational Training Cycles were designed (levels 2 and 3). The methodology used can be consulted at: **MEC (1997)**: *Metodología para la definición de las Titulaciones Profesionales (Desarrollo del Sistema de Profesionalidad de la LOGSE)*. Madrid.

largely the specific competencies:[2] that is to say, the competencies required by an individual to successfully carry out a particular job. Although this reform (re)structured, (re)defined and improved the level of vocational training, it was by no means free of criticism —much of which was levelled by universities— of its utilitarian nature, its focus on the job market and its excessive pragmatism.

The definition of competence that underlies this approach was first put forward by Bunk (1994): Individuals have professional competence if they have the necessary knowledge, skills and aptitudes to practise a profession, they can solve professional problems in an autonomous and flexible fashion, and they are qualified to collaborate in their professional environment and the organisation of work.

2. GENERAL COMPETENCIES

Moving on to another domain, general competencies can be defined as

"A set of wide-ranging skills, attitudes and knowledge that affect different task types and which can be carried out in different situations so they are readily generalizable and transferable. They can be acquired from experience and they result in effective professional performance" (ALECOP, 1999).

And we should add they can be developed in both the world of work and in such other contexts as academia, family, social activity, etc.

Following this definition, we can now go on to discuss the steps involved in developing general competencies:

- Identification
- Selection
- Operationalization
- Development
- Evaluation

As the graph below shows, these steps are not linear but cyclical, and thanks to the monitoring system they can be continuously evaluated and improved.

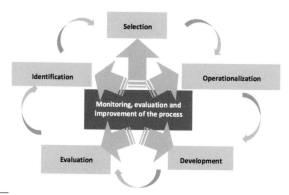

---

2. If there is not complete agreement about the concept of competence, neither is there about the "types of competence". A wide variety of types can be found: basic, key, general, specific, instrumental, interpersonal, systemic and so on. At the risk of simplification, on the basis of our work at the University of Mondragón and the social and labour-related environment in which we operate we shall use the terms specific and general competencies (for vocational and university education) and basic and key competencies (for compulsory education).

Let us take a look at each one of these steps:

- **Identification of general competencies**

  The first step is to identify the general competencies that are to be developed by a particular institution. In this regard, many lists can be used for reference purposes, but the logical move would be to start with the lists in the nearest and/or most relevant context. The existing lists are extensive,[3] cover a wide range of aspects (not all of which are regarded as general competencies by all authors) and are highly generic (and therefore need to be precisely defined). This means that it is necessary to select the general competencies that are to be worked on and developed by a particular institution.

- **Selection of general competencies**

  As has been pointed out above, once the possible general competencies to be developed have been identified, a selection has to be made. This is by no means an easy task, but it must be done by the whole of the teaching staff and a consensus reached (and implemented by those responsible for running the school). The selection of the competencies to be developed can be facilitated (and, paradoxically, complicated if people do not work flexibly and with open minds) because many of them are not independent from one another; rather, work on one competency can reinforce another and/or require a second competency to be worked on.

  Moya and Luengo (2011: 44-45), in their work on basic education, state three criteria that may be of use when selecting general competencies for other educational settings.

  - The competencies selected are attainable by most people and, therefore, the aim is not to selectively differentiate but to construct a common culture.
  - The competencies selected are relevant for a wide range of areas of life and the associated social practices.
  - General competencies make a contribution to lifelong learning and, therefore, on the whole, can be regarded as instrumental to much more specific competencies.

Another criterion of considerable importance is that the selection of these general competencies should be in tune with the educational and social ideas of the particular institution; that is to say, they should integrate naturally and solidly with the education project (or with the curriculum or even, at university level, with the university's strategic plan).

---

3. For an example, see:
   http://tuning.unideusto.org/tuningal/index.php?option=content&task=view&id=217&Itemid=246
   http://www.unizar.es/ice/images/stories/calidad/ResumenEjecutivoEstudioCompetencias.pdf

Our work and experience at the University of Mondragón has led to the development of seven general competencies in the various faculties and degrees. At the Faculty of Humanities and Education Sciences, we have reduced these seven to five:

Mendeberri Project (2000-2001)	New proposal (2008-2009)
Learning to learn	Learning to learn
Teamwork	Teamwork (and leadership)
Effective communication	Effective communication
Problem solving	Problem solving (and decision making)
Decision making	Overview
Leadership	
Overview	

- **"Operationalization" of general competencies**

  This process involves defining as closely as possible what we understand by each of the general competencies that are to be developed. In this regard, some of the tasks that can/must be carried out are the following:
  - Agree and share the meaning of each of the general competencies.
  - Determine the sequence in which they will be presented.
  - Identify the various components/aspects that are involved in developing each general competency.
  - Identify all the possible levels of development (learning outcomes) that can emerge from each of these components/aspects.
  - Identify the contexts in which these general competencies can be developed.

  The Annex contains a simple of the results obtained after the tasks mentioned above had been completed.

  Plans should also be made about how each of these general competencies is to be developed: that is to say, decisions should be taken as to whether they are to be developed independently, whether they are going to be worked on from within each of the different areas, whether they are going to be developed on the basis of interdisciplinary work, whether this work is going to be institutional, etc.

  Other issues that should also be borne in mind are how they are going to be evaluated, what tools will be used, the extent to which they will be reflected in the grades (if at all), etc. And, of course, what training do the teaching staff require, what is the starting point going to be, where is it all going to end up and what support will be provided? And essential to everything is that teachers share the educational significance and meaning of the various general competencies.

- **Developing general competencies**

  General competencies are largely developed outside educational spheres, although the attempts by educational processes to systemise and reflect on them can lead to better results. In this regard, we should remember the competency development cycle (valid for both general and specific competencies), which we could represent in the following way:

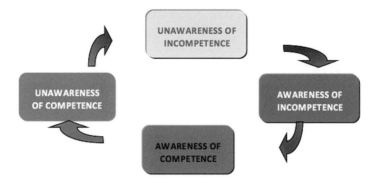

The aim, then, is for the tasks and activities to make students aware of the process, internalise it, work on it and develop it, which means using situations that are as real as possible and which require the general competencies selected.

Also, going deeper into this process enables us to find relations between some concepts that have often been thought to be mutually exclusive: content, abilities and competencies.

The competency development cycle is based on ignorance both of the contents that one has and that are required to activate a competence (be competent) and abilities.

The first step in bringing "awareness of incompetence" seeks to activate the content that makes it possible to develop the competence, and to analyse and identify the relevant abilities already acquired.

The next step –the awareness of competence– involves working on the content that has been identified (which will be largely procedural for the development of competencies) and extending abilities. All this must be contextualised for the competencies that are to be achieved, in such a way that the content and cognitive processes that are activated enable the abilities (potentialities) to be transformed into competencies.

Finally, to bring "unawareness of the competence" at the particular level we are working on, the content needs to be worked on in different contexts (learning transfer) and at increasing levels of difficulty so that the competence becomes internalised and largely automatic. At this point, a new and higher level of achievement can be established and a similar process initiated.

As can be seen from the above, content is essential if both general and specific competencies are to be developed so it must be carefully selected as a function of these competencies. Competencies also require contexts/situations in which they can be developed. If progress is to be made, the type of tasks that are to be presented to students at every educational level must be analysed and identified, and their purpose taken into account.

As Moya and Luengo point out (2011: 77-78), "In the process of teaching, evaluation and learning , tasks play a central role... The problem we have to solve in our quest for a shared task structure that facilitates the attainment of the basic competencies is not only how to achieve the appropriate use of the knowledge acquired but also how to ensure that the knowledge acquired generates a competence."

Our own experience identifies various spaces and strategies in and by which general competencies can be developed. For example:

- Integration into the curriculum
  - Class-based projects worked on from a knowledge area
  - Interdisciplinary and general projects within the institution
  - Institutional projects
  - Entrepreneurial projects
- Projects external to the institutions
- Practical experience in real contexts
- Work-training alternation
- IT-mediated training (independent of or supplementary to the above)

Therefore, an initial analysis identifies a range of areas in which the general competencies selected could be developed. We believe that those spaces, contexts and situations that provide an overview, require knowledge from different disciplines and encourage the use of different types of content have greater potential for developing a variety of general competencies than single-discipline approaches that restrict content to a single type.

All the above (procedural nature of developing general competencies that are valid in a range of contexts, integrate different content-types, and are related and applicable to real situations) leads on to a final reflection on the methodology to be used. Assuming that the teachers' task is to generate situations −preferably from real life or as close as possible to it− that enable this sort of competence to be developed, it is necessary to break away from the idea that a single methodology (whatever it might be) can be sufficient for work in the classroom. Only in contexts that integrate various methodologies (projects, case studies, simulations, lectures, etc.) and adopt curricular approaches of an interdisciplinary nature, can students use and develop the various aspects/components of each of the general competencies selected.

The educational model that all these issues lead us to implement in our particular context can be summarised in the following points:

Classical Model	MU Model
Essentially rote learning	Based on constructivist theories
Focus on cognitive contents	Focus on a range of content
(Almost) exclusive prominent role of the teacher	Prominent role of teachers and students
"Bulimic" teaching	Active and participatory methods
Students work individually	Students work alone and in teams
Text-book based	Based on various information sources
Great importance of the final exam	Process and product are important
Development of specific competencies	Development of specific and general competencies
Teachers work individually/in isolation	Teachers work as a team

As Weinberg points out (2006: 28), the aim is to "place the focus on the subject who learns in order to: a) restore to the educational process, and reinforce, those competencies that pervade a range of performances throughout the life cycle and in a variety of fields of employment, and b) review the explicit and concealed messages of curricular planning and educational practice (which, in some cases, strengthen the real potential of subjects but in other cases does precisely the opposite) in order to generate and manage institutional knowledge so that the knowledge of individuals can be combined, valued and promoted."

- **Evaluation of general competencies**
  Evaluation is the final step that closes the aforementioned cycle (and opens up a new one) for the development of general competencies.[4] It is a complex, controversial and never-ending issue that teachers, nevertheless, have to cope with in all educational processes.

  An initial, obvious premise when adopting a particular approach to evaluation is that it must be relevant to and consistent with, all that has been done up to that point: that is to say, it should give valid and truthful information about the extent to which the students have developed the general competencies selected by the institution. In this approach, which assumes that the development of a competence is a gradual process of improvement, a second premise is that it should provide information so that achievement can be improved in those cases that this is necessary.

  For the first premise, we need to have defined the learning outcomes,[5] which mark the point we wish to reach. In turn, confirming that these learning outcomes have been achieved requires tools and criteria to evaluate all the tasks[6] required of the students. This means that every single one of the tasks contributes to the development of general competencies (or some of them) and will therefore be evaluated as part of the process and as the final product.

  The above requires such strategies and techniques as observation of class dynamics, the analysis of student "production", the evaluation of any presentations that may do, the use of exams when necessary, etc. These techniques can be used only by the teacher or, as is increasingly being suggested, also include the students (either in the form of self-evaluation or co-evaluation).

---

4. Here we focus on evaluating the students' general competencies: their relevance, the processes followed by the teachers, compliance with initial plans, etc. These evaluations take place throughout the process, and are part of the general evaluation and monitoring of the process.

5. "Learning outcomes can be defined as the knowledge, skills and attitudes that students develop in a particular competence throughout a course/module/subject. They must be observable and help to define the competence that is to be evaluated. Depending on the bibliographic sources consulted they may be referred to as learning outcomes, competence descriptors, learning objectives, etc.
    The aim of setting learning outcomes is to ensure that there is shared agreement about what a particular competence means. Therefore, they should be defined in such a way that they encourage teachers to work together, teaching coordination and the consistent design of competence-based subjects" (Universitat Rovira i Virgili, 2009).

6. We understand tasks to mean a sequence of activities that has a clearly defined beginning and end (and, therefore, make sense as a whole), that is designed to develop a series of competences, and that, normally, ends up with some sort of "product" (presentation, technological artefact, dossier on an ecosystem, etc.). Other terms can also be used: teaching unit, project, work proposal, etc.

All the above enables us to evaluate the process by which general competencies are developed and to generate a process of educational evaluation with, and about, the students so that the final results are in accordance with the expected learning outcomes. This formative evaluation (which can also be included in the final grade) is carried out on each and every one of the tasks and its main function is to "situate" students in their educational reality so that they are aware of which aspects are being developed as expected, which should be improved, which should be changed, etc. This formative evaluation can be carried out exclusively by the teacher but, in this case –perhaps with even greater relevance than in summative evaluation– self-evaluation by the students themselves and evaluation by other colleagues can be considered.

Evaluation should be taken into account from the very beginning of the process of designing the subject and, to this end, the scheme on the next page can be used. This scheme also enables the achievements of the students on the various tasks to be analysed and shows the extent to which the development and evaluation of competences selected has been valid and effective.

The scheme also reveals some of the critical points involved in developing competency-based educational processes:

♦ As has been mentioned above, it is essential that both the general and the specific competencies be selected with great care. This first step affects all the following steps.

♦ The learning outcomes need to be correctly defined if the educational process –which is designed to achieve these outcomes– is really to be competency based. If these learning outcomes do not match the previously defined competencies, the following steps may generate education, but it could hardly be described as competency-based.

♦ This step is very similar to the previous one, both in its procedure and "criticity". It involves specifying the learning outcomes defined for the cycles, courses and semesters of a particular educational stage. It is not the same to speak of the development of teamwork at a particular stage of primary education or in middle education and higher education.

♦ In many cases, subjects are imposed by the educational authority and their content often needs to be developed. However, the educational stage in which the subject is to be taught and the defined learning outcomes make it necessary to interpret and select the content, define how this content is to be approached, identify contexts in which the content can be used, etc. And throughout, of course, the aim is to develop and achieve (some of) the learning outcomes specified in the point above for this particular educational stage.

♦ The definition of tasks or work proposals also plays a key role in consolidating competency-based education. These proposals need to have sufficient potential to develop the competencies desired and to be adapted to the social and employment context of the environment.

♦ The evaluation criteria make it possible to further specify the learning outcomes by fitting them to the tasks that are given to the students. What is critical at this stage is that these criteria are correctly defined and that they evaluate the learning outcomes as a whole.

♦ The learning outcomes that will be achieved as the result of the various tasks or work proposals can be of various types (conceptual, procedural, attitudinal, etc.) and therefore require different forms of work and classroom dynamics. In this regard, the most relevant −and potentially most effective and efficient− methodologies need to be selected (or combined) if the learning outcomes of each of the proposed tasks are to be achieved.

♦ Finally, the evaluation tools and techniques need to be selected with care so that they match the methodologies used throughout the teaching/learning process and, in conjunction with the previously-established evaluation criteria, can be used to re-liably determine the extent to which the learning outcomes associated with the task in question are being achieved.

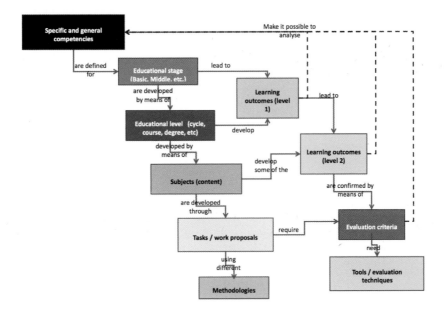

REFERENCES:

Arnold, R (2001): *Formación Profesional: nuevas tendencias y perspectivas*. OIT-CINTERFOR. Montevideo.

Bunk, G. P. (1994): La transmisión de las competencias en la formación y perfeccionamiento profesionales en la RFA, en *Revista Europea de Formación Profesional*, nº 1. CEDEFOP. Tesalónica.

Catalano, A. M.; Avolio de Cols, S.; Sladogna, M. (2004): *Diseño curricular basado en normas de competencia laboral: conceptos y orientaciones metodológicas*. BID. Buenos Aires.

Garagorri, X. (2007): Curriculum basado en competencias: aproximación al estado de la cuestión, in *Aula de Innovación Educativa* nº 161. Graó. Barcelona.

Moya, J.; Luengo, F. (coords.) (2011): *Teoría y práctica de las Competencias Básicas*. Graó. Barcelona.

Ott, B. (1999): Características estructurales y categorías de destinatarios para una formación profesional integral, in *Revista Europea de Formación Profesional*, n° 17. CEDEFOP. Tesalónica.

Sarasola, L. (1996): *Cualificación y formación profesional en la Comunidad Autónoma Vasca*. Universidad del País Vasco. San Sebastián.

SENA (2001): *Estado del Arte de las Competencias Básicas o Esenciales*. SENA-Corpoeducación. Santa Fé de Bogotá.

SENA (2006): *Orientaciones para entender e implementar la integración de Competencias Básicas y Transversales en los Módulos Específicos, el cambio en el Desarrollo Curricular y la ejecución de Programas de Formación*. Santa Fé de Bogotá.

Weinberg, P.D. (2006): *El trabajo en el Siglo XXI. Panorama actual y desafíos para la formación profesional y el empleo de los jóvenes*. Document presented at the International Conference on Education, Culture and Technology, Recife, 9- 1 March 2006. Cinterfor/OIT. Online, http://www.ibcperu.org/doc/isis/6199.pdf

AUTHOR

Eugenio Astigarraga, *Universidad de Mondragón*

Description of the competence *Effective Communication* for the first two years (in the third and fourth years Situations/Contexts will be modified, though not the competence itself) of the bachelor degrees in Education at the Faculty of Humanities and Education Sciences, University of Mondragón.

EFFECTIVE COMMUNICATION

COMPETENCE (Definition)
To use, transmit and/or create information drawn from a variety of sources, comparing it and elaborating on it; to create documentation, cultivate working modes and fluid and effective relations in the context of the work to be done.

SITUATIONS/CONTEXTS	
A: Competence in certain academic activities, most of which are guided or supported by a tutor. **A**	**B:** Competence in certain academic activities and in different contexts. Some activities are complex or not habitual and there is some individual autonomy and responsibility. The support of other people may sometimes be required and work groups will be created. **B**

EFFECTIVE COMMUNICATION

COMPETENCE (Components)	STUDENTS		
	1st level	**2nd level**	**3rd level**
Ability to identify one's own strategies and competencies, and the emotions generated so that they can be regulated and adapted to the communicative context. **A**	Are not aware of the characteristics of the communicative process and, therefore, do not adapt to the context or the participants.	Are aware of some of the characteristics of the communicative process and adapt to some extent to the context and the participants.	Identify the characteristics of the communicative process, the strategy concerning the participants and the most appropriate competencies.

EFFECTIVE COMMUNICATION

COMPETENCE (Components)	STUDENTS		
	1st level	2nd level	3rd level
Ability to present one's own ideas, beliefs, emotions, etc. and defend them, actively listening to others. **B**	Have difficulty describing and defending their ideas, beliefs, emotions, etc in a particular communicative context. They cannot adapt to the work that is being done or to the people they are interacting with. **B**	Can create a coherent and reasoned discourse on their own ideas and opinions but do not actively listen to what others have to say.	Can create a coherent and reasoned discourse on their own ideas and opinions, and at the same time pay active attention to what others have to say, taking into account the reasons for and against all points of view.
Ability to analyse different communicative styles, assess the extent to which they are appropriate to the context and decide whether they need to be regulated. **B**	Are unable to identify an individual's communicative style. **B**	Can identify an individual's communicative style but do not take into account the needs of the communicative context.	Can identify an individual's communicative style, and adapt to the characteristics and requirements of a particular situation.
Ability to analyse and select the appropriate information and strategy (search, choose, create, use, etc.) required for the work to be done. **A**	Have not sufficiently sought, analysed and chosen the information required to carry out the work in the best possible way. **A**	The information has been extensively, sufficiently and appropriately analysed and chosen, but its use (that is to say, the communicative style) is not the most appropriate for the particular situation.	The information has been extensively, sufficiently and appropriately analysed and chosen, and its use (that is to say, the communicative style) is appropriate to the particular situation.
Ability to create and use useful information for the work to be done, bearing in mind the end user, the time available and the format in which the information will be presented, and using a range of technologies and media. **A**	The value of the information created is not sufficient for the work to be done. **A**	The information created is useful and appropriate for the work to be done, but it is not used appropriately.	The information created is useful and appropriate for the work to be done, and it is used effectively with a range of media, formats, technologies, etc.

Juan González Martínez
Cinta Espuny Vidal

1.3
THE DIGITAL COMPETENCE

1. THE DIGITAL COMPETENCE AND LEARNING IN SIMULATION ENVIRONMENTS[1]

The general competences (usually those that belong to the core curriculum) are competences that are common to most professions and have to do with the integrated application of aptitudes, personal development, educational background and other values. In general it is accepted that these competences should be worked on in environments that are as similar as possible to those in which they would be required in professional practice and it is precisely in this respect that simulation environments have started to find one of their most useful applications to date. Without a doubt, this is the main aim of the project Simul@: to assess the possibilities of a simulation environment for learning and evaluating such important general competences as self-management and teamwork.

Virtual 3D spaces such as Second Life, OpenSim or OpenSimulator are online communities that simulate three-dimensional physical spaces. They may be real or not and they enable users to interact and use, create and trade objects through their avatars. Indeed, there are spaces of immersion that are interactive, adaptable to the will of the user, readily accessible and programmable (Atkins, 2009). They also enable spaces to be created that resemble physical spaces and which have similar or alternative rules, synchronous or asynchronous exchange, etc. (Allen & Demchak, 2011). Finally, these spaces have numerous possibilities of considerable educational interest, which should not be ignored either by educational praxis nor research (Cela Ranilla et al., 2011). For all these reasons, simulations are a method of exceptional potential for learning general competences and skills which, otherwise, may be difficult to address (Gisbert Cervera, Cela Ranilla, & Isus, 2010). The fact is that these competences can only be exercised and demonstrated through action, and this requirement opens the door to the design of simulations in which users play an active role in solving problems that they can only cope with by mobilising the cognitive resources that the context requires (Esteve Mon,

---

1. The discussion in this chapter is based on an article submitted to the journal New Educational Review, which we qualify and extend here so that it can be included as a chapter in this work on Simul@.

Larraz Rada, Gisbert Cervera, & Espuny Vidal, 2011). In these contexts, the activity that must be carried out must be precisely designed and implemented, but we should always bear in mind that the very use of 3D software simulation is not an impediment to learning the general competences that we have decided to work on and evaluate.

As can be seen, in this process of research into simulation environments, we have encountered another general competence: the digital competence. In fact, the reflection that we make here is not aimed so much at analysing the results of the simulation experiment itself but at reflecting on the digital competence of whatever students who are chosen to take part in a learning sequence that is based on a virtual world: that is to say, we wish to pause for a moment to think of the digital competence of our informants in the project Simul@. And we wish to do so because if this teaching-learning experiment is to be as successful as possible, we believe that it is fundamental that students be competent from the digital point of view; because if they are not, we must provide them with supplementary training that makes up for these digital shortcomings. This interesting reflection is the subject of this paper.

2. WHAT DO WE UNDERSTAND BY DIGITAL COMPETENCE? DIGITAL LEARNERS AND DIGITAL COMPETENCE

There is no doubt that in recent years there has been an unprecedented technological revolution that is affecting all areas of knowledge and which, of course, has had an important effect on the educational process (Baelo Álvarez & Cantón Mayo, 2009). In this context, neither is there any doubt that university students, most of whom were born after 1980, fully belong to the so-called digital age. In this regard, we often refer to them as digital natives (Prensky, 2001), in clear reference to the fact that they are the first generation to have grown up completely surrounded by technology (Internet, video games, mobile phones, etc.) (Gallardo Echenique, 2012). And as many authors point out (Bullen & Morgan, 2011; Bullen, Morgan, Belfer & Qayyum, 2009; Gallardo Echenique, 2012), it is logical to think that for these new individuals new strategies must have emerged for accessing, managing and processing information. Likewise, it is plausible to deduce that this may also have been accompanied by new learning strategies.

However, the (academic and non-academic) reflection has focused much more on the cognitive and essential nature of these new citizens than on the consequences on their learning as digital students. For example, we found discussions on the Net.Generation (Tapscott, 1999) or descriptions of the main features of this sort of student (Oblinger & Oblinger, 2005), some of which were a certain ability to handle technology (often referred to as digital literacy), the constant use of Internet, immediacy, constant socialisation, and the ability to work simultaneously with different media. Other studies have made in-depth analyses of their wishes, preferences, habits and most frequent uses (Gallardo Echenique, 2012).

Nevertheless, as yet there is no consensus on the nature of these new citizens, which contributes to the debate remaining focused on their essence rather than on the educational implications it may have. Some authors, in fact, even dare to deny that there is such a radical separation between the subjects of the digital age and their predecessors (Selwyn, 2005). And, along these same lines, some believe that this traditional distinction between Prenski's digital natives and immigrants limits the real possibilities of the information and communication technologies (ICT) in teaching-learning processes, and not only from the perspective of the student but also from that of the teacher.

In this plethora of opinions, several authors point out the need to review the literature to determine whether the academic work done on the students of the Net.Generation has provided sufficient empirical evidence that this natural ability in technological environments (which above we have referred to as digital literacy) really helps students to learn more and more efficiently which, after all, should be our main concern as educators (Bullen et al., 2009; Bullen, Morgan, & Qayyum, 2011; Gallardo Echenique, 2012; Gisbert Cervera, Espuny Vidal, & González Martínez, 2011a; González Martínez, Espuny Vidal, & Gisbert Cervera, 2010). For example, ECAR (Salaway, Caruso & Nelson, 2008) shows that 80% of high-school students in the USA own a lap top, but they only use it in the traditional fashion in both their academic and personal lives. This undoubtedly supports the hypothesis just mentioned that their unquestionable ability to handle technology in general does not necessarily lead to learning of greater scope or with less effort. In other words, although we accept that our university students are digital natives, their digital competence is not so clear (Gallardo Echenique, 2012; Gisbert Cervera et al., 2011a).

At this point we find another of the main foci of academic reflection on the educational use of technology: the very concept of digital competence. In this regard, we accept the usual descriptive comparisons of the concept, the most common standards and the analyses of digital competence that our group has been making for some time now (Gisbert Cervera et al., 2011a; Gisbert Cervera, Espuny Vidal, & González Martínez, 2011b; González Martínez et al., 2010), and we establish the following definition of digital competente (Esteve Mon et al., 2011; Larraz Rada, Espuny Vidal, & Gisbert Cervera, 2011):

Digital competence can solve the problems of the Knowledge Society in all areas of our learning environment (personal, professional and social). This digital competence is multidimensional and involves integrating cognitive, relational and social skills in four different groups of literacies:
- Informational literacy: Digital information management.
- Technological literacy: Ability to treat data in different formats.
- Multimedia literacy: Analysis and creation of multimedia messages.
- Communicative literacy: Participation, public spirit and digital identity.

On the basis of this definition, we accept the reservations about the ability of digital natives to learn better (Bullen & Morgan, 2011; Bullen et al., 2009, 2011) and we can evaluate all the issues that we have mentioned in the introduction to this chapter: the students that take part in the Simul@ experiment generally belong to the Net.Generation, but it has yet to be proved that this means that they have an acceptable and desirable level of digital competence. And there is no evidence in the literature to suggest that they can in fact use technology to learn more and more effectively. In an attempt to make up for this lack, we propose using the tool INCOTIC-Grado to measure their digital competence at the beginning of the experiment and determine what training, and how much, students need if they are to be able to take maximum advantage of simulation environments to acquire the other general competences.

3. INCOTIC-GRADO, AN INSTRUMENT FOR DETERMINING THE INITIAL LEVEL OF DIGITAL COMPETENCE

3.1 INCOTIC-Grado: The instrument for data collection

The tool that we used to make the first diagnosis of students' digital competence is the self-perception questionnaire entitled INCOTIC.Grado, whose design process (González Martínez et al., 2010) and final validation (Gisbert Cervera et al., 2011a) have already been communicated to the academic community.

As we know, the teaching of the digital competence contains an inherent and specific challenge: it is difficult to plan and evaluate, it is complex to design the teaching-learning processes that will make students feel secure in this competence, etc. In this context, INCOTIC-Grado aims to improve these processes by implementing the fundamental initial action of getting university students to diagnose their own digital competence. This initial step, which must be carried out before the teaching is planned, will enable us to determine what knowledge students consider they have already acquired at the beginning of their university degree. Thus, the general objectives of the tool are the following:

1. To obtain systematic information about the perception students have of their level of digital competence.
2. For first-year students to make a self-diagnosis of their level of digital competence.

3.2 Procedure

Students access the INCOTIC-Grado questionnaire using Google Spreadsheets. This system not only made it easier for them to respond but also to analyse and systematise the resulting data. As a tool for the self-diagnosis of digital competence, then, INCOTIC-Grado complies with the requirement of being integrated into the Web 2.0 interface, with all the advantages that this has. In our case, the questionnaire was hosted in the forum of one of the basic subjects (and therefore done by all students) on the first-year degree course in Infant and Primary Education at the Terres de l'Ebre Campus of the Universitat Rovira i Virgili.

The sample consisted of 47 informants, which was 61.8% of the population analysed, who responded to the INCOTIC-Grado questionnaire at the beginning of the Simul@ experiment in which they were taking part and which we have already mentioned above (first week in May 2011).

3.3 Questionnaire structure

As we have mentioned above, we restructured the tool on the basis of the rubric of the C2 and C3 competences approved by the Universitat Rovira i Virgili, Storey's general reflections (2002) about the usability of IT tools, the usual consideration in relation to the process of European convergence and the ICT (Esteve Mon, 2009) and the general definition mentioned above of digital competence (Larraz Rada et al., 2011), which is understood to be an aggregate of several components (namely, informational literacy, technological literacy, audiovisual literacy and communicative literacy.)

We shall now go on to give a more detailed description of the content of the questionnaire:

- **First part.** Identification, resources and use of ICT:
  - ◆ Section A: Personal details
  - ◆ Section B: Access and availability of digital resources
  - ◆ Section C: Use of general ICT and ICT specific to students
- **Second part.** Digital competence and attitudes to IT:
  - ◆ Secton D: Specific training in IT
  - ◆ Section E: Digital competence: technological literacy; incidence of IT in our training as "competent" citizens; competence in the use of IT as a tool at the service of intellec-

tual work; competence in the use of IT as information tools; competence in the use of IT as communication tools

♦ Section F: Attitudes to IT

Now that we have briefly described the content and the structure of the tool, we move on to describe and appraise the data provided by this first use of INCOTIC-Grado with our first-year students studying the degree in Infant and Primary Education.

4. SOME DATA ON DIGITAL COMPETENCE IN SIMUL@

Now we can proceed to analyze the self-assessment indicators of digital competence. As stated in a previous report (Gisbert Cervera et al., 2011b) the tool enables various aspects of digital competence to be tested: technological literacy, communication and intellectual work among other things (further information about this calculation processes can be checked in our INCOTIC validation paper (Gisbert Cervera et al., 2011a)). So the general digital competence index (INCOTIC), with a range from 1 to 5, can be used as an initial reference. In turn, this indicator can be broken down into less important indicators with the same range: Multimodal Literacy Index, Intellectual Working Tools Index, Information Managing Index and Communication Index (see block E of the questionnaire). Finally, it will be very interesting to bear in mind the Attitudes towards ICT Index, from Section F of this questionnaire (also scored between 1 and 5).

	Mean	St. Dev.
Techological literacy	3.3932	0.69497
Instruments	3.5006	0.52042
Info. management	3.4255	0.61171
Communication	3.2911	0.73804
Attitudes	3.233	0.6637
INCOTIC	**3.3691**	**0.56386**

Table 3. Indicators of digital competence used in Simul@.

As can be seen, the students participating in the simulation experiment rate themselves using the central values of the scale, perhaps as a result of bias centrality. They can be seen to feel more competent in the technological literacy component, since the value of the indicator of technological tools is highest (3.50 points). On the other hand, they feel less competent in the communication component, which has one of the lowest values (3.29 points). It is especially interesting to see that the lowest value recorded is for the attitudinal component, when in previous uses of the same instrument it was clearly the highest, with values close to 4 as shown below (Espuny Vidal, González Martínez, & Gisbert Cervera, 2010; Gisbert Cervera et al., 2011a, 2011b; González Martínez et al., 2010). The table below indicates some of the significant differences between men and women:

		Mean	St. dev.	St. error
Attitude	*Man*	3.357	0.6841	0.1191
p-value:	*Woman*	2.939	0.5234	0.1399
< 0.05	*Total*	3.233	0.6637	0.0968

Table 4. Attitude differences by gender in Simul@

5. SOME FINAL REFLECTIONS

If the data obtained are analyzed in the light of the overall Simul@ experiment, it can be seen that they are not particularly positive, as we have subjected our students to a simulated education process in a technological environment, and they do not seem to be particularly competent in the use of new technologies, with all that this implies. Within this overall assessment, some values are especially striking because they are extremely low. We are referring, in particular, to student scores on communicative components which, in conjunction with their scores on attitude, are the lowest of all. This reveals a low level of communicative competence in a particularly demanding technological environment. If it is borne in mind that all teaching and learning activities during the Simul@ experiment are carried out in a virtual world, this communicative competence may not be enough to ensure that the learning process is fully effective.

We should also draw attention to the low value of the indicator Attitude. As we have noted above, this value was higher in earlier uses of the instrument INCOTIC-Grado, and so we must ask ourselves whether any teaching action is required to bridge this gap. Certainly, the lack of a positive attitude to the use of technology is not a particularly good for an experiment like ours.

In general, as we have said, the values of all our indicators suggest that the profile of this group is quite different from that of other users of INCOTIC. If we compare our Simul@ sample with the 1st-year Bachelor of Education students analyzed in Espuny Vidal et al. (2010), our present students show a similar level of general digital competence, but significantly worse values in attitude and technological literacy. This is noteworthy because the groups are not apparently too different. On the other hand, if we compare them with the sample of 1st-year Bachelor of Education students used to pilot the tool the year before (Gisbert Cervera et al., 2011a), our Simul@ sample is less competent in all the indicators and, of course, also overall. All this can be seen in the following table, which provides the data from Espuny Vidal (2010), labeled "2010", and Gisbert Cervera et al. (2011a), labeled "Pilot".

	Simul@	**Pilot**	**2010**
Technological literacy	3.39	3.72 ↑	3.60 ↑
Instruments	3.50	3.71 ↑	3.36 ↓
Info. management	3.42	3.69 ↑	3.41 ↔
Communication	3.29	3.76 ↑	3.19 ↓
Attitudes	3.23	3.72 ↑	3.67 ↑
INCOTIC	**3.37**	**3.72** ↑	**3.34** ↔

Table 6. Indicators in Simul@ and INCOTIC Pilot

One of our main conclusions after evaluating these data is in line with Bullen's skeptical reflections (2009) on Prenski's assertions (2001) about the natural predisposition of the Net.Generation to use technologies. Just as the Canadian author points out, mere common sense indicates significant differences between the new students and ourselves (see Oblinger & Oblinger (2005)), but no scientific evidence confirms that they are digitally competent, that they are permanently connected, or that they always prefer experiential learning, etc. Neither is there any evidence to suggest that all this affects how they learn, which is of main interest to us as educators.

A priori, then, we doubt that our Net.Generation students have the right level of digital competence, and their own assessment does not confirm that they have. So it is reasonable to conclude that success using Simul@ is at least partially affected by students' digital competence and the degree of entrenchment they show. Therefore, our thoughts about the digital competence of our students and how it affects their learning necessarily prompted us to consider what actions should be planned to supplement the educational activities provided by the Simul@ experiment for working on core competences such as teamwork and self-management. Below we discuss some of these actions.

One of the first conclusions that emerges from our work using INCOTIC-Grado is that there is a need to enhance knowledge on how tools for educational collaboration and information access can be used. As far as collaborative working tools are concerned, a specific training program can be designed to teach students not only how these computer programs work and should be used, but also how they can improve their own academic performance in environments such as Simul@, which is our real goal. Sometimes, the challenge of competence building is often not unsolvable or even difficult to undertake, particularly if there is a clear and practical vision of two starkly contrasting situations: the initial diagnosis and the competence goal. If we can initially assess our students, and determine what we want then to be able to do, we need only focus on designing the training process. Sometimes, in addition, this process does not require new resources to be designed, but can be solved by the pure economics of existing resources (Gisbert Cervera et al., 2011b).

When students have their core competences measured in a 3D environment, a lack of digital competence can be a real problem. However, if we obtain information about our students' digital competence (that is to say, their self-assessed competence at using ICT and their attitudes towards ICT), we will be able to plan specific training (integrated modules to cover their needs). So this first step helps students to take advantage of the process designed for them to learn about self-management and teamwork skills.

Therefore, we agree with Esteve et al. (2011) and their specification of the virtues of assessing digital competence through 3D environments, since simulations provide action, active roles, learning implementation, resource selection, decision making, individual processes and relationships with others, collaborative and cooperative work, searching, problem solving and knowledge transfer. Simulations allow contextualization, because their similarity and transfer to the working world is very high, as Oblinger and Oblinger (2005) and Gisbert, Cela and Isus (2010) point out. But, since simulations take place within a technological environment, we must ensure that they have the appropriate level of digital competence.

REFERENCES

Allen, P. D., & Demchak, C. C. (2011). Applied Virtual Environments: Applications of Virtual Environments to Government, Military and Business Organizations. *Journal of Virtual Worlds Research*, 4(1).

Atkins, C. (2009). Virtual Experience: Observations on Second Life. In M. Purvis & B. Savarimuthu (Eds.), *Lecture Notes in Computer Science. Vol. 5322. Computer-mediated social networking* (pp. 7–17). Berlin: Springer.

Baelo Álvarez, R., & Cantón Mayo, I. (2009). Las tecnologías de la información y la comunicación en la educación superior . *Revista Iberoamericana de Educación*, 50(7), 1–12.

Bullen, M., & Morgan, T. (2011). Digital Learners not Digital Natives. *La Cuestión Universitaria*, 7, 60–68.

Bullen, M., Morgan, T., Belfer, K., & Qayyum, A. (2009). The Net Generation in Higher Education: Rhetoric and Reality. *International Journal of Excellence in e-Learning*, 2(1), 1–13.

Bullen, M., Morgan, T., & Qayyum, A. (2011). Digital Learners in Higher Education: Generation is not the Issue. *Canadian Journal of Learning and Technology*, 37(1).

Cela Ranilla, J. M., Esteve, V., Marqués Molías, L., Gisbert Cervera, M., Arias, Í., Vaca, B. E., & Samaniego, G. N. (2011). SIMUL@: 3D spaces to learn generic skills. A pilot study with education students. *6th International Conference on e-Learning*. Canada: University of British Columbia.

Espuny Vidal, C., González Martínez, J., & Gisbert Cervera, M. (2010). ¿Cuál es la competencia digital del alumnado al llegar a la Universidad? Datos de una evaluación certo. *Enseñanza & Teaching*, 28(2), 113–137.

Esteve Mon, F. M. (2009). Bolonia y las TIC: De la docencia 1.0 al aprendizaje 2.0. *La Cuestión Universitaria*, 5, 59–68.

Esteve Mon, F. M., Larraz Rada, V., Gisbert Cervera, M., & Espuny Vidal, C. (2011). L'avaluació de la competència digital a través d'entorns de simulació 3D. In U. R. i Virgili (Ed.), *Seminario Internacional Simul@*. Tarragona.

Gallardo Echenique, E. E. (2012). Hablemos de estudiantes digitales y no de nativos digitales. *UT. Revista de Ciències de l'Educació*, 7–22.

Gisbert Cervera, M., Cela Ranilla, J. M., & Isus, S. (2010). Las simulaciones en entornos TIC como herramienta para la formación en competencias transversales de los estudiantes universitarios. *Revista Electrónica Teoría de la Educación: Educación y Cultura en la Sociedad de la Información*, 11(1), 352–370.

Gisbert Cervera, M., Espuny Vidal, C., & González Martínez, J. (2011a). INCOTIC. Una herramienta para la @utoevaluación diagnóstica de la competencia digital de la universidad. *Profesorado. Revista de currículum y formación del profesorado*, 15(1), 75–90.

Gisbert Cervera, M., Espuny Vidal, C., & González Martínez, J. (2011b). Cómo trabajar la competencia digital con estudiantes universitarios. In R. Roig Vila & L. Cosimo (Eds.), *La práctica educativa en la Sociedad de la Información. Innovación a través de la investigación* (pp. 157–174). Alcoy, Alicante: Editorial Marfil.

González Martínez, J., Espuny Vidal, C., & Gisbert Cervera, M. (2010). La evaluación cero de la competencia nuclear digital en los nuevos grados del EEES. *@tic. Revista d'innovació educativa*, 4, 13–20.

Larraz Rada, V., Espuny Vidal, C., & Gisbert Cervera, M. (2011). Los componentes de la competencia digital. In G. de C. y Educación & U. A. de Barcelona (Eds.), *Estrategias de alfabetización mediática: Reflexiones sobre comunicación y educación* (pp. 1–12). Barcelona: UAB.

Oblinger, D. G., & Oblinger, J. L. (2005). *Educating the next generation.* (Educause, Ed.)*Science & justice : journal of the Forensic Science Society* (Vol. 48, p. 196; author reply 196). Washington, D.C.

Prensky, M. (2001). Digital Natives, Digital Immigrants Part 1. *On the Horizon*, 9(5), 1–6. doi:10.1108/10748120110424816

Salaway, G., Caruso, J. B., & Nelson, M. (2008). *2008 The ECAR Study of Undergraduate Students and Information Technology , 2008* (Vol. 8).

Selwyn, N. (2005). The social processes of learning to use computers. *Social Science Computer Review*, 23(1), 122–123.

Tapscott, D. (1999). *Growing Up Digital: The Rise of the Net Generation.* New York: McGraw-Hill.

AUTHORS

Juan González Martínez. *Department of Pedagogy. Rovira i Virgili University. Tarragona, Spain.*

Cinta Espuny Vidal. *Department of Pedagogy. Rovira i Virgili University. Tarragona, Spain.*

Sofía Isus
Cristina Torrelles
Jordi Coiduras
F. Xavier Carrera
Jorgina Roure
Georgina París

1.4
TEAMWORK AND SELF-MANAGEMENT

INTRODUCTION

One of the challenges of the Simul@ project is to determine the extent to which generic competences can be learned through simulations in technological environments. Of the numerous generic competences that can be developed using simulations we shall focus on teamwork and self-management.

Developing and evaluating competences requires complex systems that mobilise students and provide evidence about how they are performing. This complexity finds technological simulation to be a particularly suitable methodological strategy. Working in these environments also implicitly involves an opportunity to develop the so-called digital competence, which is regarded as one of the keys to performance in both academic and professional environments.

Whatever the simulation is and whatever technological environment is used, instruments and strategies need to be adopted that facilitate and improve the evaluation process. Of all the tools that exist for evaluating competences, in this study we opted for rubrics because they are powerful tools as far as content and accuracy of the elements and levels of evaluation are concerned, and they can also be used for a variety of purposes.

Now we have made clear that advanced technology can be used for acquiring and evaluating competences, let us introduce the competences that we shall discuss here: teamwork and self-management.

The competence of teamwork in virtual environments helps to develop the virtual collaborative work that in recent years has become a key component of digital competence. According to Davies, Fidler and Gorbis (2011), virtual collaboration will be one of the key competences required by workers in the future. Self-management is a strategy that enables people to regulate their activity autonomously in all sorts of contexts (academic, labour, social, etc.) independently of whether there is more or less technological mediation.

After focusing on the meaning of general competences, we move on to evaluate them using rubrics. Then we go deeper into the competence of teamwork and the methodological process for designing and constructing the rubric to evaluate it. Finally we give the rubrics for evaluating the competences of teamwork and self-management and, in the second chapter, we discuss the evaluation of the digital competence in simulation environments.

1. CONCEPTUAL APPROACH TO GENERAL COMPETENCES

In recent decades both higher education and the professional world have been converging on a definition of education that responds more closely to the needs of the labour market. There has been a qualitative change in the concept of profession. The focus is no longer on capacities and qualifications; the professional world is now regarded to be fundamentally based on competences (Fernández Rodríguez, 2009). It is for this reason that in the different university scenarios, the institutions devoted to vocational, occupational and lifelong training, and companies there has arisen a concern for professional qualifications and work skills.

Authors such as Mertens (1997), Alex (1991), Le Boterf (1991), Bunk (1994) and Mazariegos et al (1999) refer to at least two major types of competence: one of these types is specific to a particular job or work function, while the other −more wide ranging in nature− refers to competences that are required in numerous different contexts. The specific competences are seen as technical competences that belong to a particular occupation and level of professional qualification. The transferable competences, on the other hand, have also been likened to the generic competences, so fundamental that Mertens (1997) has referred to them as competences for employability. This terminological diversity does not suppose a diversity of meanings (Vargas, 2000); it is more a question of semantics.

Transferable competences are those generic competences that are common to most professions and which are related to the integrated activation of aptitudes, personality features, acquired knowledge and values.

We are referring to those competences that are not specific to a particular job or profession, but are necessary for employees not only to perform competently at the level required by the job but also to adapt continuously to the changing world of work. Transferable competences can also be more broadly defined as a set of widely-ranging skills that affect various task types in different situations, which means that they are highly generalisable and transferable, and lead to efficient professional practice.

Transferable competences are, essentially, social and personal in nature, and they are directly linked to skills of this sort. Although there is no clear consensus on what the transferable competences are in the university context, some of them appear in most compilations and classifications (Van-der Hofstadt & Gómez, 2006; Blanco, 2009). Among others, these are the competences of critical thought, personal communication, conflict solving and negotiation, use of the information and communication technologies, responsibility, planning and management (or organisation) and teamwork. Once competences have been identified, they must be described so that the working relations and transactions between employees, workers and educational institutions can be established. Normally, when normalised systems are organised, there is a procedure of standardisation linked to an institutional figure in such a way that the competence identified and described by a common procedure becomes a norm, a valid reference for the institutional institutions, workers and employees.

2. THE RUBRIC AS A TOOL FOR EVALUATING COMPETENCES

Unlike other learnings and personal acquisitions, the evaluation of competences, regardless of their type, requires complex strategies to confirm the level of command attained by the individual evaluated. On the basis of the components established by Cinterfor (2003) and AQU (2009), we suggest a general system for evaluating competences made up of several components (competence content, purpose of the evaluation, context of the evaluation, evaluation activity, instruments of evaluation, levels of command, evaluating agents, proof of performance and evaluative judgement). This system can be seen in figure 1.

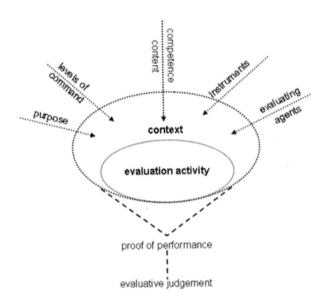

Figure 1. Components of the evaluation of competences.

Competence content is expressed by means of: a) a generic description, by way of a conceptual definition or delimitation; b) professional or academic references associated with the competence; and c) the detailed description or structure of the competence which takes into account subcompetences, dimensions, components and/or competence elements. On the basis of these minimal units of content (competence elements), the levels of command are determined. **Levels of command** are understood to be the level and the quality of the achievement attained by the person when performing the competence, and they are often identified as standards of competence, evaluation criteria or norms. The **purpose** of the evaluation depends on the context in which it is undertaken (academic or professional) and by the objectives pursued (identification of errors, improvement of performance, selection of staff, etc.). The **evaluating agents** may be the usual protagonists of the scenarios in which the competence is required (students and teachers in academic contexts or workers, bosses or management in professional contexts). As well as these internal evaluators, there may be other external ones (specialists and professionals, human resources staff, more advanced students, etc.) who occasionally become involved in the process of evaluation. The **instruments** are those techniques and tools that operationalise and systematise the process, and facilitate the collection of evidence on the performance of competences. We shall discuss these concepts below.

The design of specific **evaluation activities** requires not only the above components to be taken into account but also others such as organisation (space and time of the evaluation, or the length of the evaluation). Likewise, the context in which it takes place must also be borne in mind. Evaluation activity must envisage real scenarios or, failing that, scenarios that are as real as possible, which allow individuals to display their command of the competence.

The compilation of meaningful **proof of performance** (relevant, objective and focused on the norm, standard or criterion) must allow pertinent **evaluative judgements** to be made in quantitative or qualitative terms depending on the purpose pursued and the instruments used.

The whole process centres on the subjects evaluated and, therefore, exactly how they are required to express themselves in the evaluation activity determines the quality of the proof obtained and how this proof reflects the real command of the competence. There are three ways in which the competence can be expressed or externalised: self-perception, description and performance.

a) **Self-perception**. When people express their perception of the command they believe they have of a particular competence. It is a personal, introspective appraisal that is often affected by a certain amount of subjectivity. Personal factors such as self-esteem, the demands individuals place on themselves and critical spirit can deviate the responses given from the real level of command that people have of the competence.

b) **Description.** When people construct a narrative of how they would act if they had to apply the competence and express it verbally (orally or in writing) or by other knowledge representation languages and systems (schemes, diagrams, graphs, etc.). This evaluation focuses on the knowledge (declarative, procedural, strategic and tacit) that people have of the competence. The transformation of this knowledge into a coherent, structured and clear message determines the quality of the information received by the evaluator and whether this information corresponds to the real command of the competence.

c) **Performance**. When people execute or carry out the competence in a real context or a simulation that reproduces and resembles the real context to a greater or lesser extent. The command that they have of the competence and the quality of their performance can be evaluated. In this case, the evaluation can be affected by factors and agents external to the person evaluated. Among other things, they may interfere in the scenario of evaluation, the instrument used to record or analyse, the complexity of the competence itself, or the subjectivity and experience of the evaluator.

The quality of the process of evaluating competences is associated with the adoption and use of strategies and instruments that make the collection and analysis of the information, and the subsequent issuance of evaluative judgements rigorous, systematic and objective. On the basis of Prades (2005), Torrelles (2011) shows that there are numerous quality tools available for evaluating competences (see figure 2).

The selection of a particular evaluation instrument depends on various criteria, the most important of which are the type of competence to be evaluated, the context and the evaluation scenario, and the activity in which it is to be used. For the evaluation of performance, particularly suitable are professional practice, real problems, 360° evaluation, Miller's pyramid and rubrics. The latter is the instrument adopted to evaluate the competences of teamwork, self-management and digital competence in the Simul@ research project because, in a univer-

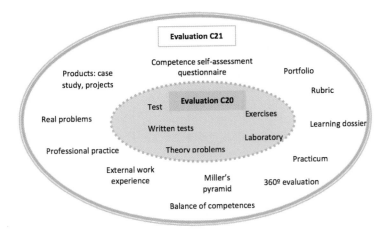

Figure 2. Instruments for evaluating competences (Torrelles, 2011: 102)

sity environment, rubrics provide a precise and objective evaluation of how students perform competences. According to Carrera (2012), they are a tool that

(a) describes the levels of execution or achievement of a competence when carrying out an activity;

(b) specifies the expected results of the work and/or learnings to be carried out by the student;

(c) enables these learnings and activity to be appraised by applying established criteria, provides students with feedback and provides proof on which grades can be based; and

(d) encourages students to constantly monitor their learning.

That is to say, rubrics can be used for a variety of reasons by teachers and students. And they can also be used in conjunction with other evaluation instruments and techniques.

Depending on their structure, rubrics can be holistic or analytical (Moskal, 2000; Allen & Tanner, 2006). Holistic rubrics aim to provide an overall evaluation of the competence by describing the proof of achievement by levels. Analytical rubrics, on the other hand, break down the competence into dimensions, criteria or aspects. For each of these, and at each level of achievement, detailed descriptions are formulated about the expected results. This higher level of specificity makes the analytical rubric particularly interesting because it provides the evaluator with a considerable amount of proof on the performance of the competence.

To construct an analytical rubric, the dimensions, components, elements and /or criteria that are to be evaluated must be determined and then the envisaged levels of achievement, performance or execution must be established. The scientific literature and professional praxis show that four or five levels of performance are usually set, although the more elementary rubrics may reduce this to three. By way of example, table 1 shows the classical structure of an analytical rubric.

Evaluation rubric		Levels of performance			
		Low	Medium	High	Optimal
Component of the competence	Criterion 1				
	Criterion 2				
	Criterion 3				
	.				
	.				
	.				

Table 1. Example of the structure of an analytical rubric

The validity, usefulness and usability of the rubric largely depend on the quality of the written descriptions for each level and aspect to be evaluated. These descriptions should always be of behaviours, performances and actions that are precise and observable. They must also be expressed clearly and precisely so that readers will unequivocally interpret the different grades of performance at each level and that these will be seen to be progressive and equidistant. Before use, it is advisable for the rubric to be revised by experts and adapted to their recommendations.

3. TEAMWORK AS A GENERIC PROFESSIONAL COMPETENCE

The considerable changes that have been undertaken in organisations in recent decades have contributed to a more collaborative and cooperative concept of professional activities. Organisational complexity, and the trans- and interdisciplinarity of activities in the different economic and knowledge fields increasingly require objectives that are shared by human teams in which results can only be achieved if different roles interact and complement each other. The need for a wide range of professional competences, a high level of knowledge, quick responses and a high degree of adaptability require roles to be complementary and actions to be integrated. This is only possible if cooperation permits the activities of various professionals to be to be carried out synchronously.

Teamwork has been regarded as a competitive advantage (Badger, Sadler-Smith, & Michie, 1997; Rousseau, Aubé & Savoie, 2006; Tjosvold, 1991) that involves significant transformations in the way in which work is done. The increasingly numerous and diverse teams in both the public and the private sectors, the aim of which is increased productivity and quality of services, innovation and user or client satisfaction can only be understood from the perspective of cooperation (Ayestarán 2005; Rousseau et al., 2006). From this viewpoint, a team can be regarded as a complex, dynamic and adaptable entity, which is part of a multi-tiered system that ranges from the individual to the team and to the organisation. In his model, Hackman (1987) defines this system as a process (input-process-output) in which the cognitive, affective and behavioural dimensions take part with the time factor.

Although it may seem paradoxical, teamwork can be studied from the individual's point of view, how the individual participates in the team. Several authors have adopted this approach to teamwork and focused on the knowledge, skills and capacities of each of the members of a team (Baker et al., 2005; Cannon-Bowers, Tannenbaum, Salas et Volpe, 1995; O'Neil, Chung, et Brown, 1997; Rousseau et al., 2006; Stevens et Campion, 1994). This approach suggests that it is necessary to know which elements make up the competence so that, on the one hand, they can be evaluated and, on the other, they can be included in vocational training for a variety of jobs. The competence of teamwork is relatively new and there are few conceptual references (Cannon-Bowers et al., 1995; Dyer, 1984; Guzzo & Shea, 1992; Salas, Burke & Cannon-Bowers, 2000; Baker et al., 2005). One of the most-cited definitions of this competence is by Cannon-Bowers et al. (1995) and it has been adapted by various researchers (Ellis et al., 2005; Lerner et al., 2009; Motsching-Pitrik & Figl, 2008; Weaver et al., 2010).

> "...the requisite knowledge, principles, and concepts underlying the team's effective task performance; the repertoire of required skills and behaviors necessary to perform the team task effectively; and the appropriate attitudes on the part of team members (about themselves and the team) that foster effective team performance".
>
> (Cannon-Bowers et al., 1995, p.336-337)

Steven & Campion (1994) discussed the importance of knowledge, skills and abilities (1) at the personal and the team level, distinguishing between the areas of communication, conflict resolution and collaborative work management, and (2) in the self-management of implementation and goal orientation, and in task planning and coordination. In a 1995 review, Cannon-Bowers, Scott, Tannenbaum, Salas and Volpe, using a multidimensional conceptualisation –in which they categorised 130 labels collected from various investigations into teamwork– obtained eight dimensions: adaptability, sharing of knowledge, process monitoring and feedback, leadership, interpersonal relationships, coordination, communication and decision making. In 2005, Baker, Horvath, Campion, Offerman and Salas mentioned four dimensions that are essential to the competence of teamwork: communication; the whole set of interpersonal abilities, which includes both the ability to collaborate and conflict solving; planning and group decision making; and adaptability or flexibility. This proposal does not include leadership –unlike Cannon-Bowers et al. (1995); Charkraborti et al. (2008); Fernández et al. (2008); Leggat (2007); Weaver et al. (2010)– because it does not consider management-related aspects.

Rousseau, Aubé and Savoie (2006) propose a competence structure based on the actions that facilitate group tasks. On the first level, they place regulating team performance and management. Regulating involves a sequence of preparation, execution, evaluation and, as a result of this latter phase, a final phase of adjustment.

To date, these authors are the most representative of research into teamwork from the individual's point of view. Table 2 summarises the similarities and differences between their proposals.

Stevens & Campion 1994		Cannon-Bowers et al. 1995	Baker et al. 2005	Rousseau et al. 2006	
KSA Self-management	Specific, challenging and accepted aims	Adaptation	Planning and decision making	Preparation of work accomplishment	Team mission analysis
		Sharing the knowledge of a situation			
	Expected tasks and roles	Decision making			Goal specification
					Planning
KSA Self-management	Task coordination	Interpersonal relationships	Abilities in interpersonal relationships	Tasks related to collaborative behaviours	Coordination
		Coordination			Cooperation
KSA Interpersonal	Communication	Communication	Communication	Tasks related to collaborative behaviours	Information exchange
KSA Self-management	Monitoring and feedback	Supervision of performance and feedback	Adaptability and flexibility	Work assessment behaviour	Perfomance monitoring
		Adaptation			Systems monitoring
KSA Interpersonal	Collaborative problem solving	Interpersonal relationships	Planning and decision making	Team adjustment behaviors	Collaborative problem solving
KSA Interpersonal	Conflict Resolution		Ability in interpersonal relationships		
				Team adjustment behaviors	Backing up behaviors
					Intrateam coaching
					Innovation

Table 2. Similarities and differences between models

4. CREATION OF THE RUBRIC FOR EVALUATING TEAMWORK

On the basis of this first analysis and the perception by Rousseau et al. (2006) and Humphrey et al. (2010) of certain difficulties in reaching an agreement on the conceptualisation of the dimensions that make up the competence of teamwork, out of a total of 163 publications we selected 75 that had been published between 1990 and 2011 because they contained descriptions about effective teamwork. On this basis, and after consulting experts, a proposal was put forward for evaluating this competence.

The process of creating the rubric took place at two different points in time (table 3). In the first step, the literature on teamwork was subject to a qualitative analysis and a model of dimensions, components, elements and indicators was defined by a discussion group. In the second, the tool was validated. Internal validity was assessed by an expert committee and, subsequently, external validation was assessed by 360º feedback.

Step 1. Definition and creation of the rubric				
Process	**When**	**Technique**	**Instrument**	**Participants**
Definition of the competence	2008-2009	Metanalysis	Categorization Labels	
Creation of the tool	2008-2009	Discussion group	Discussion group	5 experts

Step 2. Validation of the rubric				
Process	**When**	**Technique**	**Instrument**	**Participants**
Internal validation of the tool	June-July 2009	Expert committee	Questionnaire	9 experts
External validation	March-December 2010	360° methodology	Rubric	277 questionnaires 55 teams of 360°

Table 3. Process of creation and validation

The experts gave their opinion on the elements that constituted the competence, their definition and the indicators (table 4), which made internal validation possible after the modifications and after the competence had been defined (table 5).

1. Composition of the competence

Aim: To determine the suitability of the dimensions, components and sub-components that define the competence.

Belonging to the competence (P). The relationship with the competence is questioned.

Appropriateness of the name (A). The name assigned to the dimension, component, etc. is assessed.

2. Definition

Aim: To determine its precision and comprehensibility.

Drafting of the definition. The coherence, the precision and the comprehension of each definition is assessed.

3. The indicators

Aim: To determine whether the indicators of each subcomponent are relevant, comprehensible and suitably progressive.

Belonging (P). Assesses whether the indicators correspond to the element.

Comprehension (C). Assesses the comprehensibility of the description of each indicator.

Classification (G). Assesses the extent to which the indicators express the progressive acquisition of the subcomponent of the competence.

Table 4. Assessment levels of the rubric

COMPETENCE OF TEAMWORK		
Definition: Set of knowledge, abilities and attitudes that make it possible to collaborate with other people to perform tasks and achieve common objectives by exchanging information, distributing tasks, accepting responsibilities, solving problems that arise and contributing to collective improvement and development.		
	COMPONENTS	**DEFINITION**
1. IDENTITY Real and genuine idiosyncrasy that is created by the individual and group connection of all the members with the team and their sense of belonging to it, as well as their commitment and implication in the activity undertaken.	1.1. OBJECTIVE	Specific purposes for which the activities and tasks undertaken by the team are designed and which contribute to the achievement of the mission.
	1.2. BELONGING	Awareness and feeling that each member has of being part of the team.
	1.3. ROLE	Function or functions adopted by each of the members of the team or by the team as a whole to reach the objectives established.
	1.4. ADAPTABILITY	Individual and collective flexibility of the team to adjust its actions to the conditions and circumstances that arise during its activity.
	1.5. WORK CLIMATE	Atmosphere generated in the team by the attitudes of its members, their actions and the work conditions.
	1.6. COMMITMENT	Obligation undertaken voluntarily in relation to the activities, aims and purposes of the team.
2. COMMUNICATION Interaction among the team members with the aim of sharing information and enabling it to function optimally.	2.1 INFORMATION	Exchange of information inside and outsider the team for the achievement of the objectives established.
	1.2. PERSONAL INTERACTION	Relation between the members of the team established on the basis of their personal attitude and the contribution to the coordinated activity.
3. EXECUTION Implementation of the activities and strategies that the team has planned in accordance with the agreed aims.	3.1. PLANNING	Early organisation of the activities to be carried out by the team and the resources required.
	1.2. DECISION MAKING	Choice between different alternatives.
	1.3. TASK PERFORMANCE	Effective performance by an individual or the group of the tasks assigned.
	1.4. MONITORING	Systematic observation and analysis of the tasks undertaken by the team and carried out by individuals or the group as a whole.
4. REGULATION Adjustment processes that the team make permanently to advance towards its goals.	4.1. CONFLICT SOLVING	Decisions are made to provide solutions to a range of problems, difficulties and approaches that arise within the team at any moment of its activity.
	4.2. NEGOTIATION	Process of communication and interaction in an attempt to reach agreement and make decisions that are accepted and expressed by all the members of the group.
	4.3. IMPROVEMENT	Initiatives agreed to by the team to increase effectiveness, boost growth and reach higher levels of achievement.

Table 5. Definition of the teamwork competence.

The internal validation led to some modifications that were implemented in the first version of the rubric using the 360º methodology, which requires several subjects to evaluate the competence of the person in question. This allows triangulations to be made and perceptions (observers) and self-perceptions (participants) to be contrasted.

The criteria that were used to select the observers that would participate in the 360º evaluation were: (1) their job as university or firm tutor, or coordinator/colleague; (2) their professional experience of teamwork; and (3) a minimum of three months of experience working at the firm so that the participant has had enough time to adapt to teamwork. The data were analysed using descriptive statistics and exploratory factor analysis, which enabled us to change the size of the tool from 4 dimensions, 15 components, 34 elements and 136 indicators to 4 dimensions, 14 components, 15 elements and 60 indicators (see table 6).

5. RUBRIC FOR EVALUATING TEAMWORK

The rubric defines four levels of command using indicators or items that describe the degree of individual competence in each of the elements.

It can be used in various ways: all the dimensions can be evaluated or just some of them. It also envisages self-evaluation procedures which enable individuals to judge themselves on various components and elements of the competence– and heteroevaluation, in which several external observers assess the individual's degree of competence using the indicators proposed. In mixed processes of self- and heteroevaluation, self-perception can be contrasted with the perceptions of other experts or members of the same team.

The detection of weaknesses and strengths of one or more members of a team is not only useful for understanding potentialities but also for determining which dimensions need to be improved by teaching, advice or other strategies. The rubric can inform us of the team's zone of proximal development: that is to say, the domain in which it is necessary to act so that the team can improve its levels of effectiveness and efficiency.

COMPETENCE OF TEAMWORK						
COMPONENTS	**ELEMENTS**	**INDICATORS**				
			1	2	3	4
IDENTITY	**OBJECTIVE**	IDENTIFICATION OF OBJECTIVES	Has difficulty in understanding the team's mission and the objectives to be achieved.	Understands the team's mission but not his/her role.	Understands the team's mission and objectives and identifies with them.	Understands the team's mission and objectives and helps to achieve them.
	ROLE	ADOPTION	Does not adopt the role.	Adopts the role in accordance with the needs of the team.	Adopts the role in accordance with the needs of the team and his/her own potentialities	Adopts his/her role and helps to assign role to the members of the team in accordance with their potentialities.
	ADAPTABILITY	ADAPTATION TO ACTIVITY	Does not adapt.	Adapts wrongly.	Adapts in response to the needs identified.	Adapts and encourages others to adapt.
	WORK CLIMATE	INTERPERSONAL RELATIONSHIPS	Acts impersonally.	Shows respect for the other members of the team.	Shows respect and acts constructively in the team.	Acts constructively and empathetically, and encourages positive interpersonal relationships.
	COMMITMENT	IMPLICATION IN THE TEAM	Does not take part in team tasks.	Carries out his or her tasks within the team.	Carries out his/her task and supports the activity of the rest of the team.	Carries out his/her task. Supports and encourages the activity of the rest of the team.
COMMUNICATION	**INFORMATION**	EXTERNAL SEARCH FOR INFORMATION	Does not contribute information.	Contributes irrelevant information.	Contributes verified and relevant information.	Contributes verified and relevant information, and shares his/her search strategies.
	PERSONAL INTERACTION	PERSONAL ATTITUDE	Discredits or scorns the interventions of the team members.	Intervenes only from his/her point of view.	Communicates critically and empathetically.	Values the opinion of the team members positively and encourages constructive communication.

COMPONENTS		ELEMENTS	INDICATORS			
COMPETENCE OF TEAMWORK						
			1	2	3	4
PERFORMANCE	PLANNING	TASK IDENTIFICATION	Does not recognise any of the tasks to be carried out.	Identifies tasks to be developed.	Identifies the tasks that are relevant to the activity to be undertaken.	Identifies the tasks and proposes strategies to carry them out.
		SEQUENCING OF TASKS	Is incapable of sequencing tasks.	Draws up unsuitable sequences.	Draws up efficient sequences.	Draws up efficient sequences and proposes alternatives.
	DECISION MAKING	ANALYSIS OF DECISION MAKING	Does not contribute elements of analysis for decision making.	Identifies variables in the context that affect the performance of the activity.	Identifies variables and contributes alternative courses of action.	Identifies variables, provides alternatives and predicts consequences.
	TASK PERFORMANCE	EXCHANGE OF INFORMATION ABOUT PROBLEMS THAT HAVE COME UP	Does not share the problems that he/she has during performance.	Shares the problems that he/she has during performance.	Shares problems and accepts the collaboration of others.	Accepts and offers collaboration when there are problems in performing tasks.
	MONITORING	COORDINATION WITH THE TEAM	Performs tasks independently of the rest of the team.	Is coordinated by other team members.	Is coordinated with the others at his/her own initiative.	Is coordinated with the others at his/her own initiative and drives the joint work of the whole team.
REGULATION	CONFLICT SOLVING	DETECTION OF CONFLICTS	Does not identify existing conflicts.	Requires help to identify existing conflicts.	Identifies existing conflicts and the circumstances they are affected by.	Identifies existing conflicts and the circumstances they are affected by and helps others to detect them.
	NEGOTIATION	ACHIEVEMENT OF AGREEMENTS	Prevents agreements from being reached.	Helps the team to reach agreements.	Mediates proactively so that an agreement can be reached.	Mediates proactively so that an agreement can be reached and successfully closes it.
	IMPROVEMENT	PROPOASL OF ALTERNATIVES	Does not provide solutions to existing conflicts.	Formulates alternative solutions that are not suitable for solving the conflict.	Suggests valid alternatives for solving conflicts.	Uses objective criteria to discuss and select valid alternatives for solving conflicts.

Table 6. Teamwork rubric (RUTE)

6. RUBRIC FOR EVALUATING SELF-MANAGEMENT

Following a procedure that is identical to the one described above, the rubric for evaluating the competence of self-management was defined, created and validated. Tables 7 and 8, respectively, display the definition of the competence and of the four dimensions and eleven components of which it is made up, and the rubric with the 24 elements and their corresponding indicators.

<table>
<tr>
<td colspan="3" align="center">COMPETENCE OF SELF-MANAGEMENT</td>
</tr>
<tr>
<td colspan="3">Definition of the competence of self-management
To act strategically in a project, process or activity to predict the actions to be done and take the appropriate decisions.</td>
</tr>
<tr>
<td align="center">DIMENSION</td>
<td align="center">COMPONENTS</td>
<td align="center">DEFINITION</td>
</tr>
<tr>
<td rowspan="4">1. PLANNING

Predict the actions necessary in order to do a systematic and efficient job and achieve the aims established.</td>
<td>1.1. INITIAL PROPOSAL</td>
<td>Interpretation of the initial proposition that originates the activity, process or project.</td>
</tr>
<tr>
<td>1.2. REQUISITES</td>
<td>Conditions in which the tasks to be done must be undertaken.</td>
</tr>
<tr>
<td>1.3. OBJECTIVES</td>
<td>Result that is sought by doing a particular project, process or activity.</td>
</tr>
<tr>
<td>1.4. TASKS</td>
<td>Inventory and description of all the tasks to be undertaken during the project.</td>
</tr>
<tr>
<td rowspan="3">2. ORGANISATION

Sequence the tasks, assign responsibilities and predict the resources required according to the planning</td>
<td>2.1. TIMING</td>
<td>Assignation of the time required for each task and ordering.</td>
</tr>
<tr>
<td>2.2. RESPONSIBILITIES</td>
<td>Using criteria of efficiency, effectiveness and/or equity, tasks are assigned or taken on.</td>
</tr>
<tr>
<td>2.3. RESOURCES</td>
<td>Estimation of functional, material, human and any other type of resources necessary to undertake the activity. Location, selection and acquisition of the resources required.</td>
</tr>
<tr>
<td rowspan="2">3. DEVELOPMENT

Implement the planning and readjust the process</td>
<td>3.1. EXECUTION</td>
<td>Implementation of the activities envisaged in the planning stage.</td>
</tr>
<tr>
<td>3.2. REGULATION</td>
<td>Redefinition of the planning as a function of the eventualities that have arisen during the process of implementation.</td>
</tr>
<tr>
<td rowspan="2">4. EVALUATION

Identify, obtain and analyse information about the planning and the performance of the project or activity to guide the decision making, solve the problems that have arisen and make improvements.</td>
<td>4.1. EVALUATION</td>
<td>Final review of the plan, identification of its strengths, imbalances and weaknesses, and proposal of alternatives.</td>
</tr>
<tr>
<td>4.2. OPTIMISATION</td>
<td>Proposal of changes designed to improve the implementation of an activity or project.</td>
</tr>
</table>

Table 7. Definition of the competence of self-managemen

COMPETENCE OF SELF-MANAGEMENT						
COMPONENTS		ELEMENTS	INDICATORS			
			1	2	3	4
PLANNING	INITIAL PROPOSAL	MOTIVATION	Shows no interest in the activity.	Sometimes shows interest in the activity.	Always shows interest in the activity.	Makes the activity his/her own.
		ANALYSIS OF THE PROPOSAL	Does not identify the elements and variables that make up the proposal.	Identifies the elements and variables that make up the proposal.	Identifies the elements and the variables, and sees how they are related.	Identifies the elements and the variables, sees how they are related, and predicts objectives.
	REQUIREMENTS	EXTERNAL REQUIREMENTS	Does not recognise the external requirements of the tasks.	Recognises the external requirements of the tasks.	Recognises the external requirements of the tasks and predicts others.	Takes external requirements into account when formulating objectives.
		INTERNAL REQUIREMENTS	Does not recognise the internal requirements of the tasks.	Recognises the internal requirements of the tasks.	Recognises the internal requirements of the tasks and predicts others.	Takes internal requirements into account when formulating objectives.
	OBJECTIVES	FORMULATION OF OBJECTIVES	Does not formulate objectives.	Formulates objectives.	Expresses objectives clearly and precisely.	Makes the relation between objectives explicit by inter-relating them logically.
		SPECIFICATION OF OBJECTIVES	Formulates objectives that are unsuited to the request or proposal.	Formulates objectives that are suited to the request or proposal.	Formulates objectives by taking into account the elements, variables and determining factors of the request or proposal.	Formulates objectives realistically by taking into account the elements, variables and determining factors of the request or proposal.
	TASKS	LIST OF TASKS	Does not list the tasks to be done.	Lists the tasks to be done.	Lists the tasks to be done and puts them in chronological order.	Lists the tasks to be done, puts them in chronological order and predicts alternative tasks or sequences.
		DESCRIPTION OF TASKS	Does not express the content of the tasks.	Mistakenly or only partially expresses the content of the tasks.	Expresses the content of the tasks clearly and precisely.	Updates and adjusts the description to adapt to the eventualities that arise during the performance of the tasks.

COMPETENCE OF SELF-MANAGEMENT					
COMPONENTS	ELEMENTS	INDICATORS			
		1	2	3	4
ORGANISATION / **TIMING**	DURATION OF THE TASK	Does not take into account the duration of the tasks.	Does not properly predict the time required to do the tasks.	Correctly predicts the time required for the tasks to be done.	Correctly predicts the time required for the tasks to be done and takes into account possible adjustments for eventualities.
	MOMENT OF PERFORMANCE	Does not specify the time sequence required for the tasks to be performed.	Draws up a time sequence that is incomplete or disordered.	Draws up a time sequence that is complete and ordered.	Draws up a time sequence that is complete, ordered and takes into account feasible alternatives.
RESPONSIBILITIES	ASSIGNATION OF RESPONSIBILITIES	Does not assign tasks.	Assigns tasks using inappropriate criteria.	Assigns and prioritises tasks using appropriate criteria.	Assigns and prioritises tasks using criteria that encourage efficiency and including alternatives.
	ASSUMPTION OF RESPONSIBILITIES	Does not assume the responsibilities assigned.	Assumes some of the responsibilities assigned.	Assumes the responsibilities assigned.	Assumes the tasks assigned and encourages others to assume theirs.
RESOURCES	NECESSARY RESOURCES	Does not quantify the resources identifies.	Quantifies the resources required to carry out tasks.	Quantifies the resources required to carry out tasks using criteria of efficiency.	Quantifies resources using criteria of efficiency and as a function of different rates of progress.
	COSTS OF RESOURCES	Does not calculate the cost of the resources required.	Calculates the costs of the resources required for the performance of tasks.	Calculates the costs of the resources taking into account criteria of economic efficiency.	Calculates the costs of the resources taking into account criteria of economic efficiency and different rates of progress.
	LOCATION OF RESOURCES	Does not locate the resources.	Locates the resources.	Locates the resources in different suppliers.	Locates the resources in different suppliers and checks the supply conditions.
	SELECTION OF RESOURCES	Does not select resources available from different sources.	Selects resources available from different sources.	After explaining the objective criteria, selects the resources available from different sources.	Selects optimal resources after a process of objective comparison.

COMPETENCE OF SELF-MANAGEMENT						
COMPONENTS		ELEMENTS	INDICATORS			
			1	2	3	4
DEVELOPMENT	EXECUTION	ACQUIRING RESOURCES	Does not manage the process of acquiring resources.	Does not properly manage the process of acquiring resources.	Manages the process of acquiring resources properly.	Manages the process of acquiring resources in accordance with the plans made and the needs that arise.
		ACTION	Does not carry out the activities planned.	Does not fully carry out the activities planned.	Carries out the activities planned.	Carries out the activities planned, taking into account any eventualities that may arise.
		MONITORING	Does not compare the activities with the planning.	Compares the activities with the planning but does not detect any differences.	Detects differences between the activities and the planning.	Detects all the differences between the activities and the planning.
	REGULATION	ALTERNATIVES	Does not offer alternatives to any differences detected or eventualities that may arise.	Offers unfeasible alternatives to any differences detected or eventualities that may arise.	Offers feasible alternatives to any differences detected or eventualities that may arise.	Offers various feasible alternatives to any differences detected or eventualities that may arise.
		ADJUSTMENT OF THE PLAN	Does not adapt the plan.	Makes some of the adaptations required.	Makes the adaptations required.	Makes the adaptations required and improves the initial plan.
EVALUATION	EVALUATION	EVALUATION CRITERIA	Does not draw up criteria to evaluate the planning.	Does not draw up criteria to evaluate the planning.	Draws up criteria to evaluate the planning.	Draws up appropriate criteria to evaluate the planning.
		4.1.2. EVALUATION PROCESS	Does not define the evaluation process.	The definition of the evaluation process is incomplete or mistaken.	Defines the evaluation process.	Defines the evaluation process in accordance with the established criteria.
	OPTIMISATION	4.2.1 PROPOSALS FOR IMPROVEMENT	Makes no proposals for improvement.	Proposes some proposals for improvement.	Proposes suitable and feasible alternatives for improvement.	Draws up a new plan that includes the alternatives proposed.

Table 8. Self-management rubric.

REFERENCES

Alex, B. (1991). Descripción y registro de las cualificaciones. El concepto de cualificación. In Formación Profesional, *CEDEFOP*, 2, 23-27. Berlin.

Allen, D., & Tanner, K. (2006). Rubrics: Tools for making learning goals and evaluation criteria explicit for both teachers and learners. *CBE Life Sciences Education*, 5(3), 197-203.

Aronowitz R. (2008). *Framing disease: an underappreciated mechanism for the social patterning of health*. Soc Sci Med 2008; 67:1-9.

Ayestarán, S. (Coord. 2005). *Guía para el trabajo en equipo*. Private document of the chair for Quality of the UPV/EHU. San Sebastian.

Badger, B., Sadler-Smith, E., & Michie, E. (1997). Outdoor management development: Use and evaluation. *Journal of European Industrial Training*, 21, 318-325.

Baker DP, Salas E, King H, Battles J, Barach P. (2005). The role of teamwork in the professional education of physicians: current status and assessment recommendations. *Jt Comm J Qual Patient Saf*; 31 (4), 185–202.

Baker, D.P., et al., (2005). The all Teamwork Framework, in International Adult Literacy Survey. *Measuring Adult Literacy and Life Skills: New Frameworks for Assessment*, T.S. Murray, Y. Clermont, and M. Binkley, Editors, pp. 229 – 272. Minister of Industry: Ottawa.

Blanco, A. (Coord.) (2009): Desarrollo y evaluación de competencias en educación superior. Madrid: Narcea

Bunk, G.P. (1994). La transmisión de las competencias en la formación y perfeccionamiento profesionales de la RFA. *Revista Europea. Formación Profesional*. 1/94, 8-14.

Cannon-Bowers J, Tannenbaum SI, Salas E, et al. (1995). Defining team competencies and establishing team training requirements. In: Guzzo R, Salas E, eds. *Team Effectiveness and Decision Making in Organizations*. San Francisco: Jossey-Bass; pp.330–380.

Carrera, F. X. (2012): Como diseñar una rúbrica, presentación en el symposio "Enseñanza y competencia digital" - Congreso EDUTEC 2012. Las Palmas de Gran Canaria

Chakraborti, C., Boonyasai, R. T., Wright, S. M., & Kern, D. E. (2008). A systematic review of teamwork training interventions in medical student and resident education. *Journal of General Internal Medicine*, 23(6), 846-853.

CINTERFOR (2003): Gestión de Competencias in: http://www.cinterfor.org.uy/public/spanish/region/ampro/cinterfor/temas/complab/observ/vargas/intecap/gest_com/ (consultado el 20.10.2010).

Davies, A.; Fidler,D y Gobis, M. (2011): Future Work Skills 2020. Palo Alto: Institute for the Future / Apollo Research Institute

Dyer, D. J. (1984), Team research and team training: a state-of-the-art review, in F. A. Muckler (ed.), *Human Factors Review* (Santa Monica: Human Factors Society), 285-323.

Ellis, A.P.J., Bell, B.S., Ployhart, R. E., Hollenbeck, J. R., & Ilgen, D.R. (2005). An evaluation of generic teamwork skills training with action teams: effects on cognitive and skill-based outcomes. *Personnel psychology*, 58, 641-672.

Fernández Rodríguez, Eduardo (2009). El discurso de la formación basada en competencias profesionales. Un análisis crítico de la formación inicial de profesionales en la Educación Superior. *REIFOP*, 12 (1), 151-160.

Fernandez, R., Kozlowski, S. W. J., Shapiro, M. J., & Salas, E. (2008). Toward a definition of teamwork in emergency medicine. *Academic Emergency Medicine*, 15(11), 1104-1112.

Fernandez, R., Vozenilek, J., Hegarty, C.B.; Motola, I.; Reznez, M.; Phrampus, P.E.,& Koxlowski, S.W.J. (2008). Developing expert medical teams: towards an evidence-based approach. *Conference workshop session. The society for Academic Emergency Medicine*, 15:1025-1036.

Goffman E. (2006) *Frame analysis*. Los marcos de la experiencia. Madrid: Centro de Investigaciones Sociológicas.

Guzzo, R.A., et Shea, G.P. (1992) Group performance and intergroup relations in organizations. In Dunnette, M.D., Hought, L.M. (Eds.) *Handbook of Industrial and Organizational Psychology,* 3, (pp.269-313). Palo Alto: Consulting Psychologists Press.

Hackman, J.R. (1987) The design of work teams in: J.W. Lorsch, Editors, *Handbook of Organizational Behavior*, Prentice-Hall, Englewood Cliffs, NJ, pp. 315–342.

Humphrey, S.E.; Karam, E.P.; & Morgeson, F.P. (2010). Towards a typology of team effectiveness: A meta-analytic review. *25th Annual Meeting of the society for industrial and Organizational Psychology*. Atlanta GA.

Le Boterf (1991) *Ingeniería y evaluación de los planes de formación*. Madrid-Barcelona. Deusto.

Leggat, S.G. (2007) Effective healthcare teams require effective team members: defining teamwork competencies. *BMC Health Services Research*, 7:17.

Lerner, S., Magrane, D., & Friedman, E. (2009). Teaching teamwork in medical education. *Mount Sinai Journal of Medicine*, 76(4), 318-329.

Martinez Martinez, M.R. ed. (2009) *Guia per a l'avaluació de competències als laboratoris en l'àmbit de ciències i tecnología*. Agència per a la Qualitat del Sistema Universitari de Catalunya (AQU).

Mazariegos, A.; Sopena, Q.; Cervera, M.; Cruells, E. et Rubio, F. (1999) *Competencias transversales: un reto para la formación profesional*. Barcelona: SURT-FORCEM.

Mertens L. (1997). *Competencia laboral: sistemas, surgimiento y modelos.* Montevideo: CINTERFOR/OIT, disponible en http://www.oei.es/etp/competencia_laboral_sistemas_modelos_mertens.pdf [Consulta: 12.01.2013]

Moskal, B. M. (2000). Scoring rubrics: What, when and how? Practical assessment, Research & Evaluation, 7(3).

Motschnig-Pitrik, R., and Figl, K. (2008) Researching the Development of Team Competencies in Computer Science Courses. Proceedings of the *ASEE/IEEE Frontiers in Education Conference*, Saratoga.

O'Neil, H. F., Jr., Chung, G. K. W. K., & Brown, R. (1997). Use of networked simulations as a context to measure team competencies. In H. F. O'Neil, Jr.,(Ed.), *Workforce readiness: Competencies and assessment* (pp. 411-452). Mahwah, NJ: Erlbaum.

Prades, A. (2005) *Les competències transversals i la formació universitària*. Doctoral thesis. Barcelona: Universitat de Barcelona.

Rousseau, V., Aubé, C., & Savoie, A. (2006). Le fonctionnement interne des équipes de travail: Conception et mesure. *Canadian Journal of Behavioural Science*, 38(2), 120-135.

Rousseau, V., Aubé, C., & Savoie, A. (2006). Teamwork behaviors: A review and an integration of frameworks. *Small Group Research*, 37(5), 540-570.

Salas, E., Burke, C.S., & Cannon-Bowers, J.A. (2000). Teamwork: Emerging principles. *International Journal of Management Reviews*, 2 (4), 339-356.

Stevens, M. J., & Campion, M. A. (1994). The knowledge, skill, and ability requirements for teamwork: Implications for human resource management. *Journal of Management*, 20, 503-530.

Tjosvold, D., (1991). *Team Organization: An Enduring Competitive Advantage.* Chichester: Wiley.

Torrelles, C. (2011). Eina d'avaluació de la competència de treball en equip. Tesis doctoral. Universitat de Lleida [http://www.tdx.cat/handle/10803/51341]

Torrelles, C.; Coiduras, J.; Isus, S.; Carrera, X.; París, G.; Cela, J. (2012). Competencia de trabajo en equipo: Definición y Categorización.001199 - Profesorado. Revista de currículum y formación del profesorado.15 -3, (Spain): Editorial de la Universidad de Granada, 2011.

Vander Hofstadt, R.; Gómez, J. Mª. (Dir-Coord) (2006). *Competencias y habilidades profesionales para universitarios.* Madrid: Diaz de Santos.

Vargas, F. (2000). De las virtudes laborales a las competencias clave: un nuevo concepto para antiguas demandas, Boletín Cinterfor, (149), 9-23.

Weaver, S. J., Rosen, M.A., Diaz Granados, D.; Lazzara, E., Lyons, R., Salas, E. Knych, S., McKeever M.; Adler, L., Barker, M., King, H. (2010). Does teamwork improve performance in the operating room? A multilevel evaluation. Joint Commission *Journal on Quality and Patient Safety*, 36(3) 133-142.

Weaver, S.; Rosen, M.; Salas, E.; Baum, K.; et King, H. (2010). Integrating the Science of Team Training: Guidelines for Continuing Education. Journal of Continuing Education in the Health Professions, 30 (4):208-220.

AUTHORS

Sofía Isus, *Department of Pedagogy and Psychology. University of Lleida, Lleida, Spain.*

Cristina Torrelles, *Department of Pedagogy and Psychology. University of Lleida, Lleida, Spain.*

Jordi Coiduras, *Department of Pedagogy and Psychology. University of Lleida, Lleida, Spain.*

F. Xavier Carrera, *Department of Pedagogy and Psychology. University of Lleida, Lleida, Spain.*

Jorgina Roure, *Department of Pedagogy and Psychology. University of Lleida, Lleida, Spain.*

Georgina París, *Department of Pedagogy and Psychology. University of Lleida, Lleida, Spain.*

Afsaneh Sharif

1.5

QUALITY ASSURANCE IN E-LEARNING PROGRAMS

1. INTRODUCTION

The rapidly evolving nature of the technologies used for e-learning makes the quality assurance (QA) process dynamic and challenging for these programs. Useful technologies used today are likely to be replaced or significantly modified in a very short period of time, as new technologies are constantly being introduced in ways that redefine educational opportunities. If universities are to be responsive to this constant change and potential opportunities, there needs to be flexibility and openness to change. Institutions need an environment in which the processes used to design, deploy, and maintain e-learning programs are robust and effective rather than dependent on the skills of particular individuals (Marshall, 2010). This chapter will discuss the definition of e-learning as well as its current and future standings. Furthermore, to assist and support quality assurance, it will explore practices/examples and quality assurance guidelines for e-learning programs.

2. E-LEARNING: CURRENT STANDING AND FUTURE DEVELOPMENT
2.1 Defining E-Learning

Different universities and organizations can have a variety of definitions for e-learning. In a broad sense, the term refers to the use of technologies for the purpose of assisting students in achieving their learning outcomes. Latchem (2012) describes e-learning as a learning that involves the use, wholly or in part, of the Internet, an intranet, or an extranet for course or service delivery, interaction, facilitation, assessment, and evaluation. He further explains that advantages of e-learning are its flexibility, convenience, and ability to provide fast and inexpensive access to high-quality content and materials from anywhere in the world. The origin of the term e-learning is not certain because educators around the world define it differently. The majority of educators seem to define it as access to learning experiences via the use of some technology (Moore et al., 2011). Some prefer to separate the variance by describing e-learning as wholly online learning, and others refer to the context and technology medium with which it is used.

This chapter defines e-learning as a giant umbrella that covers distance education, mobile learning, blended learning, flexible learning, learner-centred learning, open educational resources, and massive open online courses (MOOCs). It can occur in or out of the classroom, can be self-paced or cohort, and can be asynchronous or synchronous learning. E-learning is suited to distance learning and flexible learning, but it can be used in face-to-face classroom situations, in which case it is generally referred to as blended learning.

2.2 E-Learning Generations

There are several milestones in the history of e-learning. When discussing the history of e-learning, some educators refer back to 1840 when Pitman taught shorthand writing to his students via correspondence and others refer back to Pressey's invention of the "Automatic Teacher" in 1924 (eLearning Industry, 2012). The 1960s marked the introduction of Programmed Logic for Automated Teaching Operations (PLATO) when the University of Illinois' scientists created a classroom system based on linked computer terminals. Implementation of computer-assisted training and courses occurred in the 1970s when people had to use computers within a school or place of employment, and online courses began emerging in the 1980s. Learners started to have the option of earning their degrees without having their instructors present in the 1990s, and private universities such as the University of Phoenix began offering full academic degree programs online within the same decade. Currently, the revolution of e-learning is emerging as connectivist theory is taken into consideration more and offering MOOCs is becoming popular (Lepi, 2012).

Downes (2012) describes a series of "generations" of technologies and approaches that have characterized the development of e-learning over the years. He states that the first three generations of e-learning represent a focus on documents. He further explains that through the first three generations, shown in Fig. 1, a familiar process of innovation occurs: first is the development and piloting of the technology, then the commercialization of the technology, and finally the amalgamation of the commercial market as large players eliminate weaker competitors.

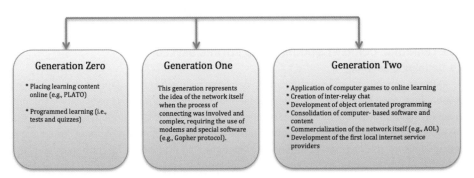

Figure 1. The first three generations of e-learning represent a focus on documents

Downes (2012) further explains that the second three generations of e-learning represent a focus on data: the content management system (CMS) is content thought of as data, web

2.0 is the network thought of as data, and the MOOC is the environment thought of as data" (see Fig. 2).

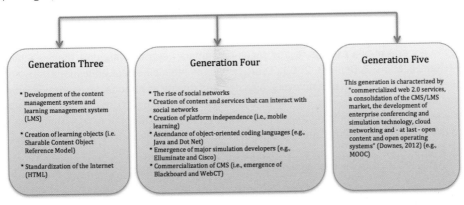

Figure 2. The second three generations of e-learning represent a focus on data.

Downes (2012) predicts that the next three generations of learning technology will be based on the idea of flow, which is when your content and your data become –too massive to store, and too detailed to comprehend. He describes that the first of these things that flow will be the outputs of learning analytics: "they will be the distillation of the massive amounts of data, presented to us from various viewpoints and perspectives, always changing, always adapting, always fluid."

Universities around the world may offer their courses in e-learning programs differently. Some universities are still in generation zero and some are attempting to adapt to the recent evolution, while others may not know how they will progress. Gibbs (1994) describes the activities of those creating software in the late 1980s and early 1990s as having "no formal process, no measurements of what they do and no way of knowing when they are on the wrong track or off the track altogether." This criticism could easily be made of e-learning activities such as MOOCs undertaken in many educational institutions today (Marshall, 2010), which also aligns with John Hennessy's (President of Stanford University) comparison of MOOCs to tsunamis that have the potential to destroy or create the areas they hit (Fairey, 2012).

Educators and universities are challenged to commit to quality in e-learning as new teaching and learning paradigms are emerging, new technologies are introduced, and more students are leaning towards e-learning programs. The next section will explore quality assurance and its practices with e-learning programs.

3. QUALITY ASSURANCE
3.1 Defining Quality

Quality is a relative concept that can be viewed differently by various stakeholders. In the case of quality of e-learning, universities and e-learning institutions may be concerned about cost-effectiveness, learner satisfaction, completion/graduation rates, and management. Instructors may be interested in the teaching aspects of online learning and intuitive course management and more concerned with the quality of learning processes and outcomes (Jung,

2011). Students may be preoccupied with different factors such as costs, flexibility, responsive teachers, accessibility, and interactions in their learning and online assessments (Ehlers, 2004; Jung, 2011).

Wang (2006) asserts that educational quality assurance is a matter of accountability and of national interest. Governments should mandate it, accreditation agencies require it, the general public expects it, and faculty members need it to support their teaching (McKenzie, Mims, & Bennett, 2003). Learners, as the main clients of educational services along with their parents or employers, also demand quality assurance, as e-learning is becoming a more consumer-driven market (Carnevale, 2000). Jung (2011) states, "the quality of e-learning is not something that can be delivered to the learner but is something that is co-developed by the learner and the provider during the teaching and learning processes" (p. 445).

Bates (2010) lists the best guarantees of quality in e-learning as

> "well-qualified subject experts also well trained in both teaching methods and the use of technology for teaching, highly qualified and professional learning technology support staff, adequate resources, including appropriate instructor/student ratios appropriate methods of working (teamwork, project management) systematic evaluation leading to continuous improvement."

The quality assurance for an e-learning program provides not only a mechanism to proactively establish and modify training and competency guidelines but also a method for continuous monitoring of current practices to correct deficiencies.

3.2 Benchmarks and Guidelines Supporting Quality Assurance

With more students moving towards e-learning programs, universities and educators are becoming more cautious and concerned about the quality of their offerings as well as the quality of learners' experiences. In response to these concerns, educators and a number of accreditation agencies (such as Sloan-C Quality Framework, and The Best Practices developed by C-RAC92000) have developed sets of guidelines, standards, and benchmarks in an effort to support and assist quality of e-learning (Barker, 2002; Bourne & Moore, 2004; Quality Matters, 2011; Wang, 2006). Although these organizations vary in their benchmarks regarding quality standards for e-learning programs, the following elements are evenly stressed in their guidelines: strong institutional commitment, adequate curriculum and instruction, peer review, effectiveness, faculty-to-student ratios, attrition rates, student support, sufficient faculty support, instructional materials, technology appropriateness, accessibility, and consistent learning outcome assessment (Chao, Saj, & Tessier, 2006; Quality Matters, 2011; Wang, 2006).

Benchmarks for e-learning quality assurance aim to encapsulate the best practices, experiences, and objectives involved in teaching and learning. Therefore, they need to be continually updated as the learning and teaching paradigms shift in this ever-changing environment. The following section presents some best practices and quality assessment design for e-learning programs around the following elements: administrative leadership and support, ongoing program concerns and support, web course development, student concerns and support, and faculty concerns and support.

4. QUALITY ASSURANCE IN PRACTICE FOR E-LEARNING PROGRAMS

4.1 Administrative Leadership and Support

Yang (2012) asserts that to ensure quality e-learning programs, administrators must be planners, motivators, promoters, and supporters. She further explains that in order for administrators to take major steps toward achieving quality e-learning programs for students, they need to understand clearly what their roles are and the impact their contribution has on the quality of e-learning programs.

At the University of Central Florida (UCF), the budget reflects the importance of distance learning programs; the university funds the technical infrastructure, faculty development, learner support, and research and development in distance learning. There are dedicated servers for e-learning programs and online courses, and the technical infrastructure is made up of wired and wireless network connections to every building. The university offers a technical and infrastructure design that provides administrative leadership, structures faculty development, and assesses course delivery service (Cavanaugh, 2002). To offer and maintain high-quality e-learning programs within a university, e-learning and its components need to be included as part of the core business.

4.2 Ongoing Program Concerns and Support

The decision to develop an e-learning program involves discussion, planning, and evaluation at different levels, including administrative and departmental. Administrators of the department and the university should support the program in order to offer and maintain a high-quality e-learning program. E-learning programs' planning and development should be based on established standards and guidelines from accrediting associations as well as national and local professional organizations. Developers should review similar existing e-learning programs and courses as well as involve faculty and students in the development of the programs. Ongoing evaluation of individual courses as they relate to the overall program is needed to maintain curriculum continuity. Alignment of outcomes among the courses as well as the overall program outcomes needs to be supported and evaluated. Program design, requirements, and evaluation should be based on comments from outside reviewers, student input and evaluations, current online research, existing similar programs, and professional literature. Program promotion, program study, program flexibility, student enrollment, and currency of the program are among ongoing concerns that should be examined closely and acted upon constantly (Lee & Dziuban, 2002).

The most common method used for assessing quality in e-learning programs is questionnaire-based research, although not everyone follows the same approach. A combination of mid-course questionnaire, end-of course surveys, end-of course focus group meetings, and students' feedback and interviews together with monitoring of student performance and drop-out rates should be instituted (Eaton, Reynolds, Mason, & Cardell, 2008).

4.3 Course Development

Chao et al (2010), building on previous literature, believe collaborative course development is the best approach to designing quality online courses. A good example of this collaborative course development is seen at the Centre for Teaching, Learning and Technology (CTLT) at the University of British Columbia (UBC). CTLT is a central service department that provides a broad range of services to the university in leadership, innovation, and the application and integration of learning technologies. Within CTLT, the organizational model for online course development and e-learning programs is a project-team-based structure consisting of instructional designers/project managers, web programmers, graphic designers, librarians, and multi-media producers. During course development, the team is joined by a faculty-appointed subject matter expert referred to as the "Course Author". The role of the Instructional Designer (ID) is diverse and multi-faceted, ranging from project team facilitation to understanding teaching epistemologies, budgeting, scheduling, and the selection of learning technologies. Within this context, the ID works with the course author to set learning outcomes, selects appropriate technologies that enable learning, implements interactive activities such as discussion forums, wikis, and blogs, ensures appropriate copyright use, and develops course evaluation processes (McCracken et al., 2011).

In the development process, the ID works with the course author to conduct a comprehensive course analysis relative to the program, focusing on course prerequisites, program sequencing, assessment strategies, and instructional methodologies. The content is designed to encourage critical thinking, be relevant and meaningful, support independent learning, and accommodate the cultural differences among students as well as the special needs of some students. Online course development is coherent, clear, and consistent and follows the World Wide Web Consortium standards for accessibility purposes. For complex programs, the team pilots a course to be reviewed by a focus group before opening it to students. Eaton et al. (2008) stress that the distance learning material and e-learning courses should be independently assessed (pre-piloted) before distribution to learners. After the first offering of the course and after receiving students' evaluations of the course, the course development team meets to reevaluate the course for the next offering.

4.4 Student Concerns and Support

To make informed choices, learners planning to register in an e-learning program should have clear information about the program aims, outcomes, structure, support, criteria for admission, and assessment regulations as well as method of evaluation (Eaton et al., 2008). They also need to be informed of financial aids and awards available within the program. Access to an online course through a guest account can be an effective tool to give learners an idea of how a course is set in the program.

UCF is a good example of how an institution can support students registered in an e-learning program. After admission to an e-learning program, students at UCF are given an email account and have access to the Internet, online course orientation, library online and tutorial, necessary software and technologies, technical support, online resource directory, and WebCT orientations (Lee & Dziuban, 2002). Access to an academic advisory committee, online program planning, graduation checklist, plagiarism regulations and resources, online netiquette and policy, and exam information are considered to be key resources for students registered in e-learning programs. After completion of the program, access to the alumni community and courses or their outlines is recommended.

4.5 Faculty Concerns and Support

Cavanaugh (2002) explains the best practices for faculty support at UCF. Instructors have access to a faculty development course, training, and workshops, such as Summer Institute, where faculties from across campus meet to create innovative teaching approaches including e-learning instructions and strategies. The instructors receive a laptop computer and are given release time and extra pay for course development. They are assisted in all phases of course design and delivery by trained "Tech Rangers". At UBC, as a support to instructors involved in the design, development, implementation, and evaluation of e-learning courses and programs, the university has provided faculty development, educational support, and production support through CTLT and different departments. Resources to assist these processes and how to use different technologies for e-learning programs have been developed and made available online.

Access to an online orientation through which the instructors are able to work with materials and tools in the same manner as their students is one of the strategies used at UBC. Different focus groups and communities of practice across disciplines enable faculty to discuss strategies for coping with the additional workloads, write cross-discipline grants, peer review, discuss/determine academic credit and recognition for online course delivery, and develop assessment and evaluation procedures.

5. CONCLUSION

E-learning is incredibly dynamic and constantly driven by changes in learners' demands/behaviours and technology. Marshall (2010) asserts that the challenge facing universities engaging in e-learning is not so much about innovation as it is about implementation and the need to rapidly evolve to sustain change at the pace technology is evolving and affecting our lives, including our education. Institutions need to be ready to reinvent themselves and make purposeful and directed changes in response to new technologies and pedagogies in order to offer high-quality e-learning programs. Benchmarks for e-learning quality assurance aim to encapsulate the best practices, experiences, and objectives involved in teaching and learning; therefore, they need to be continually updated as learning and teaching paradigms shift in this ever-changing environment.

REFERENCES

Barker, K. (2002). *Candian Recommended E-Learning Guidelines*. Retrieved January 20, 2012, from www.futured.com/pdf/CanREGs%20Eng.pdf.

Bates, T. (2010). In search of quality in e-learning. *Online Learning and Distance Education Resources*. Retrieved November 2012 from http://www.tonybates.ca/2010/06/22/in-search-of-quality-in-e-learning/.

Bourne, J. and J. C. Moore (Eds.) (2004). *Elements of Quality Online Education: Into the Mainstream*. The Sloan Consortium, Volume 5. Retrieved December 21, 2011, from sloanconsortium.org/publications/books/vol5summary.pdf.

Carnevale, D. (2000). Shopping for an online course? Kick the tires and check the mileage. *The Chronicle of Higher Education*, February 2.

Cavanaugh, C. (2002). Distance education quality: Success factors for resources, practices and results. In R. Discenza, C. Howard & K. Schenk (Eds.), *The Design & Management of Effective Distance Learning Programs* (pp. 171–189). Hershey, PA: Idea Group Publishing.

Chao, T., Saj, T. & Hamilton, D. (2010). Using Collaborative Course Development to Achieve Online Course Quality Standards. *International Review of Research in Open and Distance Learning*. Volume 11, Issue 3.

Chao, T., Saj, T., & Tessier, F. (2006). Establishing a quality review for online courses. *Educause Quarterly*, 29(3), 32–39.

Downes, S. (2012). *E-Learning Generations*. Retrieved November 2012 from http://halfanhour.blogspot.ca/2012/02/e-learning-generations.html.

Eaton, A. K., Reynolds, A. P., Mason, R., & Cardell, R. (2008). Assuring quality. *British Dental Journal*. 205 (3), 145–150.

Ehlers, U.-D. (2004). Quality in e-learning from a learner's perspective. *European Journal of Open and Distance Learning*. I. Retrieved November 2012 from http://www.eurodl.org/materials/contrib/2004/Online_Master_COPs.html.

eLearning Industry (2012). *The History of eLearning Infographic 2012*. Retrieved January 2013 from http://elearningindustry.com/history-of-elearning-infographic-education-2012.

Fairey, A. (2012). *Online education a 'tsunami' of change*. Retrieved November 2012 from http://www.thecord.ca/?p=11713.

Gibbs, W. (1994). Software's chronic crisis. *Scientific American*, 271(3): 86–95.

Jung, I. (2011). The dimensions of e-learning quality: from the learner's perspective. *Educational Technology Research and Development*. 59, 445–464.

Latchem, C. (2012) *Quality Assurance Toolkit for Open and Distance Non-formal Education*. Commonwealth of Learning. Retrieved December 2012 from www.col.org/PublicationDocuments/QA%20NFE_150.pdf.

Lee, J., & Dziuban, C. (2002). Using quality assurance strategies for online programs. *Educational Technology Review*, 10(2), 69–78.

Lepi, K. (2012). The history of online education. *Edudemic*. Retrieved November 2012 from http://edudemic.com/2012/10/the-history-of-online-education/.

Marshall, S. (2010). A quality framework for continuous improvement of e-learning: The e-learning maturity model. *Journal of Distance Education*. 24(1), 143–166.

McCracken, J., Cho, S., Sharif, A., Wilson, B., Miller, J., Crowley, C., & Scalzo, D. (2011). Articulating assessment design practice for online courses and programs: cases in assessment strategy design and development. *Proceedings of the International Conference on e-Learning*. pp. 226–235.

McKenzie, B., Mims, N., & Bennett, E. (2003). Successful online assessment, interaction and evaluation techniques. *Society for Information Technology and Teacher Education International Conference*. 2003(1), 426–431.

Moore, J. L., Dickson-Deane, C., & Galyen, K. (2011). E-Learning, online learning, and distance learning environments: Are they the same? *Internet And Higher Education*, 14(2), 129–135.

Quality Matters (2011). *Quality Matters Rubric Standards 2011–2013 edition*. Marylandonline. Retrieved November 22, 2011 from www.qmprogram.org/files/QM_Standards_2011-2013.pdf.

Wang, Q. (2006). Quality Assurance – Best Practices for Assessing Online Programs. *International Journal on E-Learning*. 5(2), 265–274.

Yang, Y. (2012). Roles of administrators in ensuring the quality of online Programs. In Paolucci, R. (Ed.) *Quality Assurance of Online and Distance Learning*. The Interlearning Company, LLC 2012. pp. 1–8.

AUTHOR

Afsaneh Sharif, *Centre for Teaching, LEarning and Technology, University of British Columbia*

CHAPTER 2:

NEW STRATEGIES AND NEW TECHNOLOGICAL ENVIRONMENTS FOR UNIVERSITY EDUCATION

Mercè Gisbert Cervera

José María Cela-Ranilla

2.1

ADVANCED TECHNOLOGY ENVIRONMENTS TO SUPPORT THE TEACHING/LEARNING PROCESS IN THE UNIVERSITY

1. INTRODUCTION

The Eurostat database (2011) reveals that 32% of the Spanish population and 27% of Europeans aged between 16 and 74 years old have good computer skills. A total of 68% of Spanish young people (16-24 years old) and 30% of adults (25-54 years old) state that they use the Internet for playing, and downloading games, images, films, music, etc. Furthermore, 76% of individuals with a high or medium level of formal education (38% in each case) also use Internet for the same reasons.

These figures show how the groups of people in the higher education context use Internet. They seem to be ready to take part in training processes that use advanced technology as an educational environment.

In parallel, during the last decade ICT has been playing an increasingly important role in terms of daily and educational use. In this latter case, it is often used to manage teaching and learning processes, for which teachers are ultimately responsible. This should be sufficient reason for encouraging teachers' ICT competences and ICT use in the classroom (SWD, 2012).

A recent EU document (2012) describes several traits that justify the use of emerging and advanced technology in educational processes: it improves the quality, access and equity of teaching/learning processes; it encourages active, practical and personalised learning; it facilitates engagement and collaboration; and it transform teachers and learners into creators of learning contents.

From an institutional point of view, ICT is regarded as one of the core axes of university education in both teaching/learning processes (Johnson et al., 2011) and productivity (Yonghong & Meyer, 2011).

Higher education may be the context in which students consolidate their use of technology from an intentional and technological perspective. However, the coexistence of education and technology does not automatically mean that technology is correctly implemented in the educational process. Educating thE nEt gEnEration: a handbook of Findings for Practice and Policy (2009) provides some guidelines for promoting good practices in this setting: "[1] Offering students the opportunity to use new technologies does not guarantee student engagement with the task. Additional steps may need to be taken to encourage student engagement. [2] Learning technologies need to be clearly integrated with curriculum and assessment. [3] The learning objectives of the activity and its educational value should be made explicit to students to help align differing expectations. [4] Implementing new technologies and learning activities requires students to develop new skills in using the technology and often in participating in new types of learning activities. Students will therefore need both time and guidance to develop these skills, and educators should allow for this when planning the timing and length of the implementation."

Berlanga et al (2010) state that the future of higher education institutions will depend on the extent to which they can provide open and adaptable models to diversify teaching/learning processes.

The report Universitic (Uceda & Barro, 2011 & 2010) points out that in the last decade Spanish universities have made the effort to incorporate ICT effectively into the teaching-learning processes by investing in infrastructure to provide the resources required for new teaching methodologies.

However the teaching/learning environments are managed in higher education, the advanced technologies provide different ways of approaching teaching processes. This difference leads to greater complexity, which should be understood from a positive perspective. This complexity accepts that there is no single ideal technological solution for creating training environments that offer processes such as construction, immersion, self-direction and interactivity in terms of collaboration (Konstantinidis et al., 2010).

2. ADVANCED TECHNOLOGY ENVIRONMENTS

In socio-constructivist terms, learning is a complex process of constructing interaction with others and the context. This process, although complex, is a natural and often unintentional process. In formative terms, technologies are advanced when they developing artefacts that facilitate the natural learning process in all its complexity.

When technology and teaching use a student-centred instructional approach, the design should include some holistic expertise. In terms of the TPACK model (Koehler & Mishra 2008), this comprehensive view requires the integration of at least three kinds of knowledge: technology, discipline and teaching (see figure X). This triadic structure enables practitioners to capitalize on the potentialities of ICT as tools for promoting learning processes based on action, activity, participation and student centrality.

Nowadays, the latest generation technologies are being used to develop the Internet and artefacts based on simulation, virtual worlds, digital games and three dimensional technologies. Research is working on finding borders between these technologies (Mayer, nd) , but the main task is to give them an educational intention. Likewise, it is not easy to find a standard categorization of digital games; in fact, there are several definitions (Kirriemuir, 2004) and ways of classifying educational games, serious games and their relationship to virtual worlds and simulations (Aldrich 2009; Sawyer & Smith 2008).

A good illustration of the difficulty of finding such a definition was the attempt made two decades ago by the American Society for Training and Development (ASTD, 1987) to list the specific features of game and simulation. A game was defined as "A structured activity in which two or more participants compete within constraints or rules to achieve an objective. One of these participants can be a computer." And simulation was defined as "An operational model, using selected components, of a real or hypothetical process, mechanism or system. A simulation game combines the characteristics of games and simulations.

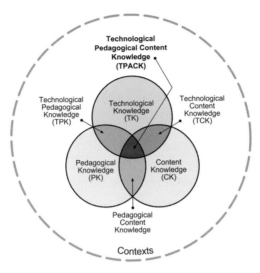

TPACK model by Koehler & Mishra (2008)

While developing these statements, Mayer (nd) proposed the additional conceptualization that simulations are essentially models of reality defined as systems. This model is dynamic and simplified, yet faiithful, accurate, and valid. The essential characteristics of a game, however, include a player or players, conflict, rules, predetermined goals, and the fact that it is often fictitious or artificial.

3. ADVANCED TECHNOLOGY AND EDUCATION OPPORTUNITIES

More than 10 years ago, Jonassen & Land (2000) suggested that, in terms of specific spaces for training, advanced technology could be used to create a variety of informal, distributed, active, and immersive learning environments in which simulation activities, collaboration opportunities and social experiences could lead to rich learning opportunities. In sum, this technology can be used to create environments with the following characteristics: active learning, collaboration, challenge, immersion, fun, entertainment, multiple disciplines, problem solving and problem posing skills, multidisciplinary problems, and opportunities for reflection.

Likewise, Peters et al. (1998) proposed some factors that should be taken into consideration when validating a learning process in a complex technology environment: congruency of situations, realistic scenario, coherence between tasks, and consistency between activities and outcomes.

It is increasingly evident that effective learning processes are those that involve testing, building, experimenting, making decisions, solving problems, etc.: in short, all those processes that require students to be active. These learning situations enable students to acquire skills and knowledge more easily (Prensky, 2001).

Several authors have stated the principles and key points to be observed during learning processes based on advanced technology such as virtual worlds or 3D simulation.

Principles of the effective use of technology (Spector, 2001)
▶ Learning is fundamentally about change *the Learning Principle*.
▶ Experience is the starting point for understanding *the Experience Principle*.
▶ Context determines meaning *the Context Principle*.
▶ Relevant learning contexts are often broad and multifaceted *the Integration Principle*.
▶ We know less than
Key points (De Freitas, 2006)
▶ Ensure there is an alignment between learning objectives, and the use of metaverses and 3D virtual worlds and assessment so that the most effective learning outcomes can take place.
▶ Ensure that the learning activities which take place within the metaverse are integrated with face-to-face learning.
▶ Provide opportunities for reflection by means of dialogue and discussion and feedback loops.
▶ Place aspects of learning within immersive environments so that learners can take control over and know how to get engaged with them.
▶ Consider the level of immersion as part of the learning design to ensure that learning is most effective.
▶ Design role-plays to allow students to empathise and reflect upon situations from real life.
▶ Develop realistic scenarios to allow transfer from rehearsal to real life contexts.
Principles in curricula (Chang et al. 2010)
▶ Challenges: The contents of the game need to be challenging in order to arouse students' curiosity.
▶ Competition: So that students' motivation remains high, either individual students or groups need to compete with each other.
▶ Cooperation: The design of the game should help students to develop a sense of 'work as a team and win as a team'.
▶ Authentic tasks: The game should incorporate authentic, real-world cases, etc.

Now that the general conditions for building an advanced technology environment have been described, let us move on to explore the benefits that have been observed after more than ten years of research in the field. One decade is not a long period of time to unequivocally determine the impact of learning processes. Nevertheless, the speed at which technology has evolved facilitates not only the development of learning processes but also the management of the assessment.

Recent research has explained many of the reasons why advanced technology can be used in learning processes. Dalgarno (2010) speaks in terms of affordances and suggests that 3D VLEs can facilitate the following processes: [1] learning tasks that lead to the development of enhanced spatial knowledge representation of the explored domain; [2] experiential learning tasks that are impractical or not possible to undertake in the real world; [3] learning tasks that lead to increased intrinsic motivation and engagement; [4] learning tasks that lead to improved transfer of knowledge and skills to real situations through contextualisation of learning; and [5] tasks that lead to richer and/or more effective collaborative learning than is possible with 2-D alternatives.

Likewise, Rich (nd) gives us several reasons for using virtual worlds in education: [1] as repositories to support information; [2] as places to communicate and share information [3]; as spaces to develop ideas and products in a realistic and visual environment with a collaborative spirit; and [4] as workspaces to develop reflective analysis.

De Freitas (2008) describes virtual worlds as environments in which students potentially govern the process that is characterized by: teamwork, joint construction, comprehensive communication, immersive and interactive participation and real or simulated planning.

Despite its potential benefits in learning processes, advanced technology also has several limitations. Atkins (2009) expresses some of these limitations, which can condition the design of activities: unfamiliarity with the environment and the high learning curve, the high level of technical requirements, and the level of reliability, trust and security of the system.

4. CONCLUSION

Whatever the learning environment, the space designed must contain a set of activities that activate the cognitive processes that are required by most professional tasks nowadays. Emerging technologies enable specific situations to be simulated that are very similar to the reality of the world of work. In fact, the evolution of technology means that there are a wide range of resources available for converting technological experience into learning experience.

These activities must follow the tenets of instructional models based on the social construction and transformation of knowledge by means of activities such as modeling, action, interaction, collaboration, experience, discovery and discussion.

Educational experiences in these environments must give a sense of "naturalness" to the activity, and at the same time provide a system for collecting, using and analyzing data in accordance with a previously defined model. This means that each learner can use his/her own learning style. The sense of autonomy and independence depends on the fact that learners interpret and carry out the activities using an approach that is consistent with their own way of performing.

The role of the person in charge of providing feedback on learners' activities is also important. Content expertise is not so essential as the ability to give support and feedback during the activity. In this regard, several supervisor profiles may intervene in this kind of learning scenario.

In sum, learning environments based on advanced technologies are prompting new ways of delivering learning actions, new ways of mediating as teachers in instructional processes, new tools for monitoring the learning processes and richer ways of assessing the resulting products.

REFERENCES

Aldrich, C. (2009). Virtual worlds, simulations, and games for education: A unifying view. *Innovate: Journal of Online Education, 5*(5).

ASTD (1987). *Training and development handbook: a guide to human resource development*. New York: McGrawHill.

Atkins, C. (2009). Virtual Experience: Observations on Second Life. In Purvis, M. & Savarimuthu, B. (Eds.), *Lecture Notes in Computer*

Berlanga. A. J., Peñalvo. F. G. & Sloep. P. B. (2010). Towards Learning 2.0 University. *Interactive Learning Environments. 18*(3), 199-201.

Chang, Y. C., Peng H. Y. & Chao, H. C. (2010). Examining the effects of learning motivation and of course design in an instructional simulation game. Interactive Learning Environments, 18(4), 319-339

Dalgarno, B., & Lee, M. J. W. (2010). What are the learning affordances of 3-D virtual environments? British Journal of Educational Technology, 41(1), 10–32. doi:10.1111/j.1467-8535.2009.01038.x

De Freitas, S. (2008). Serious virtual worlds. A scoping guide. UK: JISC e-Learning Programme, The Joint Information Systems Committee (JISC).

Educating thE nEt gEnEration a handbook of Findings for Practice and Policy. (2009). Higher Education.

Eurostat

Freitas, S. (2006) "Learning in Immersive Worlds". A review of Game-Based Learning. London: JISC

Johnson, L., Smith, R., Willis, H., Levine, A. & Haywood, K. (2011). The 2011 Horizon Report. Austin, Texas: The New Media Consortium.

Kirriemuir, J. (2004). Literature Review in Games and Learning. Futurelab. Retrieved September 7, 2012, from http://telearn.archives-ouvertes.fr/docs/00/19/04/53/PDF/kirriemuir-j-2004-r8.pdf

Koehler, M.J. & Mishra, P. *Handbook of technological pedagogical content knowledge (TPCK) for educators*. AACTE Commitee on Innovation and Technology. Routledge.

Konstantinidis, A., Tsiatsos, T., Demetriadis, S., & Pomportsis, A. (2010). Collaborative Learning in OpenSim by Utilizing SLoodle. 2010 Sixth Advanced International Conference on Telecommunications, 90–95. doi:10.1109/AICT.2010.75

Mayer, I. (n.d.). *Learning in a Virtual World: Reflections on the Cyberdam. Learning.*

Peters, V., Vissers, G. & Heijne, G. (1998). The validity of games. Simulation and Gaming, 29(1), 20-30

Prensky, M. (2001). The digital game-based learning revolution. *Digital game-based learning.*

Rich, J. (n.d.). Best Practices for Instructors to Facilitate Learning in Virtual Worlds. Retrieved March 25, 2011, from Jim Rich: http://www.jimrich.com/pdf/BestTeachingPracticesfor-VWs.pdf

Spector, J. M. (2001). An Overview of Progress and Problems in Educational Technology. Interactive Educational Multimedia, 3, 2737

SWD Education & Training Monitor 20.11.2012

Uceda, J. (2011). Un nuevo modelo educativo. In: Michavila, F.,Ripollés, M., Esteve, F. *El día después de Bolonia*. Madrid: Tecnos.

Uceda, J. & Barro, S. (2010). *Universitic 2010: Evolución de las TIC en el sistema universitario español 2006 - 2010.* Conferencia de Rectores de las Universidades Españolas (CRUE).

Yonghong, X. & Meyer, K. A. (2007) Factors explaining faculty technology use and productivity. Internet and Higher Education 10. 41–52

AUTHORS

Mercè Gisbert Cervera. *Department of Pedagogy. Rovira i Virgili University. Tarragona, Spain.*

José María Cela-Ranilla. *Department of Pedagogy. Rovira i Virgili University. Tarragona, Spain.*

Janaina Minelli de Oliveira,
Eliana Gallardo-Echenique
Annachiara del Prete

2.2

CYBORGS AT THE UNIVERSITY: GAMING FOR EDUCATIONAL PURPOSES

1. INTRODUCTION

Norbert Wiener, the coiner of the term "cybernetics", based his theory on the assumption that there is an analogy between the organic and technologically regulated systems that transmit and process information (Wiener, 1954). In the mid 1980s, William Gibson, an American cyberpunk science fiction author, used the word "cyberspace" in his book Neuromancer. The term refers to the global network of interdependent information technology infrastructures, telecommunications networks and computer processing systems. Gibson's novel was an important milestone, and since then the prefix cyber has been used in all kinds of combinations (for example, cyberbody, cybersex, cybermoney and cybercafé).

Another graphic representation is Donna Haraway's "a cyborg is a cybernetic organism, a hybrid of machine and organism, a creature of social reality as well as a creature of fiction" (Harway, 1991b: 117). For Haraway, the moment cyber technologies start to work on and penetrate the bodies of people, they begin to generate new kinds of subjectivities and new types of organisms: cybernetic organisms, cyborgs (Haraway, 1991a). "We are all chimeras, theorized, and fabricated hybrids of machine and organism" (Haraway, 1991b: 118). In short, we are all cyborgs in today's society, with all the advantages and disadvantages that this entails. To Clark (2003: 3) we "are natural born cyborgs" and our technologies are both extensions of our bodies and minds and enhancements or modifications of the environment. Our cell phones, cars and laptops have turned us into cyborgs (Case, 2012). For Case (2010), technology is making humans evolve, as we are becoming a screen-staring, button-clicking new version of Homo sapiens. We now rely on "external brains" (cell phones and computers) to communicate, remember, and even live out secondary lives. The idea of a cell phone being a technosocial object that enables an actor (user) to communicate with other actors (users) on a network (information exchange and connectivity) changes us into cyborgs (http://case-organic.com/).

In 2004, Neil Harbisson (http://eyeborg.wix.com/neil-harbisson) became the first person in the world to wear an eyeborg: a head-mounted device that translates colour to sound. The British government confirmed Harbisson's status as the first officially recognized cyborg in history. It appears that cyborgs are beginning to move away from such futuristic fictional images as Terminator, Robocop and Blade Runner, getting ever closer to a disturbing reality that seems to be within reach (Ramírez, 2011: 3).

2. CYBORG CULTURE AND EDUCATION

"The cyborg is a potent cultural icon of the late twentieth century. It conjures images of human-machine hybrids and the physical merging of flesh and electronic circuitry" (Clark, 2003: 5). To Garoian & Gaudelius (2001), the figure of the cyborg in popular culture can lead us to think of it merely as a creature of fiction. In this present chapter, however, the concept of the cyborg is used as a metaphor of the students who have incorporated technology and its affordances as an undeniable part of their everyday lives. "What is crucial is that they live in a time and a society where computers and other forms of digital media have become central in the culture. The term cyborg, used as a sensitizing, or focusing, concept, may help to understand the conditions of children growing up in a digital world" (Hernwall, 1999: 4).

"Humans have co-evolved with their technologies. Throughout history, there are numerous ways in which technologies have deeply shaped human psychological and social capacities, traits, and values, and as our culture, knowledge base, and values have evolved we have created ever more sophisticated technologies to serve (and even articulate and evolve) our needs and ends" (Lombardo & Blackwood, 2011: 90). According to Lombardo (2009) technologies become part of us and we live in a technologically constructed reality.

In the developed world, students who have grown up in the digital age come to our educational institutions with a variety of digital technologies at their disposal. To McPheeters (2009), "this new generation sees technology as an extension of human identity; hence, the label 'cyborg' is applied indicating a kind of hybrid of human and technology (cybernetic organism). Rather than technology being applied to human identity, technology actually becomes part of the human expression itself". For Lawson and Comber (2000: 420) "the Internet creates a 'crisis of boundaries', not just between time zones and geographical spaces, but also in a blurring of the boundaries between our sense of a 'real' and 'virtual' self and the different roles we play in the real and virtual worlds". Rather than transcending reality, the Internet reflects and imitates reality, while blurring the boundaries between the real and the virtual (Lawson & Comber, 2000: 420-421).

Friedman (2005: 62) analyzes how accelerated change is made possible in a globalized world by intersecting technological advances and web protocols (e.g., cell phones, the Internet, open source software, and others). He calls this next era to come Globalization 3.0. (also Web 3.0). However, McPheeters (2009) calls its impact on learning "Education 3.0" and we will be driven there by technology whether we prepare for it or not. "Just as we moved from Web 1.0 (static web-based documents with hardware as the intersect) to Web 2.0 (social networking with software as the intersect), we are now on a collision course with Web 3.0 where the Internet itself becomes the intersect" (McPheeters, 2009). In the same way that the World Wide Web has evolved, so must education evolve. Sternberg (2008) proposes a new model that focuses on the three Rs: reasoning (comprehensive set of thinking skills that a person needs to be an engaged, active citizen of the world), resilience (persistence in achieving goals despite the obstacles life places in our way), and responsibility (covers the ethical and moral dimension of development).

3. DIGITAL COMPETENCE FOR DIGITAL LEARNERS

A new generation of students is growing up in an age in which computers, mobile phones and the Internet are part of mainstream culture and society (Kennedy, Dalgarno, Bennett, et al., 2009). Today's students are different from the students that our schools were created to educate. Today's students are digital learners participating in a cyborg culture. They literally take in the world via the filter of computing devices: the cellular phones, handheld gaming devices, PDAs, and laptops they take everywhere, plus the computers, TVs, and game consoles at home. To Gibbons (2007), they communicate differently (e.g., text messaging and instant message), use a different written language (e.g., lol, cya, l8r), interact and socialize differently (e.g., via avatars in online games and Facebook), and have a different sense of authorship (e.g., Flickr and personal blogs).

According to McPheeters (2009), 21st century society demands new ways of learning and understanding, which in turn require new ways of teaching. The human mind is a product of biological evolution, "a highly developed form of the relation between stimulus and response on the purely biological level" (Copleston, 1966) which, like a giraffe's long neck, has been developed to allow the organism to adapt and survive in the physical world (Solymosi, 2006). Also, John Dewey places education in adapting to the environment to look at the needs and desires of the students. For this reason, it is important that students learn how to use technologies that support enlightening, ethically sound, and mentally empowering capacities (Lombardo & Blackwood, 2011: 93).

In a digital era of learning cyborgs, digital competence has become a key concept in the discussion of what kind of skills and understanding people should have. The European Parliament and the Council of the European Union (2006) identified digital competence as one of eight key competences essential for all individuals in a knowledge-based society. A variety of terms can be used to refer to this concept with slight differences in meaning:

Table 1. Terms to refer the digital competence

Denomination	Author	Year
media literacy	Aufderheide & Firestone Bawden Henry J. Kaiser Family Foundation New Media Consortium	1993 2001 2003 2005
digital literacy	Gilster Eshet Eshet-Alkalai Tornero Martin Martin & Grudziecki Buckingham Jones-Kavalier & Flannigan	1997 2002 2004 2004 2005 2006 2007 2006
computer literacy	Hawkins & Paris National Research Council	1997 1999

Denomination	Author	Year
media education	UNESCO Tornero Hague & Williamson	1999 2004 2009
information literacy	Bawden Jackman, & Jones Association of College and Research Libraries	2001 2002 2000
eLiteracy	Martin	2003
digital competence	European Parliament and the Council of the European Union Calvani, Cartelli, Fini, & Ranieri	2006 2008
ICT Literacy	International ICT Literacy Panel	2007

Note: Adapted from "Competencia digital en el siglo XXI", by Gallardo-Echenique, 2012.

As shown in Table 1, the concept of digital competence is by no means stable just yet. While some perceive it as the technical use of ICT, others define it more broadly as knowledge application or as 21st century skills. If we turn to the definition proposed by professor Antonio Calvani and colleagues, we will find some of the competences we expect cyborg culture participants to have. Calvani, Cartelli, Fini and Ranieri (2008: 186) define "digital competence" as the ability "to explore and face new technological situations in a flexible way, to analyze, select and critically evaluate data and information, to exploit technological potentials in order to represent and solve problems and build shared and collaborative knowledge, while fostering awareness of one's own personal responsibilities and the respect of reciprocal rights/obligations". Calvani et. al. (2010: 162-163) add to that, emphasizing the co-existence and integration of dimensions on both the technological, cognitive and ethical levels.

Some scholars emphasise that today's students are more familiar with ICTs than previous generations (Prensky, 2001a, 2001b; Oblinger & Oblinger, 2005; Weiler, 2005; Bullen et al., 2008) and make numerous claims about their technological capabilities. However, most academic research (Bennett, Maton & Kervin, 2008; Brown & Czerniewicz, 2010, Li & Ranieri, 2010) shows that today's students appear to have a superficial understanding of the new technologies, use them for very limited and specific purposes, and have superficial information-seeking and analysis skills. It is undeniable that a growing number of higher education students use technologies in their everyday life and many may feel incomplete if their batteries run out, for example. These learners, who take in the world via the filter of computing devices but in turn only seem have superficial information-seeking and analysis skills, are many of the students enrolled in higher education today and nothing seems to suggest that their number will shrink.

4. CYBORG CULTURE AT THE UNIVERSITY

Higher education faces the challenge of satisfying the expectations of the new generations of students who have grown up with the communication technologies. In an attempt to respond to these expectations, universities have largely used virtual learning environments, but there is evidence to suggest that such environments do not meet the instant flow of communication cyborgs are familiar with, and are more like depositories for hyperlinked lecture notes and text-based case studies (Crainer & Dearlove, 1998) than real interaction spaces where identities and rules are redefined. As cyborg culture participants, the use higher education students make of technology in their everyday life is quite different from the use they are required to make by the university. A growing number of higher education students expect to engage with dynamic systems from an experiential perspective and direct involvement, all provided by the freedom to interact with, and have control over digital semiotic resources. Continuous demand is placed on educators to update pedagogical approaches and apply them in more cost-efficient ways. Rapid changes in today's labour market require suitable approaches to lifelong education. Education should embrace and incorporate the changes that result from advancements in technology rather than simply adapt the technology to maintain the status quo (De Souza & Silva, 2006; De Oliveira et al., 2010).

Many researchers, institutions and practitioners are turning to the field of simulations and games for solutions. The attractions are obvious. The promise of immersive, personalized adaptive learning experiences that are as effective as they are engaging and that achieve the flow states offered by commercial games (Chin-Lung & Hsi-Peng, 2004) is a seductive one, especially for those eager to meet the expectations of cyborg culture participants. Gaming is a fascinating option. Simulations and games make use of a variety of techniques to bring the player to a level of engagement that can promote, through participation, a greater understanding of the subjective experience of a social system. Interactivity, control and a sense of authentic experience are important distinctive characteristics of simulation games – definitely the type of experience cyborg culture participants would welcome. Through simulation, learners are engaged in rich and challenging learning environments in which they may be confronted with real-life problem situations and the consequences of their actions. In this way, learning experiences become highly personalized, and learners stay motivated.

It goes without saying, however, that university lecturers are generally unfamiliar with this engaged motivational participative approach. With the notable exception of university business schools and the corporate training sector, in which computer-based simulations and games have met with particular success (Summers, 2004), the university sector as a whole has been forced to go it alone and develop its own solutions, with an understandable lag in the development of simulation and gaming pedagogies for other subject areas and disciplines (Lynch & Tunstall, 2007). Nonetheless, lately the current thinking that young people learn in a different way is fueling research into the educational use of digital games in eLearning (Lynch & Tunstall, 2007) and how this builds on the research evidence suggesting that simulations and educational games as valid methods of instruction.

Apparently, much of the debate surrounding the possible evolution of videogames into some kind of educational tool is founded upon the notion that they might offer the type of "serious" content/experience that is contained within traditional narrative forms such as books or film (Woods, 2004). Nevertheless, videogames offer a new medium with unique structural traits that distinguish them from other interactive and non-interactive media. It is evident they deal with issues of power, violence, mystery, deceit and death but, so it seems, videogames are not the most appropriate source one should turn to if looking for the emotional and intellectual depth which might be associated to other media forms. Neither should higher educators turn to them if they expect students to concentrate on their worksheets and not on the visual aspects of the virtual environment (Kennedy-Clark & Thompson, 2011). When games are only used for mastery of these basic skills, no qualitative value is added to what currently exists beyond cost-effective efficiency (De Souza & Silva, 2006). In fact, we still know little about how students interact with and within the cyber world, and how and what they learn when videogames are used to teach the curriculum. Yet, a growing number of educators and researchers are paying attention to games. The rapid expansion of academic interest in games has led to the emergence of a new academic discipline: Ludology. The debate over the educational potential of videogames is no longer an issue; the present discussion centres on what educators need to know so they can provide appropriate scaffolding to a more meaningful and motivating learning experience.

Many games have already been designed with educational objectives in mind (Young et al., 2012). It is not our objective to list them here, but we will mention just a few. There are entire virtual worlds, such as those using active worlds (e.g., Quest Atlantis and River City), interactive spaces where players can use avatars (e.g., Second Life and Open Sim), environments that focus on science (e.g., Physicus, Geoworld, Virtual Cell, Sneeze, World of Goo), mathematics (e.g., DimensionM, ASTRA EAGLE), languages (e.g., My Spanish Coach), or history (e.g., Civilization, Oregon Trail, Assassin's Creed). Young et al. (2012) believe that by improving the way we collectively examine video games as learning and instructional tools, the educational community will be able to craft much stronger, well-founded games that really help to improve the student experience. Many higher educators, however, have already begun to try them out, in an evident effort to offer a more attractive and meaningful learning experience to cyborg culture participants.

De Souza & Silva (2006), for example, explore the relationships between mobile technologies, location-based gaming, society, and education. In their experiment, the authors use virtual environments to create more meaningful learning experiences and develop forms of assessments that measure higher order processes. What underlies their theoretical framework is that knowledge is not simply a body of facts waiting to be acquired; rather it is constructed between individuals as they negotiate meaning, primarily through the means of discourse.

Another experiment was carried out by Krom (2012), who discussed the use of the Zynga computer game FarmVille, played in conjunction with the free social networking site Facebook, in a traditional face-to-face managerial accounting course. The aim was to reduce students' nervousness of course content, improve the class environment by promoting student friendship and develop students' confidence and social networking skills. Krom (2012) explains that in FarmVille, players ("farmers") manage crops, animals, and capital investments. Every time a farmer plows a field, there is a cost involved. The author considers that this simulation is ideal for entry-level accounting students. The players have to consider what they can afford to plant, when their crops will be ready for harvest, and the profit they will make on their investment. Besides, "farmers" can only succeed and advance in the game if they help others and are helped by others; therefore, the game encourages the kind of cooperative relationships that are highly desirable in both personal and professional situations. The research results indicate that the use of these tools seemed to be successful and a worthwhile way of investing time for faculty and students. Most students reported that the FarmVille game facilitated the active learning of course content and reinforced concepts taught in class. The non accounting majors reported the greatest benefit. It should be pointed out that the pedagogical approach underlying the educational experience reinforces active learning, and promotes problem-solving skills and the comprehension and retention of complex material.

Sometimes, however, what students learn and do while using games and simulation environments doe not coincide with what academics had in mind. For example, Kennedy-Clark & Thompson (2011) present the results of a study in which university students were asked to use game-based learning to collaboratively solve inquiry-based problems related to historical disease epidemics. The study confirmed the value of using game-based learning to support students in gaining a visual understanding of a complex environment. As found in many other studies, the virtual world was motivating, interesting and engaging for students. However, students focused on the visual cues rather than engaging and solving the problems proposed by their educators. In fact, the activities have to be really well structured so that students can benefit from the fun motivational advantages of games and simulation environments and still reach the depth of intellectual development their educators expect them to.

Nadolski et al. (2007) describe a generic toolkit they call the EMERGO methodology for developing and delivering scenario-based serious games that are designed for the acquisition of complex cognitive skills in higher education. They define scenario-based serious games as simulated task environments modeled on real-life situations that often include a sequence of learning activities and which involve complex decision making, problem-solving strategies, intelligent reasoning, and other complex cognitive skills. These games are often based on professional or academic role adoption and modelled on expert behavior. Students are left in charge to deal with complex problems in accordance with professional or scientific standards. Nadolski et al. (2007) present a series of phases that case developers should follow if educational experiences are to be a success:

- Analysis – Case developers first need to consider various issues related to the case and discuss them in order to gain greater insight, find common ground and increase awareness.
- Design – This phase needs to result in a detailed scenario document via the intermediate steps of framework scenario and ingredients scenario, each step providing more detail and completeness.
- Ingredients scenario – For each activity, case developers should identify how students are to perform.
- Framework scenario – This step describes the global activities students carry out during the game.
- Detailed scenario – In this phase, case developers should describe each activity exhaustively in terms of the tools and resources required if students are to be able to carry them out.
- Development – Data entry phase. The game is accessed by students and teachers who use interactive user guides and the detailed scenario for orientation.
- Implementation or case delivery – During this phase, students perform the activities proposed by the case developers.
- Evaluation – Case developers assess whether the case fulfills the initial demands defined during analysis.

Many academics, though eager to meet the expectations of cyborg culture participants, are not familiar with their tools and semiotic elaborations. Formal training and development activities can provide academics with the knowledge and skills to use simulations and games for teaching, despite the constraints and challenges with which they are faced. For example, training can provide technical know-how relating to gaming software (Moizer et al, 2009) and faculties can invest in training sessions on methodologies like EMERGO. Hayes and Games (2008) go one step further and exhort educators to explore the full educational potential of games for learning, which includes explicit attention to design. Their research questions why academics should continue to overlook such a rich and valuable aspect of game-based learning. They invite educators to start by becoming more familiar with design theories and game design in particular.

Games and virtual environments can provide enhanced visualizations and multiple perspectives. They can also bring together large groups of students for a collaborative experience, which may be difficult to replicate in a normal classroom environment but which can lead to learners being more psychologically present (Shaffer & Gee, 2012).

5. CONCLUDING REMARK

The concept of the cyborg is used here as a useful metaphor for referring to students who live in an environment in which technology has become natural and is ordinarily used to extend senses, capabilities and possibilities. As well as feeling like cyborgs, students must be digitally literate: that is, they must have the required skills to benefit from and participate in the knowledge society. This includes the ability to use both new ICT tools and media literacy skills to critically and respectfully handle the flood of images, text and audiovisual content that constantly pour across the global networks. Higher education institutions must take into account these needs of the twentieth century students, and restructure themselves to become a modern forum in which learners can acquire the basic command of specific languages (textual, iconic, visual, graphic and sound) and also learn to apply knowledge of different types to different situations and contexts.

REFERENCES

Amber Case's official site. http://caseorganic.com/

Bennett, S., Maton, K. & Kervin, L. (2008). The 'digital natives' debate: a critical review of the evidence. *British Journal of Educational Technology, 39* (5), 775–786. doi:10.1111/j.1467-8535.2007.00793.x

Brown, C., & Czerniewicz, L. (2010). Debunking the "digital native": beyond digital apartheid, towards digital democracy. *Journal of Computer Assisted Learning, 26*(5), 357-369. doi:10.1111/j.1365-2729.2010.00369.x

Bullen, M., Morgan, T., Belfer, K. & Qayyum, A. (2008). The digital learner at BCIT and implications for an e-strategy. *Proceedings of the 2008 Research workshop of the European distance education network (EDEN) "Researching and promoting access to education and training: The role of distance education and e-learning in technology-enhanced environments"*, Paris, France, October 20-22.

Calvani, A., Cartelli, A., Fini, A., Ranieri, M. (2008). Models and Instruments for assessing Digital Competence at School. *Journal of E-Learning and Knowledge Society, 4, 3.*

Calvani, A., Cartelli, A., Fini, A., Ranieri, M. (2010). Digital Competence In K-12. Theoretical Models, Assessment Tools and Empirical Research. *Analisi: Quaderns de Comunicació i Cultura*, 40, 157-171.

Carr, N. (2010). The Shallows: What the Internet is Doing to Our Brains. New York: W. W. Norton.

Case, A. (2012). Cyborg Anthropology and the Evaporation of the Interface. Talk presented at *Frontiers of Interaction*, Rome, Italy: June 7-8. Retrieved November 23, 2012 from http://frontiersofinteraction.com/amber-case/

Case, A. (2010). We are all cyborgs now. Talk presented at *TED on technology and humans*. Retrieved November 23, 2012 from http://www.ted.com/talks/amber_case_we_are_all_cyborgs_now.html

Chin-Lung, H., & Hsi-Peng, L. (2004). Why do people play on-line games? An extended TAM with social influences and flow experience. *Information & Management*, *41*(7), 853-868. Crainer, S., & Dearlove, D. (1998). *Gravy training*. Oxford, UK: Capstone.

Clark, A. (2003), Natural-Born Cyborgs: Minds, Technologies, and the Future of Human Intelligence, Oxford University Press, Oxford.

Copleston, F. (1966). A History of Philosophy. (Vol. 8, Book 3). Garden City, NY: Doubleday Image Books.

De Oliveira, J. M.; Gallardo-Echenique, E.; Cruz, O.; Geliz, F. Games, gaming and education (2010). *The New Educational Review*, *22* (3-4), 129-143.

De Souza e Silva, A. (2006). Hybrid Reality Games Reframed: Potential Uses in Educational Contexts. *Games and Culture, 1*(3), 231–251. doi:10.1177/1555412006290443

Dewey, J. (2002). The educational situation. *Journal of Curriculum & Supervision, 17*(2), 104–118.

European Parliament and the Council of the European Union (2006, December 30). Recommendation of the European Parliament and of the Council of 18 December 2006 on key competences for lifelong learning. *Official Journal of the European Union*, L394, 10-18.

Friedman, T. L. (2005). The world is flat: A brief history of the twenty-first century. New York: Farrar, Straus and Giroux.

Gallardo-Echenique, E. (2012). Competencia digital en el siglo XXI. Paper presented at *II Congreso Internacional de Educación Superior: La formación por competencias,* Chiapas, México.

Garoian, C. R. & Gaudelius, Y. M. (2001). Cyborg pedagogy: Performing resistance in the digital age. *Studies in Art Education: A Journal of Issues and Research in Art Education, 42*(4), 333-347.

Gibbons, S. (2007) Redefining the roles of information professionals in higher education to engage the net generation. Paper presented at EDUCAUSE, Australasia. Retrieved November 8, 2012 from http://www.caudit.edu.au/educauseaustralasia07/authors_papers/Gibbons2.pdf

Haraway, D. J. (1991a). Simians, Cyborgs, and Women: The Reinvention of Nature. London: Free Association Press.

Haraway, D. J. (1991b). A Cyborg Manifesto: Science, Technology, and Socialist-Feminism in the late *20th century, in Simians, Cyborgs and Women: The Reinvention of Nature.*

Hayes, E. R., & Games, I. a. (2008). Making Computer Games and Design Thinking: A Review of Current Software and Strategies. Games and Culture, 3(3-4), 309–332. doi:10.1177/1555412008317312

Hernwall. P. (1999). Children, Cyborgs, and Cyberspace - Computer Communication in the World of Children. Stockholm University, Department of Education. Retrieved November 28, 2012 from http://inb.ans.hive.no/Documents/Patrik%20Hernwall%20Children%20cyborg.pdf

Hernwall. P. (2000). The creation of the cyborg citizen - children, cyberspace and 21st century challenges. Oslo University, Institution for Communication, Technique and Design. Retrieved November 28, 2012 from http://www.nada.kth.se/kurser/kth/2D1624/PDF/Litteratur/CyborgCitizen_Hernwall.pdf

Johnson, D. (2008). Machines are the easy part; people are the hard part: Observations about making technology work in schools. Cleveland MN: Blue Skunk Press.

Kennedy, G.E., Krause, K.-L., Judd, T.S., Churchward, A. & Gray, K. (2008) First year students' experiences with technology: are they really digital natives? *Australasian Journal of Educational Technology, 24*(1), 108–122.

Kennedy-Clark, S., & Thompson, K. (2011). What Do Students Learn When Collaboratively Using A Computer Game in the Study of Historical Disease Epidemics, and Why? Games and Culture, 6(6), 513–537. doi:10.1177/1555412011431361

Krom, C. L. (2012). Using FarmVille in an Introductory Managerial Accounting Course to Engage Students, Enhance Comprehension, and Develop Social Networking Skills. Journal of Management Education, 36(6), 848–865. doi:10.1177/1052562912459029

Lawson, T. & Comber, C. (2000). Introducing information and communication technologies into schools: The blurring of boundaries. *British Journal of Sociology of Education, 21*(3), 419-433.

Li, Y. & Ranieri, M. (2010). Are 'digital natives' really digitally competent? A study on Chinese teenagers. *British Journal of Educational Technology*, 41(6). doi:10.1111/j.1467-8535.2009.01053.x

Lombardo, T. (2007). Wisdom and the Second Enlightenment. In World Futures Study Federation, *Futures Bulletin, 32* (3).

Lombardo, T. & Blackwood, R.T. (2011). Educating the Wise Cyborg of the Future. *On the Horizon, 19*(2), 85 – 96. doi: 10.1108/10748121111138281

Lynch, M. A. & Tunstall, R. J. (2007). When worlds collide: Developing game-design partnerships in universities. Simulation & Gaming, 39(3), 379–398. doi:10.1177/1046878108319275

McPheeters, D. (2009). Cyborg Learning Theory: Technology in Education and the Blurring of Boundaries. In T. Bastiaens et al. (Eds.), *Proceedings of World Conference on E-Learning in Corporate, Government, Healthcare, and Higher Education 2009* (pp. 2937-2942). Chesapeake, VA: AACE.

Moizer, J., Lean, J., Towler, M., & Abbey, C. (2009). Simulations and games: Overcoming the barriers to their use in higher education. *Active Learning in Higher Education, 10*(3), 207–224. doi:10.1177/1469787409343188

Nadolski, R. J., Hummel, H. G. K., van den Brink, H. J., Hoefakker, R. E., Slootmaker, A., Kurvers, H. J., & Storm, J. (2007). EMERGO: A methodology and toolkit for developing serious games in higher education. *Simulation & Gaming, 39*(3), 338–352. doi:10.1177/1046878108319278

Neil Harbisson: Cyborgist and Colourologist. http://eyeborg.wix.com/neil-harbisson

Prensky, M. (2001a). Digital natives, digital immigrants, Part 1. *On the Horizon, 9*(5), 1–6. doi:10.1108/10748120110424816

Prensky, M. (2001b). Digital natives, digital immigrants, Part II: Do they really *think* differently? On the Horizon, 9(6), 1-9.

Ramírez, M. (2011). Responsabilidad en la educación de Cyborgs. XII Congreso Internacional De teoría de la Educación. Barcelona.

Shaffer, D. W., & Gee, J. P. (2012). The right kind of GATE: Computer games and the future of assessment. In M. Mayrath, D. Robinson, & J. Clarke-Midura (Eds.), Technology-based assessments for 21st century skills: Theoretical and practical implications from modern research. Charlotte, NC: Information Age.

Solymosi, T. (2006). Darwin's Dangerous Descendants: The Evolutionary Philosophies of Mind of John Dewey and Daniel C. Dennett. Unpublished master's thesis for master's degree, Southern Illinois University at Carbondale.

Sternberg, R. J. (2008). Excellence for All. *Educational Leadership, 66*(2), 14-19.

Summers, G. (2004) Today's business simulation industry. *Simulation & Gaming, 35*, 208-241.

Weiler, A. (2005) Information-seeking behavior in generation-Y students: motivation, critical thinking and learning theory. *The Journal of Academic Librarianship,* 31, 46–53. doi: 10.1016/j.acalib.2004.09.009

Wiener, N. (1954). Cybernetics in History. In *The human use of human beings: Cybernetics and society,* 15-27. Boston: Houghton Mifflin

Woods, S. (2004). Loading the Dice: The Challenge of Serious Videogames. *Game studies: the international journal of computer game research, 4*(1). Retrieved November 27, 2012 from http://www.gamestudies.org/0401/woods/

Young, M. F., Slota, S., Cutter, A. B., Jalette, G., Mullin, G., Lai, B., Simeoni, Z., et al. (2012). Our Princess Is in Another Castle: A Review of Trends in Serious Gaming for Education. *Review of Educational Research, 82*(1), 61–89. doi:10.3102/0034654312436980

AUTHOR

Janaina Minelli de Oliveira. *Department of Pedagogy. Rovira i Virgili University. Tarragona, Spain.*

Eliana Gallardo-Echenique. *Department of Pedagogy. Rovira i Virgili University. Tarragona, Spain.*

Annachiara Del Prete. *Department of Pedagogy. Rovira i Virgili University. Tarragona, Spain.*

Jens Siemon

2.3

LESSONS LEARNED ON SIMULATION-BASED LEARNING

1. THEORY OF LEARNING IN A SANDBOX

Simulations are reproductions of a sufficient number of components of real world process-es, systems, machines or creatures to achieve a specific goal. They make it possible to have experiences with the simulated object. The objective of using simulations is to predict or under-stand the behavior of a real world object by interacting with the simulated object.

Because it provides designed, controlled and risk-free experiences, simulation is a power-ful tool for supporting learning processes. There are several educational arguments in favor of using simulations in educational settings.

According to psychological and educational theories, learning is understood to be an ac-tive, self-regulated, constructive, situated and social process. To construct a learning activity, a real or artificial context needs to be created (a) that triggers a need for action, (b) in which the action takes place and (c) where the result of the action can be observed and reflected. In comparison to traditional learning situations, learning by doing or on the job training, artificially constructed contexts provide the opportunity to control and increase the density of learning opportunities.

As they become more mature, people want to become more self-directed, even in situa-tions of acquiring and practicing new knowledge and competencies. Simulations provide an opportunity to interact independently in problem-centered situations that are meaningful to learners' daily lives. Learners can immediately apply what they have learned and evaluate the outcomes (Knowles, 1975).

Learning is commonly understood as a constructive process that is organized in phases. The experiential learning approach includes the phases of planning for action, carrying out the action, reflecting on the action and creating a theory based on this reflection (Gibbs, 1988). Simulations can be used to directly support the first three phases and to evaluate the learner's theory.

From the perspective of situated cognition, the process of learning is an interaction be-tween internal person-related factors and external, situational components. Knowledge can-not be separated from the process of learning and the situation in which it is constructed

(Vosniadou, 1994). Knowledge can only be transferred if situations are sufficiently similar or if the activity can be adapted to the new situation (Greeno, Smith and Moore, 1993).

Finally, Lave and Wenger (1991) point out that learning always takes place by participating in communities of practice, in which knowledge and skills are socially negotiated.

Considering this theoretical fundament, it is clear that simulations are an efficient tool for solving problems that occur in the reality of everyday vocational education. In a variety of different projects, the author has made several experiments in the application of simulations to achieve educational goals. The sections below provide the main findings and lessons learned.

2. THREE STUDIES APPLYING SIMULATION-BASED LEARNING IN VOCATIONAL EDUCATION

First study: simulation-based learning and prior knowledge

We have often discussed with teachers in vocational schools whether it is possible to initiate a learning cycle (figure 1) with no prior vocational knowledge.

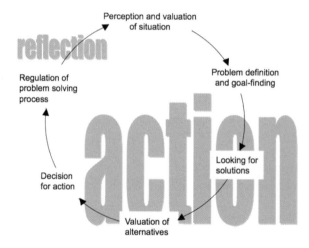

Figure 1. Learning cycle

To address this question, we developed a simulation for problem-based action in a multimedia represented enterprise (Siemon, 2001). The project was funded by the German Research Association. The sample contained 40 German apprentices in their first week of vocational training to become industrial clerks. Their task was to solve various problems presented by video. The apprentices were asked to solve the problems with no prior knowledge and no external guidance. The learning environment offered both useful and useless information. A solution could only be found by combining some central pieces of information.

We measured prior and subsequent knowledge by using a specific method of transferring verbally expressed texts into semantic networks. We found that every participant was able to solve the problem without having received any instruction prior to the task. However, the time needed to solve the problem varied considerably across the sample. This variation can only partially be explained by differences in prior knowledge. As expected, it was found that all participants increased their knowledge and drew closer to predefined expert knowledge (Siemon, 2003).

Generally it seemed that the perception that prior knowledge is required for problem solving is wrong. Every human of school age and particularly at the beginning of vocational training, has some kind of prior knowledge. The question that needs to be answered as far as future work is concerned is whether that knowledge is sufficient for generating a plan that can potentially lead to a solution and how much initial instruction is needed to activate prior knowledge.

Second study: embedding simulation-based learning in classroom settings

The problem of prior knowledge was also obvious in the next project entitled VIRTOOL – Virtual manipulation to simulate machine tool processes. It was financed by the fifth framework programme of the European Community for research, technological development and demonstration activities. The initial idea was to construct virtual reality machine tools to facilitate industrial training processes. After some initial analysis it became clear that not the practical training has to be facilitated. Teachers often struggled to transfer classroom knowledge into practical workplace action. Even if the theoretical and practical knowledge were on the same topic, they seemed to be totally disconnected (Siemon, Klockmann and Musiat, 2003).

We developed a curriculum that included transfer-lessons between mainly theoretical classroom lessons and mainly practical workshop training. These transfer-lessons used 3D-simulations of real machines found in the workshop of the participating schools (see figure 2).

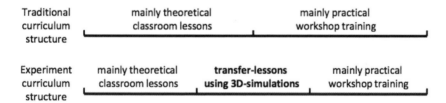

Figure 2. Curriculum structures with and without simulation

The research question was whether the gap between theory and practice could be bridged by the instructional use of 3D-simulations. We also tried to analyze whether special support for reflecting on errors is useful (Siemon, Muñoz and Berasategi, 2002; Siemon, Klockmann, Muñoz and Berasategi, 2003).

Because of specific limitations on time and other things it was only possible to give a qualitative answer to the first question. It became clear that theoretical knowledge can be applied better if students can act and experience its benefits in a risk-free environment. Because of several industrial safety limitations, the workshop itself is not always the best place for the educational transfer of theoretical knowledge. Simulations can fill this gap. As far as the second question is concerned, the results found in the schools in Spain and France were different. While in Spain the instructional reflection on errors seemed to have a positive influence on learning outcomes, we did not find the same effect in our French survey (Siemon at., 2003).

Third study: effects of simulation-based learning

Usually teachers tend to teach an entire topic before students get the opportunity to have any experience of their own. Unfortunately most simulations are not broad enough to support self-directed learning over longer periods. Consequently, the idea of the following project was to construct a dynamic and continuous (24/7) simulation with enough space for hundreds of players and educational problems that would motivate long-lasting self-directed learning processes.

This idea was put into practice by developing a business game situated in the logistics market and financed by Hamburg Authorities and companies from the Hamburg metropolitan region. The so called logistics: challenge situates learners in a job-market where they can start as store managers. Along an individual career track the players/learners gradually become more and more experienced, and finally they are able to direct the company (Siemon and Wirth, 2008).

The initial research aim was to determine which competencies are dealt with by that kind of self-directed learning process. We also wanted to know whether these competencies developed differently compared with traditional high quality vocational instruction. Consequently a research project was designed on the basis of a two group pre-post survey.

We found that the experimental group (using the simulation) had clear and significant advantages as far as their knowledge of structures and strategies was concerned. Surprisingly their declarative knowledge was also significantly better. No differences were found in knowledge of processes. An interesting gender difference was observed. In the experimental group, the declarative knowledge of the female participants developed much more than that of their male counterparts while the strategic thinking skills of the male participants were significantly better than those of the females (see figure 3).

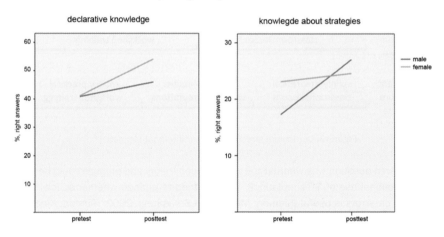

Figure 3. Gender differences in learning outcomes

Because we observed that reflection was of considerable importance during and after learning with simulations, a PhD project is currently analyzing different strategies of debriefing implemented in the learning process using the logistics:challenge simulation.

3. CONCLUSIONS

- According to psychological and educational theories, learning is understood as an active, self regulated, constructive, situated and social process. Simulations are appropriate (even the best) learning tools to support this kind of learning process.

- One of the main factors on the successful use of simulations depends is the instructional design in which simulations are embedded.
- Simulations are particularly useful for supporting self directed learning processes.
- Our empirical studies show that instructional design patterns, prior knowledge and gender have positive effects on learning outcomes.
- Further studies are necessary if our knowledge on simulations as a learning tool is to be extended.

REFERENCES

Gibbs, G. (1988). Learning by doing: A Guide to Teaching and Learning methods. London: Further Education Unit.

Greeno, J. G., Smith, D. R. & Moore, J. L. (1993). Transfer of situated learning. In D. K. Dettermann & R. J. Sternberg (Hrsg.), Transfer on trial: Intelligence, cognition, and instruction (S. 99-167). Norwood, NJ: Ablex.

Knowles, M. S. (1975). Self-directed learning: a guide for learners and teachers. Englewood Cliffs, NJ: Cambridge Adult Education.

Lave, J. & Wenger, E. (1991). Situated learning. Legitimate peripheral participation. Cambridge: Cambridge University Press.

Siemon, J. & Wirth, K. (2008). Kompetenzen in der Logistik spielend entwickeln. Wirtschaft und Erziehung, 60 (9), 274-279.

Siemon, J. (2001). Modellunternehmen A & S GmbH. Virtuelle Betriebserkundung. Troisdorf: Bildungsverlag eins.

Siemon, J. (2003). Evaluation eines komplexen Lehr-Lern-Arrangements –Eine netzwerk– und inhaltsanalytische Studie am Beispiel der Einführung in ein Modellunternehmen. Wiesbaden: DUV.

Siemon, J., Klockmann, D. & Musiat, J. (2003). VIRTOOL –Evaluation Report. Universität Hamburg. Institut Berufs– und Wirtschaftspädagogik.

Siemon, J., Klockmann, D., Muñoz, L. M. & Berasategi, M. I. (2003). A Failure Is The Origin Of A Success – Or How To Employ Errors For Effective Learning In Vocational Education. In D. Lassner & C. McNaught (Hrsg.), Proceedings of ED-MEDIA 2003, World Conference on Educational Multimedia, Hypermedia & Telecomunication, June 23-28, 2003 (S. 924-927). Honolulu, Hawaii, USA: Association for the Advancement of Computing in Education (AACE).

Siemon, J., Muñoz, L. M. & Berasategi, M. I. (2002). VIRTOOL- a VR-based Learning Environment for the Vocational Training in Machine-Tool Processes. In N. Callaos, A. Breda & M. Y. Fernandez (Hrsg.), The 6th World Multiconference on Systemics, Cybernetics and Informatics Proceedings - Concepts and Applications of Systemics, Cybernetics and Informatics ((Vol. II, S. 267-270). Orlando, Florida: International Institute of Informatics and Systematics (IIIS).

Vosniadou, S. (1994). From cognitive theory to educational technology. In S. Vosniadou, E. D. Corte & H. Mandl (Hrsg.), Technology-based learning environments. Psychological and educational foundations (S. 11-18). Berlin: Springer.

AUTHOR

Jens Siemon, University of Hamburg.

Virginia Larraz

Francesc Esteve

2.4
EVALUATING DIGITAL COMPETENCE IN SIMULATION ENVIRONMENTS

1. DIGITAL COMPETENCE

Universities nowadays are facing new challenges largely as a result of two contextual factors: the knowledge society and the European Area of Higher Education. One of these challenges is to update the so-called traditional model of education and to implement a new model adapted to the new times and focusing on transparency and student learning.

According to Uceda (2011), this new model has eight characteristics, among which are the following: (1) focus on the ability to solve complex problems and multidisciplinary orientation, (2) generalised use of ICT, (3) student centred, (4) learning centred, and (5) the development of general competences in a structured way.

The digital competence is a part of this new educational model because of its inherent characteristics: it is multidisciplinary in the sense that it integrates cognitive, relational and social abilities from different disciplines; it is sensitive to the sociocultural context; and it is technological because it is involved in the use of technologies and production by means of technologies.

Digital competence is regarded as a key competence for lifelong learning. The European Parliament and Council define the competence as involving the confident and critical use of Information Society Technology (IST) for work, leisure and communication. It is underpinned by basic skills in ICT: the use of computers to retrieve, assess, store, produce, present and exchange information, and to communicate and participate in collaborative networks via the Internet (European Commission, 2006).

One of the first definitions of digital competence was put forward by Paul Gilster in 1997. He defined it as the ability to understand and use information in numerous formats from a wide variety of sources when it is presented through computers (Lankshear and Knobel, 2008). From this point on many authors and institutions have provided their own definitions, creating a terminological chaos caused by the number of terms and concepts used (Pasadas, 2010). The fact that the first definitions are often in English, and these are then translated into other languages with varying degrees of success, has also contributed to this chaos (Ferreiro, 2011).

It is for this reason that we believed it was necessary to draw up a definition of digital competence to act as a reference framework in our research. After a descriptive, comparative and statistical analysis of regulations, standards and models, we arrived at the following definition of digital competence (Larraz, Espuny & Gisbert, 2011):

Digital competence makes it possible to cope with the problems raised by the knowledge society from all areas of our learning ecosystem (personal, professional and social).

Digital competence is multidimensional and involves the integration of cognitive, relational and social abilities that we have grouped in four literacies:

- *Informational literacy: management of digital information.*
- *Technological literacy: treatment of data in various formats.*
- *Multimedia literacy: analysis and creation of multimedia messages.*
- *Communicative literacy: participation, public spirit and digital identity.*

On the basis of this definition, we shall determine the criteria that should guide how digital competence is evaluated.

2. THE EVALUATION OF DIGITAL COMPETENCE

As an intrinsic part of the teaching-learning process, evaluation requires a systematic procedure of data collection and proof of the level of acquisition of the student. On the basis of the data collected, teachers will be in a position to be able to take decisions on the accreditation of the planned level of competence.

Above all, the evaluation of competences should be based on the genesis of the competence itself. With this in mind we consider Perrenoud's definition of competence (2004:11): a competence is the ability to mobilise various cognitive processes to cope with situations. Within this framework, five aspects can be established that must be taken into account when evaluating competences:

1. Competences mobilise and integrate knowledge, abilities and attitudes, which must be worked on and evaluated in an integrated fashion.
2. Competence is complex and, therefore, needs to be made concrete in identifiable and tangible product, which can be used as a reference to demonstrate that it has been acquired (Martínez & Echeverría, 2009: 144). These products are known as the learning outcome and it can be described gradually by means of the indicators that show the extent to which the competence has been acquired.
3. Mobilisation is only relevant in one particular situation, so learning situations must be designed that represent approximations to reality.
4. Learning situations must allow for and require the following four mechanisms (adapted from Zabala, 2008: 46-47): (1) an analysis of the complexity of the situation, (2) a review of the most appropriate action plans learned, (3) selection of the most appropriate action plan, and (4) action: that is to say, adapting the plan to reality and putting it into practice in a flexible fashion.
5. Evaluation requires information to be collected using instruments that must be varied, complex and, above all, aligned to purpose (Biggs, 2005:45).

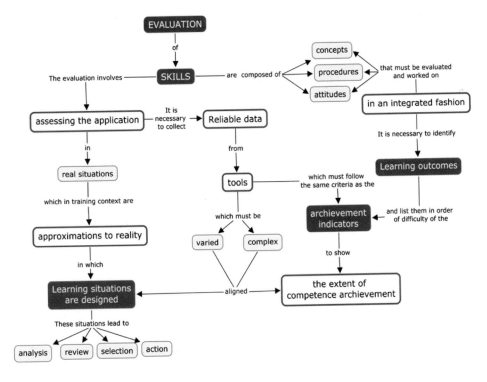

Figure 1. The evaluation of competences

Evaluation strategies and instruments must, then, be correctly chosen to ensure that data are collected and guarantee the acquisition of the set learning outcomes.

2.1 A variety of tools

In recent years a wide variety of tools have been designed for evaluating digital competence or some of its components. In the framework of the project Digital Competence: Identification and European-wide validation of its components for all levels of learners, Ala-Mutka (2011:36) states that three main types of tool are used to evaluate digital competence: (1) questionnaires, which are used to collect data from the users themselves about use, knowledge, perception, opinion and self evaluation, (2) analysis of digital tasks to measure performance and behaviour while carrying out the tasks, and (3) collection of secondary data, which is used to collect information about the availability and uses of digital tools, analysis of national policy documents, funding principles, details of curricula, etc.

Several authors (Prades, 2005; Van Deursen, 2010 and Ala-Mutka, 2011) have already spoken of the difficulties involved in the two types of tool that are most appropriate for our research into evaluating the digital competence of university students: questionnaires and drawing up digital tasks that enable competences to be evaluated through observation.

To understand which tools are most commonly used to accredit digital competence or some of its components, we analysed three studies on this issue:

- The first study, by Esteve et al (2011), analysed five instruments (INCOTIC-GRAU[1], iDCA[2], ICDL[3], PISA[4], ISkills[5]) using five indicators: author or institution, type of instrument, educational level for which the instrument is designed, evaluation strategy, elements evaluated and main literacies evaluated. The main conclusion drawn by this study is that the types and features of the instruments are quite varied. Some of them are simply on-line questionnaires, while others also include simple web or desk-top simulations that require respondents to carry out some sort of activity. These instruments often put greater emphasis on the technological and informational aspects of the literacies than on the multimedia or communicative aspects.

- The second study, by Larraz et al. (2012) analysed 22 instruments (to the five analysed in the study mentioned above it added ACTIC,[6] BEBRAS,[7] C2I,[8] CABRINI,[9] COBADI,[10] ECDL,[11] ISKILLS,[12] IC3, iDCA, INCOTIC-GRAU, ICPE,[13] ILAS,[14] ILS,[15] ILT,[16] ILTo,[17] ISST,[18] IEAd,[19] OFCOM,[20] SAILS[21] and VAN[22]). This study uses the five indicators designed by Esteve et al. and adds four more: availability, standards, types of question and times. The main conclusions of the study are that the tools do not respond to the needs for accrediting digital competence since they do not measure in the same way all the components of digital competence (informational literacy, technological literacy, multimedia literacy and communicative literacy) and neither do they work on them simultaneously.

- The third study, by Ferrari (2012), analysed 15 digital competence frameworks, of which 9 incorporate criteria or tools for the evaluation of digital competence (ACTIC, BECTA,[23] CML,[24] DCA, ECDL, IC3, ISKILLS, NCCA[25] and ILPScotland[26]). The main conclusion of

1. http://redalyc.uaemex.mx/redalyc/src/inicio/ArtPdfRed.jsp?iCve=56717469006
2. http://www.digitalcompetence.org
3. http://www.icdlus.org
4. http://www.oecd.org/document/57/0,3746,en_32252351_46584327_48265529_1_1_1_1,00.html
5. http://www.ets.org/iskills/
6. http://www20.gencat.cat/portal/site/actic
7. http://www.bebras.org
8. https://www2.c2i.education.fr/
9. http://www.cabrini.edu/Library/literacypretest/
10. https://spreadsheets0.google.com/viewform?formkey=dGhDX2RYeGRaTW9PZnBObk5jdUxVUGc6MQ
11. http://www.ecdl.org
12. http://www.ets.org/iskills/
13. http://www.topsy.org/ICAP/TestSpecs.pdf
14. http://web1.desales.edu/assets/desales/library/survey3.htm
15. http://informationr.net/ir/15-3/paper436.html
16. http://www.madisonassessment.com/
17. http://www.nilrc.org/IMLS/assessment_instrument.asp
18. http://www.jmu.edu/gened/info_lit_general.shtml
19. http://edutec.rediris.es/Revelec2/Revelec35/pdf/Edutec-e_n35_Carrera_Vaquero_Balsells.pdf
20. http://stakeholders.ofcom.org.uk/binaries/research/media-literacy/media-lit-2010/adult_questionnaire.pdf
21. http://projectsails.org/
22. http://www.alexandervandeursen.nl/serendipity5/uploads/pubs/Dissertation_VanDeursen.pdf
23. http://www.timmuslimited.co.uk/
24. http://www.medialit.org/cml-framework
25. http://www.ncca.ie/uploadedfiles/publications/ict%20revised%20framework.pdf
26. http://caledonianblogs.net/nilfs/

this study as far as evaluation tools are concerned is that most of them are designed to accredit the use of particular computer tools. And there are very few tools designed to develop digital competence, critical capacity, thinking skills and cognitive approaches at a level that is more advanced than the simple use of a particular technology.

The review of the three studies enabled us to establish the criteria and requisites that an instrument designed to evaluate digital competence must comply with. They are the following:

1. The instrument must allow complex learning situations to be designed so that:
   a. The three components of any competence −knowledge, procedures and attitudes − can be evaluated.
   b. The four components of digital competence −informational literacy, technological literacy, multimedia literacy and communicative literacy− can be evaluated in an integrated fashion.
   c. The performance of a particular student in the processes of analysis, review, selection and execution of the activity can be evaluated.
   d. Individual and collective processes can be evaluated.
2. The instrument must be sufficiently flexible to:
   a. Create various situations in which digital competence can be developed.
   b. Adapt the context in such a way that it is meaningful for students on different degree courses.
   c. Allow students to take different routes to achieve the final objective.
   d. Allow different final results.
3. The instrument must collect reliable data that can be compared and contrasted with the acquisition indicators.
4. The instrument must make it possible to design learning situations.

On the basis of the above analysis of the existing instruments for evaluating and accrediting digital competence, of their potential and shortcomings, and of the criteria and requirements that an instrument must have if it is to correctly evaluate the acquisition of the competence in accordance with the complexity of our definition, we now go on to examine a set of technological 3D simulation environments that can respond to this situation.

3. 3D SIMULATION ENVIRONMENTS FOR EVALUATING DIGITAL COMPETENCE

3D simulation environments such as Second Life or OpenSimulator are on-line communities that simulate physical spaces in three dimensions. They may be real or not and they enable users to interact with one another through their avatars, and use, create and exchange objects. Atkins (2009) points out the following features of these environments: (1) they are environments that involve immersion, since they give the sensation of being present in a simulated environment, (2) they are interactive and users can communicate in writing or orally, in real time, and also listen to multimedia items by streaming, (3) they can be personalised by users, who can add or construct new features, scenarios or objects by themselves or in a group, (4) they are readily accessible because the tools are free and open, and(5) they can be programmed; they are not games that have a particular set of instructions but allow users to establish their own rules and schedule their own objectives.

The simulations that can be carried out with this type of 3D environment are activities that facilitate learning, and create effective learning environments not only because they can be fun but because they require the user to take frequent decisions, relate to others, make searches, solve problems and transfer knowledge (Oblinger, 2006). Simulations are a highly valuable methodology for learning general competences because they resemble working environments (Gisbert, Cela & Isus, 2010). Below we list seven reasons that justify the use of these 3D simulation environments for evaluating competences and, in particular, digital competence:

1. Competences are shown to have been acquired by action and simulators enable situations to be designed in which users take on an active role with which they solve the problems raised.

2. Competences need to mobilise cognitive resources and simulators present situations that must be managed by the user.

3. If competences are to be developed and evaluated, learning must be contextualised and simulations represent real and fictitious situations that lead to experimental learning by discovery.

4. Competences are shown to have been acquired in a variety of situations by transferring learning to particular situations. Simulators enable learning to be transferred from the virtual world to the real one (with the added advantage that situations that are not viable or too costly in the real world can be represented in the virtual world).

5. The acquisition of competences is an individual process and simulators require individual tasks to be executed.

6. Competences enable citizens to be able to take effective part in the political, social and cultural life of society, and simulators make it possible to design cooperative learning situations.

7. Any learning, competences included, is speeded up by motivation. Simulators are a game that challenges and motivates students.

In conclusion, these 3D simulation environments provide new educational possibilities for learning, experimentation and even evaluation. They enable not only knowledge but also skills and attitudes to be evaluated simultaneously, and in accordance with the complexity of the multiple literacies involved in digital competence, which we defined above. At present, there are some experiences that are beginning to examine these possibilities (for example, the SIMUL@ project, which is described in some chapters of this book. Undoubtedly, it will be interesting to continue exploring the potential of these tools.

REFERENCES

Ala-Mutka, K., (2011). Mapping Digital Competence: Towards a Conceptual Understanding, IPTS-JRC 67075, European Commission, Luxembourg.

European Commission (2006). Recomendación del Parlamento Europeo y del Consejo sobre las competencias clave para el aprendizaje permanente. (2006/962/CE). Brussel·les: European Commission. http://eur-lex.europa.eu/LexUriServ/LexUriServ.do?uri=OJ:L:2006:394:0010:0018:ES:PDF (Last accessed 16/04/2009).

Ferrari, A., (2012). Digital Competence in practice: An analysis of frameworks. JRC 25351, European Commission, Luxemburg.

Ferreiro, E. (2011). Alfabetización digital ¿De qué estamos hablando?. Educação e Pesquisa, São Paulo, 37, 2, 423-438.

Gisbert, M., Cela, J. & Isus, S.: (2010). "Las simulaciones en entornos TIC como herramienta para la formación en competencias transversales de los estudiantes universitarios". In De Pablos Pons, J. (Coord.) *Buenas prácticas de enseñanza con TIC* [on-line essay]. Revista Electrónica Teoría de la Educación: Educación y Cultura en la Sociedad de la Información, 11, 1. 352-370. [Last accessed: 15/09/2011].
http://revistatesi.usal.es/~revistas_trabajo/index.php/revistatesi/article/view/6309/6322 I

Lankshear C. and Knobel, M., (2008). Nuevos alfabetismos su práctica cotidiana y el aprendizaje en el aula. Madrid: Morata.

• Larraz, V., Espuny, C. & Gisbert, M. (2011). *Los componentes de la competència digital.* I Congreso Comunicación y Educación: Estrategias de Alfabetización Mediática, Barcelona, 11-13 May 2011.

Larraz, V., Espuny, C., Gisbert, M. and Saz, A. (2012). Las herramientas para la evaluación de la competencia digita. Análisis y componentes. Congreso EDUTEC: "Canarias en tres continentes digitales: educación, TIC, NET-Coaching. Las Palmas de Gran Canaria, 14-16 November 2012.

Martínez, P. & Echeverría, B. (2009). Formación basada en competencias. *Revista de Investigación Educativa, 27, (1), 125-147.*

Oblinger, D. (2006). Simulations, games, and learning. Educas Learning Initiative *White Paper* (May), [Last accessed: 15/09/2011]. http://mobilelearningcourse.pbworks.com/f/Games+and+Learning+ELI3004

Pasadas, C. (2010). Multialfabetización, aprendizaje a lo largo de la vida y bibliotecas. *Boletín de la Asociación Andaluza de Bibliotecarios,* n° 98-99, pp. 11-38

Prades, A. (2005). Les competències transverals i la formació universitària. Doctoral thesis, University of Barcelona.

Perrenoud, P. (2004). *Diez nuevas competencias para enseñar.* Barcelona: Graó.

Uceda, J. (2011). Un nuevo modelo educativo. In Michavila, F., Ripollés, M., Esteve, F. *El día después de Bolonia.* Madrid: Tecnos.

Van Deursen, A. (2010). *Internet Skills. Vital assets in an information society.* Enschede, the Netherlands: University of Twente

Zabala (2008) Cómo aprender y enseñar competencias. Barcelona: Ed. Graó

AUTHORS

Virginia Larraz, *University of Andorra.*

Francesc M. Esteve Mon, *Department of Pedagogy. Rovira i Virgili University. Tarragona, Spain.*

CHAPTER 3:

3D VIRTUAL ENVIRONMENTS IN EDUCATION

Mar Camacho

Vanessa Esteve-González

3.1
MOVING BEYOND LEARNING: THE POTENTIAL
OF IMMERSIVE ENVIRONMENTS IN EDUCATION

1. BACKGROUND

At a time when our educational system is constantly questioned for being disconnected from the real world, authentic experiences that can lead students to real academic achievement are becoming increasingly necessary. The affordances of virtual worlds as tools that connect students to the real world through technology are manyfold and go beyond authentic learning. Virtual worlds not only make it possible for students to practice, play and be creative but also enable many different learning styles, with opportunities for "just in time" learning. It is in this context that this technology needs to be leveraged in ways that enable students to become autonomous and aware of learning outcomes, fundamental if they are to be lifelong learners. Virtual worlds are changing the way information is accessed and experienced and the way information is communicated and learned. Although few experiences in higher education contexts have explored in any great depth the potential of virtual worlds in education, good practices –which will probably be the key to future innovation within educational institutions– need to be spread.

The aim of this article is to provide an overview of the potential of virtual worlds and metaverses in education, paying special attention to their pedagogical affordances. For this reason there is an extended review of concepts and terminology, which may sometimes be confusing, and a broad overview of the key points for effective practice.

2. AN INTRODUCTION TO THE USE OF IMMERSIVE ENVIRONMENTS

Three-dimensional environments are natural environments for students. Most of the games that they use in their leisure time use this technology and are known as massively multiplayer online role-playing games (MMORPG). They are a genre of role-playing video games in which a very large number of players interact with one another within a virtual game world. These should not be confused with MUVEs, which are online, multi-user virtual environments, sometimes called virtual worlds. MUVEs provide students with the opportunity to participate in interactive educational experiences at different stages of the physical classroom. These spaces allow students to "be together at the same time and the same place," so that they can interact with each other. They tend to use 3D technology, both hardware and software, such as virtual reality, allowing users to have unique experiences, the virtual reality systems ranging from immersive systems in large spaces where the user physically goes Avatar immersive systems to desktop and persistent virtual worlds where users socialize and the user manipulates the avatar with devices input from the computer. With the development of learning technologies, students can communicate synchronously and asynchronously with other participants.

2.1. 3D virtual worlds and metaverses

Typically, virtual worlds are also known as metaverses, a concept taken from the Sci-fi novel "Snow Crash", written by Neil Stephenson in 1992. Although these terms are not exactly synonymous and there is still considerable debate in the literature, we shall agree with Castronova (2005) and assume that they can be used interchangeably.

Virtual worlds are the simulation of a space, a representation in three dimensions of geographic features and cities, and the digital simulation of real surroundings. Second Life (SL) is a 3D environment that allows users to interact through a representation known as an avatar. Their main characteristics are that they are simple to use, they provide a series of collaborative facilities and they have attractive 3D features. All in all, their new and highly immersive sensation have made virtual worlds interesting scenarios in which to test innovative educational environments or to apply new data mining techniques. Participants in a successful virtual world have a deep sense of presence in that world.

The metaverse is a more complex concept. In recent years, the term has grown beyond Stephenson's 1992 vision of an immersive 3D virtual world to include aspects of physical world objects, actors, interfaces, and networks that construct and interact with virtual environments.

Between 2007 and 2008, the Acceleration Studies Foundation (ASF) – a US-based non-profit organization with an international advisory panel - and partners explored the virtual and 3D future of the World Wide Web in a first-of-its-kind cross-industry public foresight project: the Metaverse Roadmap (MVR).

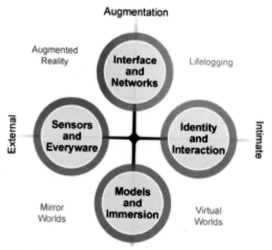

Figure 1. The Metaverse Roadmap (Smart, Cascio and Paffendorf, 2007)

The most important message given by this figure is the four scenarios, which emphasize different functions, types or sets of metaverse technologies:

- Lifelog. A digitally stored and electronically accessible record of various aspects of the experience history (GPS, time, and audio, visual, etc.) of physical objects (an object lifelog; Bruce Sterling "spimes"), or of human users (a user lifelog).
- Virtual worlds. A digital version of narratives set in "other realities" – these first existed in text form through text-based games and have evolved in many ways. Virtual world-based games are goal-oriented and take place within limitations of the rules of the game. Social-focused virtual worlds provide various levels of freedom in terms of avatar (the digital representation of a participant) customisation and the ability to build and/or create.
- Mirror world. A literal representation of the real world in digital form. It attempts to map (or mirror) real-world structures, like geography, or the stock market, in 2D or 3D form. GIS systems are often 2D mirror worlds. Google Earth is an example of a 3D mirror world.

As far as the typology of metaverses and virtual worlds is concerned, and from the standpoint of learning processes, the 3D training space is close to the constructs of what is called Web 2.0. In particular, Second Life (SL) can be analysed from the perspective of a "theatrical metaphor" that develops (Tu, Blocher & Roberts, 2008) from the four dimensions in this approach. The main contributions of SL can be analysed from the standpoint of the training process:

- Cognitive / scripts: We need to structure the training process so that SL can help students develop meaningful learning processes immediately and in a social way. Not only students have an identity and a role; teachers do, too.
- Social / actors: The avatars allow us to help students define their digital identity and assume a role within the world of SL. Teachers must also create their digital identity and assume the corresponding role in this world that represents the training environment (Dwyer, Hiltz & Passerini, 2007; Tu et al., 2008). In the same way, standards of operation and patterns of behaviour must be created in order to ensure the success of the teaching-learning process.
- Networking / stages: The same communication tools that SL offers help create a climate that is suitable for communication at a time that will implement the various roles that the actors (avatars) have taken during this training process and in this 3D environment (Boyd & Ellison, 2007, Jin, 2010).
- Integration / acting: The educational process is basically a communication process that takes place in a social environment. For this reason the 2.0 tools, including SL, have such potential in terms of promoting the learning process. "Social acts that bring out identities, awareness, relationships, connections and interactions among and between learners are necessary for interactive learning" (Thomanssen & Rive, 2010). Finally, the principles of social networks will be used to design and develop space for university education.

Professor Edward Castronova affirms (2001; 2005) that virtual worlds are 3-dimensional, digital environments in which a great number of people interact with one another by means of an avatar - a digital representation of self (Castronova, 2003). Therefore, the founding features of virtual worlds are:

- **Interactivity**: they exist on one computer but can be accessed remotely (i.e. by an Internet connection) and simultaneously by a large number of people, in such a way that the command inputs of one person affect the command results of others.
- **Physicality**: people access the program through an interface that simulates a first-person physical environment on their computer screen. The environment is generally ruled by the natural laws of Earth and is characterized by a scarcity of resources.
- **Persistence**: the program continues to run whether anyone is using it or not. It remembers the location of people and things, as well as the ownership of objects.

3. GOING BEYOND THE LEARNING EXPERIENCE: WHY VIRTUAL WORLDS MATTER?

The use of metaverses for learning can change not just what is learnt but, significantly, how we learn. It is for this reason that it is important to consider all the implications of integrating them into learning processes and to observe all the possible drawbacks and pitfalls of this integration.

Virtual worlds can be used to create very effective learning spaces. Since they are generalized rather than contextual, they can reach all disciplines. The social aspects of virtual worlds are extremely relevant to education. They lend themselves to role playing and scenario building, allowing learners to temporarily assume responsibilities without incurring real-world consequences. Businesses and universities have recognised the learning possibilities available in metaverses and 3D virtual worlds as spaces that offer both freedom and playfulness to create and collaborate while learning.

Metaverses and 3D worlds in education: traits and achievements

Virtual worlds

- provide a unique training and knowledge sharing environment,
- expand the understanding of both cultural and social experience,
- provide great opportunities for group interaction and allow meta reflection to support activities and achieve learning outcomes,
- enhance collaboration and communicative skills,
- allow learners to transfer learning from a learning context to a real life context more readily,
- encourage learners to gain experience working in flat organisational structures,
- develop students' ability to build networks and communities of practice,
- promote problem-solving and negotiating skills,
- help learners become goal-oriented, envisage outcomes and work towards them,
- generate the ability to produce knowledge,
- promote learning through simulations and role-playing,
- support creativity, exploration and the development of identity through open ways of learning,
- develop skills and experience in understanding other cultures and people,
- offer unique possibilities for expression.

---

4. FRAMEWORKS FOR SELECTING AND USING METAVERSES AND 3D WORLDS IN PRACTICE

The design, development and use of metaverses and immersive environments in education are closely interwoven. These interactive technologies, which are becoming more participatory, also affect the way in which learning activities are designed, developed and used in practice, and the whole process of learning. In order to ensure that activity theory and pedagogical approaches are suitably mapped it is important to analyse the frameworks and approaches that have been developed to suport the design and study of learning in metaverses and immersive worlds. Our starting point is the framework model for practitioners provided by Freitas and Oliver (2006) which picks up four generic principles: context, mode of representation, pedagogical approach and learner specification. This framework could become a starting point for practitioners who wish to start using metaverses and virtual worlds in their learning practices:

Context: the context of the metaverse is crucial to how effectively it is used. Contextual factors include where the metaverse is used, the technical support that is needed, the requirements, etc.

Pedagogical model: According to Mayes and Freitas (2004, 2006) learning processes are supported by associative (instructivist and often task-centred), cognitive (constructivist) and situated (learning in communities of practice) models of learning. The pedagogical model is particularly important since simulation or gaming are not learning experiences in themselves; rather they are integrated within a set of activities or processes according to the approach selected. In this regard, the role of debriefing is central to immersive worlds when used to pursue educational objectives through discussion, reflection, etc.

Learner specification: integrates aspects such as age, stage, learning needs, level of digital literacy, etc.

Representation: Young learners are acquiring high levels of immersion and interactivity in virtual worlds. The representation is the level of immersion and familiarity of interface with the learning group and the world which has multiple effects upon learning.

---

5. METAVERSES AND 3D VIRTUAL WORLDS IN THE CLASSROOM: SOME KEY POINTS FOR EFFECTIVE PRACTICE

Simulations and virtual worlds engage students in high-level cognitive thinking such as interpreting, analyzing, discovering, evaluating and above all problem solving. According to De Freitas (2006), a number of key points can be of help to educators, practitioners and other stakeholders when they implement their experiences using metaverses and 3D virtual worlds. They must

- ensure learning objectives are aligned with the metaverses, 3D virtual worlds and assessment so that learning can be most effective.

- ensure that the learning activities that take place within the metaverse are integrated with face-to-face learning.
- provide opportunities for reflection by means of dialogue and discussion.
- place aspects of learning within immersive environments so that learners can control them and engage with them.
- consider the level of immersion as part of the learning design so that learning is most effective.
- design role plays that allow students to empathise with and reflect upon situations from real life.
- develop realistic scenarios that allow transfer from rehearsal to real life contexts.
- align assessment with learning activities so that they are effective.
- ntroduce a feedback loop into learning activities so that learning remains effective.

6. CONCLUSION

Metaverses and 3D virtual worlds are increasingly being used in education and training to create authentic learning experiences that are immersive, authentic and media rich. In particular, they provide opportunities to structure remote learning in engaging ways and are fast becoming part of the learning landscape in general. While there is growing interest among practitioners and researchers in the training and knowledge sharing potential of these unique learning environments, current virtual world technologies offer a range of capabilities that need to be further developed. Higher education institutions need to see the potentialities of these technologies and integrate them in their day-to-day teaching and learning practices.

REFERENCES

Antonacci, D. M. & Modaress, N. (2008). Envisioning the educational possibilities of user-created virtual worlds.*AACE Journal, 16*(2), 115-126.

Barab, S.A., Gresalfi, M.S., & Ingram-Goble, A. (2010). Transformational play: Using games to position person, content, and context. *Educational Researcher*, 39(7), 525-536.

Boyd, D.M., & Ellison, N.B. (2007) "Social network sites: Definition, history, and scholarship". *Journal of Computer-Mediated Communication*, Vol 13, No. 1, pp 210-230.

Castronova E., (2001), "Virtual Worlds: A First-hand Account of Market and Society on the Cyberian Frontier", CESifo working Paper, n. 618, December.

Castronova E., (2003), "Theory of the Avatar", CESifo Working Papers n. 863, February.

Castronova E., (2005), Synthetic Worlds: the Business and the Culture of Online Games, University of Chicago Press, Chicago

De Freitas, S. (2006) Learning in immersive worlds. *A review of game-based learning*. The report is available at: www.jisc.ac.uk/whatwedo/programmes/elearning_innovation/eli_outcomes

Dwyer, C., Hiltz, S. R., & Passerini, K. (2007). Trust and privacy concern within social networking sites: A comparison of Facebook and MySpace. Proceedings of AMCIS 2007, Keystone, CO.

Gisbert Cervera, M.; Cela-Ranilla, J.M.; Isus Barado, S. (2010) "Las simulaciones en entornos TIC como herramienta para la formación en competencias transversales de los estudiantes universitarios". *Teoría de la Educación. Educación y Cultura en la Sociedad de la Información*, Vol 11, No. 1, pp 352-370

Jin, Seung-A. Annie (2010) "Leveraging avatars in 3D virtual environments (Second Life) for interactive learning: the moderating role of the behavioral activation system vs. behavioral inhibition system and the mediating role of enjoyment", *Interactive Learning Environments*

Johnson, L., Smith, R., Willis, H., Levine, A., and Haywood, K., (2011). The 2011 Horizon Report. Austin, Texas: The New Media Consortium.

Livingstone, D.; Kemp, J., (2008). "Integrating Web-Based and 3D Learning Environments: Second Life Meets Moodle". UPGRADE (European Journal for the Informatics Professional) 9 (3): 8–14.

Livingstone, D; Kemp, J. (2006) Proceedings of the First Second Life Education Workshop, Part of the 2006 Second Life Community Convention, August 18th-20th 2006, Fort Mason Centre, San Francisco, Ca

Mayes, T. and De Freitas, S. (2004). Review of e-learning theories, frameworks and models. JISC e- learning models study report. London. The Joint Information Systems Committee.

Mayes, T. and De Freitas, S. (2006). Learning and e-learning: the role of theory. In H. Beetham and R. Sharpe (Eds), Rethinking Pedagogy in the Digital Age. London. Routledge.

Minocha, Shailey and Reeves, Ahmad John (2010) "Design of learning spaces in 3D virtual worlds: an empirical investigation of Second Life", *Learning, Media and Technology*, Vol 35, No. 2, pp 111-137

Smart, J.M., Cascio, J. and Paffendorf, J. (2007), Metaverse Roadmap Overview.

Thomassen, Aukje and Rive, Pete (2010). "How to enable knowledge exchange in Second Life in design education?", *Learning, Media and Technology*, Vol 35, No. 2, pp 155-169

Tu, Chih-Hsiung, Blocher, Michael and Roberts, Gayle (2008) "Constructs for Web 2.0 learning environments: a theatrical metaphor", *Educational Media International*, Vol 45, No. 4, pp 253- 269. Discussion of how World of Warcraft can be used as a learning environment in education. Presented at the American Educational Studies Association, October, 2007.

Adaptation Camacho, M.; Esteve, V.; Gisbert, M. (2011). Delve into the deep: Learning potential in metaverses and 3D worlds.(eLearning Papers).

AUTHORS

Mar Camacho. *Department of Pedagogy. Rovira i Virgili University. Tarragona, Spain. Email: mar.camacho@urv.cat*

Vanessa Esteve-González. *Department of Pedagogy. Rovira i Virgili University. Tarragona, Spain. Email: Vanessa.esteve@urv.cat*

Luis Marqués

Cinta Espuny

Noemí Rabassa

3.2

PLANNING THE LEARNING OF GENERAL COMPETENCES USING 3D VIRTUAL ENVIRONMENTS

1. STRUCTURE OF THE EDUCATIONAL PROPOSAL

To carry out the experience in the 3D World, the three teachers who took part drew up an educational proposal. The three proposals had the same structure and stages, and the only difference was the subject that was being taught. The subjects were:

- "The Fundaments of Sports I". Free elective subject of 6 credits on the Diploma for Physical Education Teachers (1997 curriculum). A total of 11 students took part (4 women and 7 men).
- "School Organisation". Core subject of 4.5 credits on the Diploma for Infant Education Teachers (1997 curriculum). A total of 33 students took part.
- "Marketing Management". Compulsory subject of 6 credits on the Master's Degree in Strategic Business Management taught at the Universitat Rovira i Virgili.

Below we shall describe the main features of the work carried out in the three subjects.

1.1 The environment

The environment used was OpenSim, a platform that enables users to create virtual worlds. One of the aspects that most interested us was the integration of this 3D platform with the University's virtual campus, Moodle, because this would allow us to record all the activities undertaken in the virtual world for the participants. To this end we used the module known as Sloodle. OpenSim contains tools for personalising avatars, chatting with other users and modifying the terrain so that 3D spaces can be created that simulate different work areas and environments.

1.2 Avatar

The users represent their identities and characteristics by transforming their avatars and interacting with the avatars of other users (Suler, 2002; Wood et al., 2005; De Lucia et al. 2009). One of the first things participants had to do in this experience was personalise their avatar. They all had a default avatar and they could change its appearance, move it and communicate with it by using the options of the environment (Figures 1 and 2).

Figure 1. Avatar-world interaction   **Figure 2.** Interaction between avatars

1.3 Resources

Each group had access to a central island and an empty island, which they could access by means of a teleporter. The island is the region (virtually physical) in which the avatars move and interact. On each island there was one dispenser with basic resources and another with extra resources. By doing the activities, students could win points and then exchange them for extra objects. The central island had a resource centre that provided information about the topic of the project.

1.4 Educational proposal

The educational proposal for the three subjects was designed on a project based learning structure (PBL).

The project that the students had to carry out for the subject "Fundaments of Sports I" was to organise a five-day School Sports Event, with both sporting competitions and social activities. It was prepared over a period of four weeks, students had unlimited access to OpenSim, and it had to be presented to a sports committee. The project was both competitive and collaborative: three groups competed to make the best proposal and the members of each team were all responsible for a particular area of the project.

Table 1 lists and classifies the activities to be carried out as part of the educational proposal. It shows where the related 3D object can be found and the Moodle activity it represents.

Table 1. Categories of the activities carried out

Category	Activity	Instruction	Space	Sloodle object	Moodle activity
Personal organisation	My team: people in charge and aims of each area	Determine the people in charge and the aims of each area.	Meeting point /Island group	Note + Chat	Task assignment
Spatial organisation	Public address system	Decide where the public address system is to be installed.	Island group	Chat	Chat
	Publicity	Decide where the advertising hoardings are to be located.	Island group	Chat	Chat
	Sports facilities	Decide where the sports facilities are to be located and how they are to be oriented.	Island group	Chat	Chat
Documents	Access points	Set up control points for access to the sports areas.	Island group	Chat	Chat
	Identity cards	Establish an identity system for spectators and athletes.	Central island	Sphere	Task assignment
	Spectators	Draw up a list of ways to encourage attendance.	Sports hall /Island group	Note + Chat	Task assignment
Lists	First-aid kit	List of things required for a first-aid kit.	Island group	Note	Task assignment
	Sponsors	List of possible sponsors what they are expected to contribute.	Central island	Sphere	Task assignment
Budgets	Security budget	Draw up a basic budget of income and expenditure for security issues.	Central island	Sphere	Task assignment
	Advertising budget	Draw up a basic budget of income and expenditure for advertising.	Central island	Sphere	Task assignment
Schedule	Competition schedule	Draw up a preliminary competition schedule.	Central island	Sphere	Task assignment
Planning/ predicting	Miscellaneous	Individual questionnaire on all areas	Meeting point	Desk	Questionnaire
	Information	List of all the information that must be provided before and during the event. Describe the content of the advertising messages.	Central island	Sphere	Task assignment
	Sports/competition equipment	Draw up a list of all the resources (sports material and equipment) that will be required for the event.	Central island	Sphere	Task assignment
	Sequence of actions	Individual questionnaire on all areas	Sports hall	Desk	Questionnaire
	True/False	Individual questionnaire on all areas	Dressing room	Desk	Questionnaire

Explaining/ arguing	Legislation (Professional football)	Describe the legislation and regulations governing security measures that must be taken into account when organising a first- or second-division football match.	Island group	Chat	Chat
	Visit	Presentation of the model to the sports committee.	Island group		

The students of the subject School Organisation were asked to plan a school symposium to be held in a rural area and involving three schools of different types. In groups of five members each, they had to organise a meeting of teachers and students, and plan a series of activities taking into account the level of the students and the spaces available. They also had to plan and design their proposal and present it to the other groups.

The items that had to be included in the proposal are listed below together with their weights and deadlines:

- Decide what sort of school is required (choose the various spaces bearing in mind the students, activities, needs, etc.) and the focus of interest. Justify the decision. 15%, 1 June.
- Review the presentation on Moodle:
  - ♦ Reflect on the different spaces required
  - ♦ Make a small drawing-model of what you aim to construct
  - ♦ Transfer the project to the virtual world
- Activities:
  1. Read the instructions for organising and running a school provided by the Department of Education of the Catalan Government:
     The number of teachers for a particular number of infant or primary students.
     The need to inform the Inspectorate of Education.
     Decide what to do with those students who are not allowed to go on the excursion.
  2. Draw up the Annual Plan and get approval from the School Council.
  3. Relate outcome targets to competences / skills.
  4. Plan the activities to be carried out: order, spaces, people in charge, etc.
  5. Consider the possibility of applying for subsidies and funds.
  6. Present the organisation of the activity to the staff council.
  7. Draw up an information leaflet for families.
  8. Organise a meeting for families.
  9. Prepare a first-aid kit.
  10. Arrange for all the necessary authorizations and telephones.
  11. List the necessary materials (camera, signed permission to use students' images, list of students who are not going on the excursion, allergies, sun cream, mobile phone, etc.). Suggest a person in charge.
  12. Plan the meals and drinks (timetable, food, etc) of the students and teachers.
  13. Evaluate the activity.
  14. Draw up a flow chart of what to do in the case of absence or the late arrival of students on departure day. Extraordinary situations. 15%, 12 May.
  15. Take into account the presence of a diabetic student. Things to bear in mind. 15%, 19 May.

16. Consult the instructions on organizing and running infant and primary state schools (2010-2011). How to respond and what to do when there are accidents or incidents. Choose a practical case and act as teachers. 15%, 26 May.
17. Add any other material, activities or remarks you feel to be appropriate.
18. Prepare a presentation of about 10 minutes to tell the class what has been planned. 20%, 1 June.

For the subject Marketing Management, the aim of the project was to prepare a proposal entitled Participation in a Trade Fair that was to last about 4 days. At this professional trade fair, which was open to the general public at the weekend students had to present and provide a new product and/or service.

Three different areas were identified:

- Creative. In this area decisions need to be taken about preparing and designing promotional material to be used at the trade fair
- Financial. In this area, decisions need to be taken about the programme and the budget
- Logistics and infrastructure. In this area decisions need to be taken about reserving and designing fair space.

A programme with a range of activities was drawn up.

Code	Activity	Space	Sloodle object	Moodle activity
1	Questionnaires: Questionnaire on competences (general and digital) Questionnaire on learning patterns (LML)	Class		Face-to-face
2	Virtual tour	Class		Face-to-face
3	Act. 1: My team: people in charge and objectives per area	Moodle	Chat + Nota	Task assignment
4	Act. 2: Development of the new product	Moodle		Task assignment
5	Act. 3. Design of promotional material	Moodle		Task assignment
6	Act. 4. Selection of trade fair	Moodle		Task assignment
7	Act. 5. Budget proposal	Moodle		Task assignment
8	Act. 6. Reservation of fair space	Moodle		Task assignment
9	Act. 7. Distribution of the stand			Chat
10	Act. 8. Construction of the stand	3D		3D
11	Visit from the evaluating committee	Class		Face-to-face presentation

Table 2. Tasks to be carried out in the teaching activity proposal

1.5 Criteria governing the projects.

The following criteria had to be taken into account when drawing up each project: a) each group was responsible for managing their own island; b) all the members of the group communicated by means of the island's chat room and a special room called "meeting point"; c) the resources available depended on the organization of the event and a limited budget assignation; and d) each member of the group headed a particular work area.

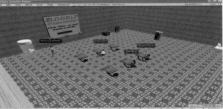

Figure 3. Island or region in the virtual environment.   **Figure 4.** Meeting point.

1.6 Project stages

Figure 5 shows the different stages of the experience. The preliminary stage, the only one that was face-to-face, and the activities involved installing and getting to know the 3D environment, personalising the avatar and creating groups. In the planning stage, each work group designed their proposal and their organizational model by carrying out tasks or activities. In the development stage, each group constructed the project model that they had planned in the previous stage within the 3D environment. The result of this stage was the final design of the island. In the evaluation stage, the groups presented their proposals in public.

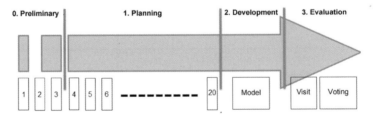

Figure 5. Stages of the project

2. TEACHING PERSPECTIVE

This section summarizes the personal perceptions and reflections resulting from the teaching activity described in the section above from three points of view:

2.1 The teacher

The teacher must be digitally competent and guide the students. The activity must be planned in detail if learning is to be autonomous and the teacher should only intervene to clear up doubts and encourage constructive learning.

If these initiatives are to be developed and applied in teaching, the schools and students must have access to the hardware and platforms, and also have the necessary advanced computer techniques. In teaching innovation projects, it is essential to have institutional support to provide the extra infrastructure that is not required for face-to-face teaching in the classroom.

The teacher needs to have a good command of all the issues to be able to respond to any unforeseen questions. If the simulation is to be evaluated as part of the subject, the teacher must be aware that getting used to a new virtual environment can take time, and this should be borne in mind when planning the subject. On- and off-line arrangements should be made by teachers while the activity is being carried out so that they can respond to any doubts and incidents that may arise. Teacher-student communication competences are developed not only in the academic sphere but also in the social and personal spheres.

Virtual scenarios make it possible to vary the complexity to match the various degree courses and the years in which they are taught. However, we required technical assistance to adapt our proposal to the simulator. Having to rely on a computer technician in the preliminary stages prevents total control over the planned teaching activity.

2.2 The virtual world

The choice of the simulator took some considerable time. Analysing different simulators and finding just one to which a range of teaching proposals could be adapted was the biggest challenge. Once the decision has been made, the adaptation of the tasks and activities depends on the technical requirements of the simulator. Controlling waiting and connection times is fundamental to the success of a pedagogical proposal such as this one.

Although the simulator is free, instruction manuals and tutorials are essential to the teaching activity, as is technical support to install the program on the students' and teachers' computers. It should be pointed out that the educational proposals were presented and put into practice for a four-to-five week period, which makes it very necessary to include some time for students to adapt to the simulator if the educational proposal is to be a success. Educational proposals that are spread over longer times should not really need to incorporate a period of adaptation to the simulation program.

2.3 Students

The students were very positive about taking part in this teaching innovation experience. They regarded it as a way of developing general and specific competences that would help them to develop as individuals and professionals.

The environment encouraged group work and the use of technology to learn. It enabled ideas to be presented attractively and in an organised way, and the display was an aid to understanding. However, it does have some drawbacks: it requires a broadband connection to Internet and sometimes there are problems when several users try to log on at once.

The digital competence of the students has been observed in an intuitive environment, but the interface was in English, which was an added difficulty for those least competent in the language.

The figure of a group delegate or coordinator encourages different roles within the group. The continuous assessment activities require considerable effort to be made by the students. It is important to plan the time spent on these activities carefully and to focus on their real aims because the tool can be used at different levels of complexity. It is the teacher's task to make these levels clear. And, because there is a considerable creative component to the simulation proposal, it is particularly important to clearly state the dates on which all activities start and finish.

One of the most important activities carried out by the students was the personalisation of their avatars, which reflect their personality and can even be regarded as their professional presentation.

Teamwork is essential if the proposal is to be successful and it is also very helpful to have mechanisms to help create teams with complementary learning profiles and ways of working. As proposed by Wolfe and Chacko (1983) and Jaffe and Nebenzahl (1990), the average number of students in a group was 3, which is just the right number to make an efficient, cohesive group. We believe that this composition was highly effective and fundamental to the preparation of the proposal, and it helped create the expected cohesion and co-responsibility.

By assigning different roles for the different decisions to be taken we have been able to develop specific competences for all the roles, which should reflect the professional realities of each subject area. Both students and teachers should be aware that during the various activities conflicts will arise between participants and will need to be solved. However, the solution to these conflicts was regarded as a part of the learning process and the formation of professional competences.

In this sort of initiative it is important to be aware that there may be initial objections by students who are not so technologically competent and it may be necessary to provide extra support and tutorials to prevent dropout. It is very important to prevent students from being discouraged by not knowing how to work the simulator.

It should be pointed out that the final presentation in public was very important because it enabled things to be shared, and showed what the simulator had contributed and how it had been used by each of the work groups. It also provided students with the opportunity to reflect and explain the objectives they had reached and what they had learned during the experience. Many students pointed out the need for some sort of help to find their way around the environment.

3. SYNTHESIS

To sum up, decision making in the professional world must be quick, dynamic and adaptable to new situations. Virtual experiences now make this dynamism both possible and motivating.

If these tools are to be used properly and teaching innovation initiatives are to be successful, the work teams must be interdisciplinary, technical staff must be available and the institution must provide support. Teaching staff must also be provided with institutional training in the field of educational innovation.

We do not wish to finish our description of the experience without pointing out that the level of group motivation, commitment and cohesion was considerable, and that the extent to which the academic objectives were achieved was assessed very positively.

We should also say that 3D environments are a very useful tool for training future professionals independently of the field or the subject area because they provide a form in which they can apply the competences required of them. In this teaching activity, the students used their knowledge to design three projects. They were members of a team but also had individual responsibilities. They worked on the competences as future teachers or professionals in their professional field.

The students received no previous training on how to use the program. They freely learned how to use the environment, how to construct their avatar and how to interact with their avatar, their colleagues and the environment. Despite the complexity of the virtual world, they managed to overcome the obstacle of having to cope with an unknown environment and acquired a good command of it with hardly any technical help.

In short, the use of a simulation process in a virtual world encouraged students to plan and to be more creative.

Before entering a virtual world of this sort, teachers must be clear what their aims are and must plan their activity on the basis of the criteria of evaluation: that is to say, the environment should not be the objective but the resource. The relation between the amount of time spent and the learning outcome should also be evaluated. The analysis should include the competences, not only the objectives achieved.

Using this environment and with the support of the teacher, the students will carry out a project that will require them to organize themselves, take on tasks and make decisions as a group throughout the process. If this proposal is to be implemented successfully, students must have the external support and advice of professional experts in virtual worlds and the encouragement of participation.

Therefore, if a proposal of this sort is to be undertaken, the stages described below should be followed:

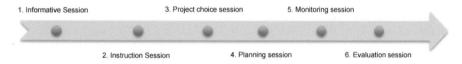

Figure 6: Proposal of project stages

i
1. **Information session:** Presentation of the environment In this session, the tutor explains the 3D program to the students: the stages, the objectives, the methodology, and, most importantly, the role and tasks of the teaching staff and students. It is, therefore, in this session that the teaching staff will decide whether to take part in the programme or not and they will decide exactly what they commit themselves to for the rest of the course

2. **Instruction session:** Introduction to the environment. In this session the 3D program is put into context: the concept of participation, the rules on participation, ways of participation, the functions of delegates, participatory bodies and the development of the programme.

3. **Project choice session.** This session is fundamental to the development of the programme because students have to choose the project on which they will work throughout the course. The choice of project will involve diagnosing classroom needs and it must be taken jointly by teaching staff and students.

4. **Planning session.** In the third session, the project chosen is analysed, the tasks are planned and the roles of each of the students assigned. In this session, concepts of participation are discussed: cooperative work, team work, dialogue, collective decision making, commitment and responsibility.

5. **Monitoring session.** In the fourth session, the tutor monitors how the projects are developing and the extent to which both teachers and students are internalizing the participation competences. If necessary, delegates are provided with new participation tools.

6. **Evaluation session.** This session presents and analyses the various projects carried out during the course and evaluates the participatory processes that have taken place and the learning and competences acquired.

To sum up, simulation in 3D virtual environments is a challenge that can improve learning in teaching scenarios on both undergraduate and postgraduate courses. Teaching platforms such as Moodle are essential to the development of such initiatives and prepare students for new learning scenarios. We should point out that one of the most important results of this empirical application of simulation is that students have the perception of having learned content in a more dynamic way and that it is the perfect complement to a face-to-face course.

REFERENCES

Baruch, Y. (2006). Role-play teaching: acting in the classroom, *Management Learning*, Vol. 37 (1), 43-61.

Daly, S. P. (2001). Student-operated Internet businesses: True experiential learning in entrepreneurship and retail management. *Journal of Marketing Education, 23*, 204-215.

De Lucia, A., Francese, R., Passero, I., & Tortora, G. (2009). Development and evaluation of a virtual campus on Second Life: the case of Second DMI. *Computers & Education, 52*, 220 - 233.

Faria, A. J., Hutchinson, D., Wellington, W. J., & Gold, S. (2009). Developments in business gaming: A review of the past 40 years. *Simulation and Gaming, 40*(4), 464-487.

Jaffe, E.D., Nebenzahl, I.D. (1990). Group interaction and business game performance,*Simulation and Gaming*, Vol. 21(2), 133-46.

Kennedy, E.J., Lawton, L. and Walker, E. (2001). The case for using live cases: shifting the paradigm in marketing education, *Journal of Marketing Education*, Vol. 23 (2), 145-51.

Li, T., Greenberg, B. A., & Nicholls, J. (2007). Teaching experiential learning: Adoption of an innovative course in an MBA marketing curriculum. *29*(1), 25.

Pearson, M.M., Barnes, J.W., Onken, M.H. (2006). Development of a computerized in-basket exercise for the classroom: a sales management example, *Journal of Marketing Education*, Vol. 28 (3), 227-36.

Porter, T. S., Riley, T. M., & Ruffer, R. L. (2004). A review of the use of simulations in teaching economics. *Social Science Computer Review, 22*(4), 426-443.

SLOODLE: <http://www.sloodle.org/>

Smith, L.W., Van Doren, D.C. (2004). The reality-based learning method: a simple method for keeping teaching activities relevant and effective, *Journal of Marketing Education*, Vol. 26 (1), 66-74.

Suler, J. R. (2002). Identity management in cyberspace. *Journal of Applied Psychoanalytic Studies, 4*(4), 455–460.

Vos, L., & Brennan, R. (2010). Marketing simulation games: Student and lecturer perspectives. *Marketing Intelligence and Planning, 28*(7), 882-897.

Wolfe, J., Chacko, T.I. (1983). Team-size effects on business game performance and decision making behaviours, *Decision Science*, Vol. 14 (1), 121-33.

Wood, N. T., Solomon, M. R., & Englis, B. G. (2005). Personalization of online avatars: is the messenger as important as the message? *International Journal of Internet Marketing and Advertising, 2*(1/2), 143–161.

Wright, L.K., Bitner, M.J., Zeithaml, V.A. (1994). Paradigm shifts in business education: using active learning to deliver services marketing content, *Journal of Marketing Education*, Vol. 16 (3), 5-19.

AUTHORS

Luis Marqués, *Department of Pedagogy. Rovira i Virgili University. Tarragona, Spain.*

Cinta Espuny, *Department of Pedagogy. Rovira i Virgili University. Tarragona, Spain.*

Noemí Rabassa, *Department of Business Management. Rovira i Virgili University. Tarragona, Spain.*

Vanessa Esteve-González
Byron Vaca
Nicolay Samaniego

3.3

MAKING 3D OBJECTS IN VIRTUAL LEARNING ENVIRONMENTS

1. INTRODUCTION

This chapter reviews the software tools that are used in the field of virtual education and which, thanks to Internet, facilitate teaching and learning processes. The programs associated with the learning environments and the tools that work with augmented reality (in 3D environments) are described. What is more, it also explains how to make 3D objects for learning activities using Sloodle, which links to a multi-user virtual environment (MUVE) such as OpenSim with a learning management system (LMS), in this case Moodle.

2. VIRTUAL LEARNING ENVIRONMENTS (VLES)

VLEs are computer applications that have been developed to manage and administer learning processes through Internet. They aim to provide the tools required to manage the various e-learning initiatives designed to develop the attitudes and aptitudes of the participants of an educational process. A VLE must be designed, constructed and integrated into the educational process from a pedagogical point of view to guarantee not only that it incorporates technology but also a mediating interface that facilitates learning (Suárez, 2003).

2.1. Learning Management Systems (LMSs)

LMSs are computer applications that integrate management- and administration-oriented functions for users, virtual classrooms, content and learning activities. An LMS is not only a software application: it is designed and constructed on a sound pedagogical basis that makes learning possible by displaying content, and managing and administering the educational process. LMSs must provide and integrate a set of web tools that facilitate learning and course management. What makes LMSs different is the pedagogical orientation that they give to these tools so that they can be more useful (Malikowski, Thompson, & Theis, 2006).

An LMS is structured in such a way that it shows students how to learn. It provides an environment that makes it possible to organise information and the architecture to display it; a set of tools that facilitate interaction between the actors in the process, and between the actors and the content; and a set of interfaces that facilitate the integration, participation, action, communication and collaboration of the students engaged in educational activities and research. It also contains a wide variety of tools that enable students to find different ways of doing, thinking and feeling (Dillenbourg, 2000).

According to Sánchez (2009), the most widely used term to refer to this sort of software application is learning management system. Nevertheless, there are other related terms: virtual learning environments (VLE), course management systems (CMS), mediated learning environments (MLE), integrated learning systems (ILS), learning support systems (LSS) and learning platforms (LP).

The first of these tools to emerge was the course management system (CMS), designed to manage learning-oriented content and which is not necessarily a software application limited to the web. They were used to provide support to distance education. CMSs also facilitated the generation of dynamic websites for some types of content (Boneu 2007).

After CMSs came LMSs, software applications that can work on both intranet and extranet levels: that is to say, they were developed for internet and make it possible to update and accumulate dynamic content, and also improve the possibilities of collaboration, interaction and communication of the platform users.

Learning and content management systems (LCMS) have a repository of learning objects, which are stored as a database of the digital content and information and learning objects that make up the lessons, teaching units and courses generated from the learning objects. The LCMS can be defined as a web-based system that uses the web to create, approve, publish, administer and store educational resources and on-line courses (Rengarajan, 2001).

2.1.1. Moodle

Moodle is an LMS based on the philosophy of free and open source software and it is one that is in widespread use by teaching staff and students all over the world, as can be seen in the statistics that are available on its website. It enables courses to be managed and distributed on Internet and it is based on a "social constructivist pedagogy" (SCOPEO, 2011).

3. VIRTUAL REALITY

Virtual reality (VR) is the science that studies and develops the various components of both hardware and software that aims to simulate reality and the sensation of presence through a medium of communication. "Virtual reality is a three-dimensional simulation, commonly computer-generated or assisted, of some aspect of the real or fictional world, in which the user has the feeling of belonging to the synthetic environment or of interacting with it. Virtual reality makes it possible to interact with three-dimensional worlds in a more natural way: for example, a user can perform actions within a virtual model, travel, move, walk through it or lift things and thus experience situations that resemble the real world." (ISEA, 2008).

In the context of VR, virtual worlds simulate real worlds, or not, in three dimensions (3D) using software platforms installed in a computer (Grané, Frigola, & Muras, 2007)

3.1. Multi-user virtual environments (MUVEs)

On-line virtual worlds known as MUVEs integrate resources that enable users to communicate, interact and collaborate from a new perspective (ISEA, 2008).

For Camacho, Esteve & Gisbert (2011), a virtual world is a simulation of a space, a three-dimensional representation of geographical features, cities and digital simulation of the real environment. Second Life, for example, is a 3D environment that enables users to interact by means of a graphical representation that is known as an avatar.

MUVE applications are classified in two large groups depending on the functions available to users and the administration options available to organizers. Client MUVEs are platforms that are available and which are administrated by a company or organization. MUVE servers are platforms that can be downloaded or purchased to be installed and configured in other servers.

3.1.1. OpenSimulator

OpenSimulator (OpenSim) is an open-source, cross-platform, multi-user software application. It is a 3D-applications server. It can be used to create a virtual environment that can be accessed by various clients using different protocols (http://opensimulator.org/wiki/Main_Page). The development of OpenSim is closely connected to the platform SecondLife owned by Linden Labs. It has two main components:

- The **client,** which is a software application consisting of a window or interface by which the user navigates through a three-dimensional space. This interface also enables the user to make searches, view maps, manage the inventory, communicate by chat, configure and personalize the interface, and administer clients.
- The **server**, which is the software application that communicates with the client by accepting requests and sending responses. The server application is connected to one or more databases in which all the user's assets and the inventory articles are stored

It has three operation modes:
- **Independent mode:** Clients authenticate themselves to the server before they are teleported to the virtual world. The server has all the basic services integrated into an executable image that dynamically invokes libraries
- **Network mode:** This mode has a range of specific services: **U**ser, **G**rid, **A**sset, **I**nventory, **M**essaging (UGAIM). The authentication service is responsible for managing the users who connect to the grid. The grid service understands the general layout of the grid including the Internet addresses associated to each region. A grid consists of regions and includes everybody. The assets service manages all the assets (basic geometry, texture maps, audio files, terrain geometry) in the regions. The inventory server administrates the goods that are linked to a particular agent, in such a way that when users authenticate themselves as agents they are automatically linked to a set of inventory articles. The messaging service is responsible for the text chat.
- **Hypergrid mode:** The hypergrid mode is a set of simulators connected without a global grid manager. In many respects it resembles the Internet's hypermedia platform. The equivalent of the web link for OpenSim is teleporting from one region to another.

Image 1 shows the typical interface of a virtual world in OpenSim.

Image 1: OpenSim interface.

Fuente: An introduction to opensimulator and virtual environment agent-based M&S applications (Fishwick, 2009).

3.1.2. Simulation-linked object-oriented dynamic learning (SLOODLE)

Sloodle is an open-source Project that was developed with the purpose of integrating a web-based LMS (Moodle) and the wide variety of interactions made possible by the MUVEs (OpenSim) (http://www.sloodle.org/moodle/).

Image 2 shows the integration between LMS and MUVEs through Sloodle.

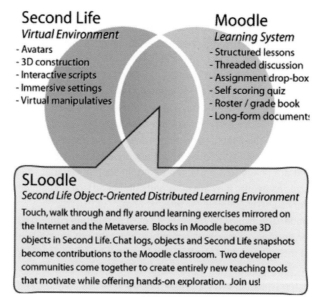

Image 2: Sloodle project

Source: Configuration of learning objects in 3D virtual environments (Samaniego, et al., 2011).

Sloodle increases educational possibilities synergically by creating the potential for immersion and immediacy, which improves Internet-based processes.

Image 3 shows Moodle's 2D activities, its corresponding 3D objects in OpenSim and their integration and interaction through Sloodle.

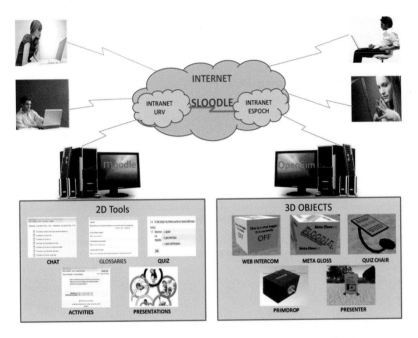

Image 3: 2D tools and 3D objects integrated through SLOODLE
Source: author

4. INTEGRATION OF MOODLE AND OPENSIM USING SLOODLE

To integrate Moodle and OpenSim, Sloodle must first be installed and configured in the two platforms. Image 4 shows the layered architecture of the platforms.

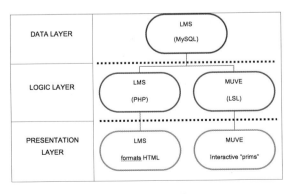

Image 4: Layered arquitecture

The data layer stores the data of the system and the users.

The logic layer executes the functions and operations requested by the user, processes the information and sends the responses after the process. This layer communicates with the presentation layer to receive applications and present results, and with the data access layer to store and retrieve data.

The presentation layer is the user's interface: it is responsible for the system interacting with the user and viceversa, it shows the system to the user, it presents information to the user and obtains information from the user

5. 3D OBJECTS AND 2D ACTIVITIES

A set of important Tools have been developed for MUVEs that enable the content and activities to be displayed in a 3D context. However, not all the tools available in Moodle have a corresponding tool in the 3D environments. The table below shows the interaction between the 3D objects and 2D tools made available by Sloodle.

Table 1: Interaction between 3D objects and 2D tools through Sloodle.

3D object	Description	2D tool
Sloodle Set 	This 3D object connects or links the MUVE environment to the Moodle environment.	**Connect con Moodle**
Web Intercom 	This object links the chat sessions that are carried out in the 3D environment to the Moodle chat module and records all the interaction that takes place in the 3D environment in the Moodle platform.	**Chat**
Presenter 	This object displays the content of websites, pdf documents and videos uploaded to Moodle as presentations in the 3D environment.	**Web, pdf, videos**

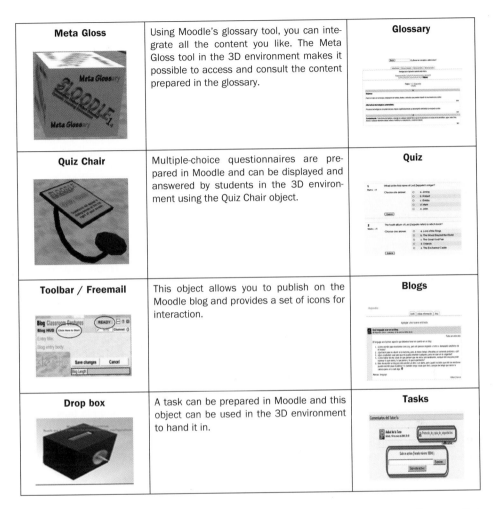

Meta Gloss	Using Moodle's glossary tool, you can integrate all the content you like. The Meta Gloss tool in the 3D environment makes it possible to access and consult the content prepared in the glossary.	Glossary
Quiz Chair	Multiple-choice questionnaires are prepared in Moodle and can be displayed and answered by students in the 3D environment using the Quiz Chair object.	Quiz
Toolbar / Freemail	This object allows you to publish on the Moodle blog and provides a set of icons for interaction.	Blogs
Drop box	A task can be prepared in Moodle and this object can be used in the 3D environment to hand it in.	Tasks

Source: author

6. CONCLUSIONS

With the passage of time, more and better tools are becoming available for promoting and supporting learning using the new information technologies. Virtual worlds are one of the many alternatives and, if they are used appropriately, they can increase the teaching possibilities enormously and democratize and improve the quality of educational processes.

Learning objects in a 3D space can be configured and used for such specific needs as reality simulations in educational and training situations.

Most Moodle activities can be represented in a 3D environment such as OpenSim, in which the data on the interaction of users are recorded in Moodle, thus allowing them to be subsequently analysed and evaluated.

REFERENCES

Boneu, J. (2007). Plataformas abiertas de e-learning para el soporte de contenidos educativos abiertos. Revista de Universidad y Sociedad Del Conocimiento, 4, 36-47.

Camacho, M.; Esteve, V.; Gisbert, M. (2011). Delve into the deep: Learning potential in metaverses and 3D worlds. (eLearning Papers).

Dillenbourg, P. (2000). Learning in the new millennium: Building new education strategies for schools. Virtual Learning Environments in EUN Conference 2000, 1-30.

Fishwick, P. (2009). An introduction to OpenSimulator and virtual environment agent-based M&S applications. Orlando, Florida. (Proceedings of the 2009 Winter Simulation Conference) 177-182.

Grané, M.; Frigola, J.; & Muras, M. (2007). Second life: Avatares para aprender. Buenos Aires, Argentina.

ISEA. (2008). *Internet 3D, análisis prospectivo de las potencialidades aplicaciones asociadas a los mundos virtuales.* Innovación en Servicios Empresariales Avanzados.

ISEA. (2009). 3D - LEARNING, análisis prospectivo de las potencialidades de la realidad virtual en los procesos de enseñanza - aprendizaje. Innovación en Servicios Empresariales Avanzados.

Malikowski, S. R.; Thompson, M. E.; Theis, J. G. (2006). External factors associated with adopting a CMS in resident college courses. The Internet and Higher Education, 9(3), 163-174. doi: 10.1016/j.iheduc.2006.06.006.

OpenSim. (2012). Open simulador. Retrieved Octubre/19, 2012, from http://opensimulator.org/wiki/Main_Page).

Samaniego, G.; Vaca, B.; Esteve, V.; Cela, J.; Marqués, M.; Gisbert, M.; Mnelli, J. (2011). Configuración de objetos de aprendizaje en entornos virtuales 3D. Braga, Portugal.

SCOPEO. (2011). Aproximación pedagógica a las plataformas open source en la universidad española. Universidad de Salamanca Servicio de Innovación y Producción Digital

Sloodle (2012). Sloodle. Retrieved Octubre/19, 2012, from http://www.sloodle.org/moodle/

Suárez Guerrero, C. (2003). Los entornos virtuales de aprendizaje como instrumento de mediación. Teoría de la Educación, (4), 5.

AUTHORS

Vanessa Esteve-González. Department of Pedagogy. Rovira i Virgili University. Tarragona, Spain. Email: Vanessa.esteve@urv.cat

Byron Ernesto Vaca Barahona. Department of Pedagogy. Rovira i Virgili University. Tarragona, Spain. Email: byronernesto.vaca@estudiants.urv.cat

Gonzalo Nicolay Samaniego Erazo. Department of Pedagogy. Rovira i Virgili University. Tarragona, Spain. Email: gonzalo.samaniego@estudiants.urv.cat

Josep Holgado García

Ramon Palau Martín

3.4

DESIGN OF LEARNING ACTIVITIES FOR 3D TECHNOLOGICAL ENVIRONMENTS

1. INTRODUCTION

On-line teaching and technology broaden the spectrum of educational options and are a qualitative leap forward. The digitalisation of educational spaces involves changes to both professional activity and educational needs. Going beyond the physical conception of a university educational space to a more conceptual conception opens up new, more diverse, possibilities for teaching, more in tune with students nowadays. This new teaching model is not based on control by those who teach but on self-management by those who learn, and it requires a scenario to be designed in which students direct their own activity towards what they really need.

The graphic design of visual communication in a three-dimensional environment is an incipient but essential field for the presentation of digital contents in any discipline since the scenarios, the setting, the graphics, the models, the sounds and the colours will largely determine whether users will decide to remain in the 3D environment. Therefore, it is important to establish a design methodology that will establish the technological instruments to be used; defining a team with specific roles and functions; optimising development time, reaching agreements about design and, therefore, avoiding reprocesses and achieving the desired product.

2. MODELS FOR DESIGNING LEARNING ACTIVITIES IN 3D ENVIRONMENTS

When designing educational spaces in 3D environments which largely use simulations, a range of principles must be borne in mind that, in general, should not depend on the particular content to be studied. The environment should enable students to communicate and collaborate since the environment must be connected to the network to facilitate distributed interaction and cooperation. In the 3D environment, the students are represented by avatars which, in general, simulate human figures that all have the same image and same physical structure. These avatars are the students' eyes and hands. The environment must allow for tutorials, feedback and student evaluation by means of case studies. The students and the groups in which they work must be able to speak, act, create and review their actions in order to be able to solve the problems that they are faced with. They must be able to take decisions in real time about all the situations in which they are immersed within this "invented" digital world so that it can be active, participatory and dynamic. All this is possible only of the environment has the appropriate symbols and tools that enable them to interact and "live" in this simulated world.

Various things need to be borne in mind when designing the activities. Firstly, the virtual environments and settings for teaching and learning need to be designed and developed from a multidisciplinary point of view and they also need to be linked to the uses that teachers and students make of IT to achieve their learning objectives. And secondly, these activities need to be able to adapt to the virtual environments for teaching and learning in the short and the long term, and the evolution of social software, the Web 2.0 and the 3D immersive environments or virtual worlds.

One other thing that it is essential to take into account is that the design of a virtual environment for teaching and learning does not end with the selection of the technological resources and the plans for using them. The use that the participants make of these resources and their evolution must also be monitored, the extent to which the educational objectives for which they were designed are achieved must be evaluated, and they must be accordingly reconstructed and adapted. In this regard, collaboration and exchange between end users (mainly teachers and students), instructional designers and technological developers is fundamental if virtual environments for teaching and learning are to be optimised (Onrubia et al., 2006).

3D virtual environments must include the following elements:

1) a space for creating, managing and delivering sequences of learning activities with proposals made by teachers that students can select and develop;

2) a range of mechanisms that enable students to identify the characteristics and variables of the task proposed so that they can adapt their approach individually and collectively;

3) a range of automatic functions that provide information to both teachers and students about who does what, how, when, with whom and with what results, so that self-regulatory processes can be implemented and learning support can be offered at both an individual and a group level;

4) a dynamic structure that enables students to move quickly and efficiently from individual to group work, maintaining the identity and specificity of both work spaces.

Various models have been put forward to explain the process that must be followed to design activities for 3D virtual environments. For example, Baños and Rodríguez García (2012) proposed the scheme below (see table 2) at the 5th Symposium of Societies faced with the Digital Challenge.

Process for designing and setting up e-activities in 3D virtual worlds
1. Choice of a virtual world
2. Construction and/or management of appropriate spaces in the immersive environment
3. Creation and management of the teaching self
4. Design and development of a learning strategy for the immersive experience: design of suitable activities
5. Training of students in the essential competences for controlling the immersive environment

Table 2. Scheme for designing activities in 3D virtual environaments
Source: 5th Symposium of Societies faced with the Digital Challenge

Salmon (2004), on the other hand, proposed a different model that has a similar structure and which also has five stages.

Stage 1. Access and motivation

In this stage the participants access the virtual environment and acquire the competences required to use it. In the virtual world they need to acquire some basic competences so that they can manage their avatar's interaction with the environment and with other users. These competences are very similar to those required in the real world: mobility and communication. The presence in this phase of a teacher or tutor who can move around the virtual environment with ease is fundamental if orientation problems that may lead to a loss of motivation ar to be solved. Teaching support must be designed so that asynchronous and synchronous solutions can be provided.

Stage 2. Socialization

In this stage, the students configure their identities in the virtual World and begin to interact among themselves and with the teachers. Participants get used to using the tools of the virtual world to relate to their peers and a learning community starts to take shape that allows on-line, geographically disperse students to feel that they are working together on a common task. The technologies that support these platforms of communication and social relations generate or facilitate instances of socialization, which is the first step in configuring a coherent work community. For a teaching-learning activity to be constructed in the virtual world, there must also be a tangible interaction by the teacher.

Stage 3. Sharing information

This is the moment at which students are presented with the content of the forum and begin to exchange information about the main activity proposed. Salmon (2004) points out that the increasing amount of information in this phase and the need to work with it can cause a feeling of saturation in the students. They begin to develop a variety of strategies to cope with the requirements and the time involved in understanding the material.

Stage 4. Construction of knowledge

According to Salmon's model (2004), in this stage the group members relate to one another through discussion and communication. The students do not limit themselves to receiving or providing information but take active part in the process of constructing knowledge. Interaction is highly participatory and wholly learning oriented. They record their ideas, argue and counter argue about the proposed content, and there is an exchange of messages that take the form of a dialogue and whose outcome is active learning. And it is precisely in this stage, the most important one in the teaching-learning process within an e-learning system, that an immersive activity to be carried out synchronously in a virtual graphic environment becomes an educational tool that has features that make on-line teaching richer and more functional. In the present experiment, it is at this point that the main immersive activity is carried out: a synchronous debate about a particular topic that has been worked on in the teaching units and applied to a case.

Stage 5. Development
In this last stage, the students are asked to find advantages of the technological platform they have used and how it could be applied in other contexts. They are also asked to provide a critical vision of the environment and how it works.

Zapata, Marín and Vélez (2012) also put forward the following methodology for designing virtual environments for educational purposes.

1. Composition of the team
The team needs to be interdisciplinary so that it can cope with all the pedagogical, technological and visual communication issues involved in creating an educational environment; therefore, the following roles need to be defined: – Graphic designer for 3D educational environments. This person is in charge of creating, digitalising and editing two-dimensional images, as well as diagramming and illustrating all the pieces required. He/she is also responsible for making sketches and models of the three-dimensional environments and pieces, joining them up in such a way that the whole visual composition helps the 3D virtual environment users to have a pleasant and aesthetic experience. – Thematic expert. This person understands the subject that is to be taught in the 3D virtual environments. He/she is in charge of drawing up the content of the knowledge unit and illustrating the concepts to be developed that may become graphic elements in the virtual world. – Instructional designer. This person accompanies and guides the thematic expert in planning, designing learning activities and defining teaching resources. – Technological consultant for 3D virtual environments. This person decides which virtual world platform is to be used for the project and is in charge of coordinating the integration of the elements provided by the graphic designer for 3D virtual environments and the work done by the programmer. – Programmer for 3D virtual environments. This person is in charge of developing the software components for the platform in accordance with the objectives of the project.

2. Recognition of the technology to be used
The aim of this stage is to understand the possibilities and the limitations of the platform selected so that in the subsequent stages the functionalities that the technology provides can lead to the outcomes that the project was designed for.

3. Familiarity with the interface
The graphic designer for 3D virtual environments must explore and use the modelling tools available in the technology chosen in order to understand all of its possibilities and strike a balance between functions, imagination and creativity. It is essential for functionality to prevail over aesthetic aspects: design should not hinder function. In this stage it is important for the designer to investigate and explore other software that can supplement the 3D design and which is compatible with the technology that is to be used.

4. Definition of scenarios

In this stage the thematic expert and the instructional designer meet to decide how many scenarios are required to comply with the needs and expectations of the project, the context, the period and the style that will be simulated in the 3D virtual environment. Three essential scenarios have been defined for teaching and learning environments in virtual worlds:

– Presentation of content. This scenario is the avatar's entrance to the 3D virtual world (home) where the elements for displaying the content are defined (the architecture, the graphics and the setting). During this stage, the thematic expert and the instructional designer present the visual communication requirements for the content of the knowledge unit, and define how users navigate the site and the resources to be published (images, texts, animation, links to documents or websites, etc.).

– Activity environment. This space is used to list the activities that the students must do in the knowledge unit to fulfil the learning objective. The scenario and the setting of this environment will depend on the theme chose by the teacher. The activities can be put forward in the content scenario or a separate scenario, depending on the teacher's preference.

– Meeting space for participants. This is the place where the avatars can interact socially. It can be used by teachers to meet with students at pre-arranged dates and times.

5. Sketches and white paper

It is suggested that in this stage at least three sketches are made: top view, front view and side view. They will be checked, adjusted and approved by the thematic expert and instructional designer. The concept art must include a map of the land on which the 3D scenarios are going to be designed. The map must be a bird's eye view and take into account the relief that the scenario will have, the architectural design of the constructions and the design of the setting elements. The white paper must be based on the special features of each project (in this case a knowledge unit).

6. Preparation for the production of scenarios

Before the scenarios can be produced, the avatar must be personalised and the land on which they are to be built levelled.

7. Production of scenarios

Before the setting elements that are to go in each scenario can be created, the pre-determined area of the 3D virtual world must be modified.

8. Construction of the setting elements

Graphics must be produced that can be part of the scenery or setting.

9. Final adjustments

Before the product can be finalised, it must be reviewed by the thematic expert, the instructional designer and the technological consultant.

Bustos and Coll (2010) point out that the design of a teaching and learning virtual environment does not end with the selection of the technological resources and the planning of these resources. The use that the participants make of these resources must be monitored and the degree to which the objectives for which they were designed have been fulfilled must be assessed. Subsequently the original design must be adapted. In this regard, Onrubia (2006) considers that it is fundamental for the end users (teachers, students, instructional designers, technological developers, etc.) to collaborate and interact if virtual teaching and learning environments are to be optimised.

Bustos and Coll (2010) consider that 3D immersion environments must incorporate:

1. A space for creating, managing and displaying sequences of learning activities put forward by the teachers so that students can select them and carry them out.
2. Mechanisms that enable students to identify the task proposed so that they can carry it out individually or in a group.
3. Automatic functions that provide information about who does what, how, when, with whom and with what outcome.
4. A dynamic structure that enables students to move readily from individual to group work.

2.1. The role of symbols and learning tools

From the users' point of view, it is essential to analyse the roles and functions of the different symbols and objectives that are to be part of the 3D world

Development of the signifier: a variety of 3D mechanisms (authors, objects, etc.) are designed to fulfil the objectives of human beings. Some of them are means to advance towards the objective of human activity while others are designed to reflect ion this activity.
Exchange processes: some 3D mechanisms and human actions and knowledge among the students that participate in 3D environments. Other 3D mechanisms are means for object exchange.
Role taking processes: some 3D environments mediate the division of such tasks of responsibility as joint decisions, commitments and work plans.

Krange (2000) identified three relationships that characterise the 3D environment:

Actor-object relationship: makes it possible for students to act on objects in the 3D environment. They directly manipulate objects by clicking, lifting or moving them. The actor-object relationship provides information on how a task has been completed. This allows students to internalise the images, which reduces the need to metacommunicate all the interactions.

Object-object relationship: the manipulation of one artefact affects the position of another artefact. The object-object relationship has a twofold effect on collaborative learning. On the one hand, the results of individual actions on an object are displayed, which gives significant information that affects future actions on the division of tasks and discussion of these tasks. On the other, it is essential to create a good collaborative environment, which is always much better than an environment that only permits tasks to be executed. It provides teachers/trainers with information about how students interact with the environment, how they have completed all the actions and how they have taken the decisions at the very moment they do so.

Actor-actor relationship: is based on social interactions and an extension of what Gutwin (1995) called social conscience. Krange (2000) also argued that the efficient execution of a task is not sufficient to improve the learning effects of 3D environments. In other words, the effects of collaborative learning begin to be optimal when the virtual environment provides opportunities to discuss the tasks that are being or have been carried out. The possibilities of interaction in the environment need to be optimised to stimulate students permanently, to encourage personal responsibility and to prompt discussion of the whole decision-making process. If these environments are to be used in educational processes we must define exactly what their role is to be in this process so that it can be guaranteed that students will acquire the predicted competences-

2.2. Types of tools to be used in simulation activities for teaching

Most of the technological devices that students use from an early age have more to do with an active process of interaction with the tool than with processes of passive reading. Likewise, they have all become technologically literate on the basis of the image. EDUCAUSE (2006) published an interesting report on this issue and identified six areas that must be taken into account when systematising tool types:

Social computing: computer applications designed to facilitate interaction and collaboration

Personal broadcasting: based on audio and video. This has been made possible thanks to the greater simplicity of the tools used to treat audio and video and the improvement in technological infrastructures.

Mobile telephones: have brought educational content and services closer to users.

Educational games: have considerable educational potential.

Augmented reality: in widespread use in such fields as medicine, engineering, archaeology, etc. Its greatest contribution is the creation of 3D realities and spaces using abstract data that make it possible to accurately reproduce real spaces in digital format.

Context-Aware: environments and devices developed to respond to voice, movements or any other type of subtle signal made by the occupants of a context.

All this technology is present not only in educational spaces but also in daily life. The fact that is integrated into daily life for decision making, communication and access to information means that young people feel comfortable in a technological environment. This is what the university should use to generate other spaces for learning. These spaces in face-to-face universities can lead to blended learning projects that take full advantage not only of our experience in face-to-face projects but also the potential of IT (Dziuban et al., 2004).

3. CONCLUSIONS

Some of the advantages of including activities in 3D settings over traditional teaching are the following:

1.	The learning curve of the 3D platform is short and effective.
2.	They are efficient resources for online teaching because they motivate students to participate.
3.	They improve communication and interaction among the course participants, both teachers and students.
4.	This technology needs to be taken into account as an innovation in the media used to support the process of teaching and learning.
5.	In the creation of three-dimensional virtual worlds, technology must be used to give rise to immersive and fun teaching and learning spaces that are attractive to participants and conducive to the fulfilment of the learning objective.
6.	In order to develop a teaching and learning environment in a 3D virtual world, there must be an interdisciplinary team consisting of graphic designers, thematic experts, instructional designers, technological consultants and programmers.
7.	It is important for the design not to contain many distractions because the main aim of the world is to be used in the field of education.
8.	Virtual simulations in 3D facilitate the learning of theoretical processes and abilities and professional skills.
9.	The use of 3D environments favours the creation of collaborative pedagogical strategies that generate communicative and innovative alternatives for students.

The use of advanced technological environments for education is a challenge that represents a qualitative leap forward in the field of teaching. This challenge can be divided into two parts: firstly, changes can be made to some elements that are the driving force behind the transition to a student-centred educational model; and, secondly, there is a need to overcome the idea that teaching is little more than the individual action of the teacher who focuses on controlling the classroom and the specific content of the subject.

In a recent report published by New Media Consortium and EDUCAUSE Learning Initiative, Johnson et al. (2010) show that the central themes in education will continue to be closely linked to IT issues. Some of these are clearly related to digital contents and electronic books (e-books), and 3D simulations and environments.

REFERENCES

Aldrich, C. (2009). Virtual worlds, simulations, and games for education: A unifying view. Innovate, 5 (5). Retrieved from http://www.innovateonline.info

Alexander, B. (2008). Deepining the chasm: Web 2.0, gaming, and course management systems. *Journal of Online Learning and Teaching, 4*(2), 198-204.

Almaguer, T. y Elizondo, A. (2002) *Fundamentos sociales y psicológicos de la educación*. México, D. F.: Trillas.

Arredondo. E. (2009). El Uso de Mundos Virtuales de Aprendizaje en el CECyTEZ (MVA-CECyTEZ) Univ. Interamericana para el Desarrollo

Retrieved from http://www.cecytez-emsad.net/mundo_virtual/mundo_virtual.pdf

Baños G. M., Rodríguez G., T.G. (2011). E-learning en mundos viortuales 3D. Una experiencia educativa en Second Life. Revista Icono 14. Year 9 Vol. 2, pp. 39-58.

Bronack, S., R. Sanders y otros cuatro autores. (2008). Presence Pedagogy: Teaching and Learning in a 3D Virtual Immersive WorldInt, J. Teaching and Learning in Higher Educ., 20(1) 59-69 (2008).

Bustos S., A., Coll S., C.(2010). Los entornos virtuales como espacios de enseñanza y aprendizaje. Una perspectiva psicoeducativa para su caracterización y anàlisis. Revista Mexicana de Investigación Educativa, Vol. 15, No. 44, January-March, 2010, pp. 163-184. Mexico: Consejo Mexicano de Investigación Educativa.

Castranova, E. (2001). Virtual Worlds: A First-Hand Account of Market and Society on the Cyberian Frontier (December 2001). *CESifo Working Paper Series*. Nº 618. [on-line] Retrieved from http://ssrn.com/abstract=294828

Dickey, M.D. (2005). Three-dimensional virtual worlds and distance learning: two case studies of Active Worlds as a medium for distance education, British J. Educ. Technol., 36(3), 439–451

Dziuban, C. D. *et al.* (2004). *Blended Learning. Boulder*, Colo. EDUCAUSE. Center for Applied Learning, research bulletin, issue 7.

Edirisingha, P., Nie, M., Pluciennik, M. and Young, R. (2009). Socialisation for learning at a distance in a 3-D multi-user virtual environment. *British Journal of Educational Technology.* 40, (3), 458–479. doi:10.1111/j.1467-8535.2009.00962.x

Graván, R (s/f) Los entornos de trabajo colaborativo y su aplicación a la enseñanza. Universidad de Sevilla. Retrieved from http://tecnologiaedu.us.es/nweb/cursos/asig-nntt/html/pedro-colaborativo/2-2.htm#

Gros, B. (2002). Videojuegos y alfabetización digital. Publicado originalmente en la Revista Enredando.com. Retrieved from http://www.diegolevis.com.ar/secciones/infoteca.html

Gros, B., Miranda, J. (2008). Con el dedo en la pantalla": El uso de un videojuego de estrategia en la mediación de aprendizajes curriculares. Revista Electrónica Teoría de la Educación. Educación y Cultura en la Sociedad de la Información, 9(3). Retrieved from http://www.usal.es/teoriaeducacion.

Gros, B., Lara, P. (2009). Estrategias de innovación en la Educación Superior: El caso de la Universitat Oberta de Catalunya, Rev. Iberoamericana de Educ., 49, 223-245.

Hanna, D. (2002). *La enseñanza Universitaria en la era digital*. Barcelona: Octaedro.

Jara, G. (2004). Hacia la construcción de competencias para la informática educativa.

Retrieved from http://www.somece.org.mx/simposio2004/memorias/grupos/archivos/006.doc

Jonassen, D. and Carr, C. (2000). Mindtools: Affording Multiple Knowledge Representations for Learning. In S. P. Lajoie (Ed.). Computer as cognitive tools. Mahwah, NJ: Lawrence Erlbaum Assosiates.

Krajcik, J., Soloway, E., Blumenfeld, P., Marx, R. (2000). Un andamiaje de herramientas tecnológicas para promover la enseñanza y el aprendizaje de Ciencias. In C. Dede (Comp.). Aprendiendo con tecnologías. Buenos Aires: Paidós.

Krange, I. *et al.* (2000). Collaborative Learning in Schools by distributed use of interactive 3D technology. FoU Report 18/2000.

Lévy, P. (2007). *Cibercultura: la cultura de la sociedad digital.* Mexico: Anthropos-Universidad Autónoma Metropolitana.

Onrubia, J.; Bustos, A.; Engel, A. y Segués, T. (2006). "Usos de una herramienta de comunicación asíncrona para la innovación docente en contextos universitarios", comunicación presentada en el Congreso Internacional de Docencia Universitaria e Innovación.

Pavón, F. (2005). Educación para las nuevas tecnologías. *Pixelbit* (25). Retrieved from http://www.sav.us.es/pixelbit/articulos/n25/n25art/art2501.htm.

Pontes P., A. (2005). Aplicaciones de las tecnologías de la información y de la comunicación en la educación científica. Primera parte: funciones y recursos. Revista Eureka sobre Enseñanza y Divulgación de las Ciencias, 2 (1), 2-18. Retrieved from http://www.apaceureka.org/revista/

Quinche,J., González,F. L. (2011). Entornos virtuales 3D. Alternativa pedagógica para el fomento del aprendizaje colaborativo y gestión del conocimiento en Uniminuto. Formación Universitaria. Vol. 4(2), 45-54 (2011) doi: 10.4067/S0718-50062011000200006.

SALMON, G. (2004). *e-Actividades. El factor clave para una formación en línea activa.* Barcelona: UOC.

Squire, K.D. (2008). Game-based learning: An emerging paradigm for learning. Performance Improvement Quarterly, 21 (2), 7-36. Retrieved from http://www3.interscience.wiley.com/journal/120835177/issue.

TWINING, P. (2009). Exploring the educational potential of virtual worlds—Some reflections from the SPP. *British Journal of Educational Technology. 40 (3),* 496-514. doi:10.1111/j.1467-8535.2009.00962.x.

Vander, V.F. (2008). "Identity, power, and representation in virtual environments", *Journal of Online Learning and Teaching,* 4(2) pp. 205-216.

Horizon, 2007 C.A. "Informe Horizon". New Media Consortium y EDUCAUSE Learning Initiative. EEUU.

Zapata, D. Z., Marían A.L., Vélez, P. Y. (2012). Metodología de producción de diseño gráfico para un entorno de enseñanza aprendizaje en un mundo virtual tridimensional (MV3D). Uni-pluri/versidad, Vol. 12, Nº 1.

AUTHORS

Josep Holgado Garcia. *Department of Pedagogy. Rovira i Virgili University. Tarragona, Spain. Email: josep.holgado@urv.cat*

Ramon Palau Marti. *Department of Pedagogy. Rovira i Virgili University. Tarragona, Spain. Email: ramon.palau@urv.cat*

Jose María Cela-Ranilla

Vanessa Esteve-González

3.5
USING SIMULATION GAMES TO IMPROVE LEARNING SKILLS

1   INTRODUCTION

While educators teach their students about decision making in complex environments, managers have to deal with the complexity of large projects on a daily basis. To make better decisions it is assumed that the latter would benefit from a better understanding of complex phenomena, as would students, the professionals of the future.

Virtual worlds can be used to promote higher levels of student engagement and facilitate highly interactive and multimodal learning experiences. They have the potential to radically transform education [e.g. Thomassen (2010); Kluge, S., & Riley, L. (2008); Johnson, L. & Levine, A. (2008); Freitas, (2006)]. Some virtual world technologies make use of such commercially-hosted platforms as Second Life and Active Worlds, while others extend and adapt 3D toolkit to create collaborative virtual world server platforms and open-source products such as Open-Simulator, Open Cobalt and Open Wonderland. Yet others build their own, adapted platforms and systems using a variety of programming languages and game engines to accommodate their specific needs and purposes.

In the Game Generation, computer games respond to children's contemporary needs, habits and interests (Henderson, 2005). Olson et al. (2007) pointed out that children who have never played computer games are quite rare since they regard gaming as a social activity. Game-based learning (GBL) is designed to combine learning and game playing, so it will improve the ability of the player to retain educational subjects and apply them to the real world. Educational games encompass educational objectives and subject matter that have the potential to make learning more learner-centered, easier, enjoyable, interesting, efficient and effective (Prensky, 2001; Virvou, Katsionis, & Manos, 2005).

Throughout history there has been a need to find the balance between technology and educational usefulness. The impact on users should be the main evidence of this usefulness. However, generating an educational process in a complex technological environment is a powerful journey during which we can learn from each and every decision made.

In this regard, the present document describes the final educational proposal in a 3D simulation environment. It is designed to develop generic skills –in particular, team-work and self-management– and is based on a set of decisions related to the theoretical base, the learning environment and a specific educational proposal.

The experience takes place in the framework of a research project financed by the Spanish Ministry of Education. The name of the project is *SIMUL@: Evaluation of a Simulation Technological Environment for the Learning of Transversal Competences at University* (Ref: EDU2008-01479) and is conducted by a multidisciplinary team coordinated by the Rovira i Virgili University (Spain) and which also involves the University of Lleida (Spain), the University of Hamburg (Germany), and the University of Minho (Portugal). The main topic dealt with in Simul@ is the analysis of technological environments based on simulations in work-related environments for learning generic skills at university.

In this project, we created an educational proposal to work with 68 bachelor and master students from two different disciplines: business and education. We use the same educational structure and it is this that we describe in this document.

2 STRUCTURE

This study explains each of the parts in the decision-making process: the theoretical basis, the learning environment (pedagogy and technology) and a specific educational strategy (Figure 1).

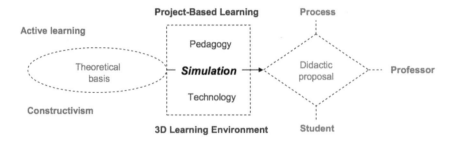

Figure 1. Decision-making process

2.1 Theoretical basis

In theory, virtual environments create particular settings and attempt to draw the participant into the setting (Gredler, 2004). Of the wide range of different approaches to learning– from the behavioural to more situational approaches –the base of the model used in simulations should be closest to constructivism. This model understands learning to be an activity in which students use their own strategies to take part. So, our starting point is an educational approach that considers learning to be an active process that is situated and contextualized in practice. This approach is consistent not only with social constructivism but also with such learning theorists as Lave & Wenger (1991) and Greeno et al. (1993), who incorporate the concept of social participation into specific activity contexts based on the situated cognition theory. These ideas can also be backed up with other social theories such as expansive learning and transfer of development (Engeström and Grohn, 2000), which states that transfer occurs when individuals involved in collective activity take action to challenge existing practice.

According to this theoretical view, the resulting didactic sequence should take into account constructivist principles of instructional design: all learning activities should be anchored to a larger problem, tasks should be authentic, learners should be supported and opportunities should be given to reflect on both the content learned and the learning process (Savery & Duffy, 1996).

This idea of construction in a specific context of practice is completed with active learning. Active learning should be regarded as an approach rather than a method (Prince, 2004) accepting that a variety of method can be applied under this generic concept. According to Meyers & Jones (1993), *"active learning derives from two basic assumptions: that learning is by nature an active endeavor and that different people learn in different ways"*. In active learning, the educational proposal should mostly target higher-order activities (analysis, synthesis, evaluation) where students can explore their own attitudes and values (Bonwell & Eison, 1991).

The didactic proposal must focus on students in such a way that they take active part in the learning process rather than merely oblige them to gather information passively from a lecture delivered in the traditional way (Slunt & Giancarlo, 2004). In other words, teaching should be based on different principles: students use resources to construct their knowledge depending on their needs and how they learn; students take responsibility for learning; students learn how to learn by developing problem-solving skills, critical thinking, and reflective thinking; learning activities take into account the various learning styles of students; teachers provide clear expectations and desired outcomes before lessons begin; teachers guide and facilitate the learning process; and teachers are responsible for students being provided with content and the learning process (Sukkum, 2002, cited by Poonruksa, 2007, p.227).

The didactic sequence should take into account the conceptual considerations made above in order to respond to the challenge of using such advanced technology as 3D simulations. In fact, this is the way in which some of the principles that define good practices in undergraduate education are put into practice: contact between students and faculty is encouraged, reciprocity and cooperation is developed among students, active learning is promoted, time on task is emphasized and different talents and ways of learning respected (Chickering & Gamson 1991).

This theoretical framework based on student action and interaction, and the context in which a product is built is particularly suitable for developing the requirements defined in the construction process of the European Higher Education Area. This process defines a curriculum in which generic skills are the main content. These skills are understood to be those that are common to most professions, and which are related to the integrated application of aptitudes, personality features, educational backgrounds and other values. Technological active learning scenarios can promote the development of generic skills, which are learnt basically in work-related environments.

2.2 The learning environment

Now it has been decided that simulation is to be the base of the educational proposal, this section describes two aspect of the learning environment: the technology and the educational strategy.

2.2.1 Technological environment: 3D virtual world

Generally, 3D virtual worlds are also known as metaverses, a concept taken from the sci-fi novel *Snow Crash*, written by Neil Stephenson in 1992. Although the notions are not exactly synonymous, they are still being debated in the literature. However, and in agreement with Castronova (2005) we will assume that virtual world and metaverse can be regarded as the same.

A virtual world is a simulation of a space, a three dimensional representation of geographical features, cities and digital simulation of the real environment. Second Life (SL), for example, is a 3D environment that enables users to interact through a representation, which is known as an avatar. The main characteristics of virtual worlds are that they are simple to use, they have a series of collaborative facilities and their 3D features are attractive and provide users with a new and highly immersive sensation. All these traits have made virtual worlds an interesting scenario in which to test innovative educational environments and apply new data mining techniques. Furthermore, participants in a successful virtual world have a deep sense of presence in that world.

Pivec (2003) explains the steps that should be taken to design a successful game-based learning opportunity:

- Determine the pedagogical approach (how you believe learning takes place)
- Situate the task in a model world
- Elaborate the details
- Incorporate underlying pedagogical support
- Map learning activities to interface actions
- Map learning concepts to interface objects

Many studies and a considerable amount of data provide evidence that SL is an environment that fosters processes of socialization (e.g. Minocha & Reeves, 2010; Koster, 2006) and learning in different contexts and with different content (e.g. Thomanssen & Rive, 2010).

After exploring several simulation environments, we decided to use SecondLife (SL) and OpenSimulator as the 3D virtual world on which to base our educational proposal. The environment and the fact that it could be integrated into a standard learning virtual environment (Moodle) were the reasons for this choice.

OS allows for interaction between simulations and games, social networking by which knowledge is shared and created, collaborative work environments, and the use of different media to meet different learning needs. Through Sloodle −a module of learning activities represented as OS objects− we integrated OS into Moodle. The student performed the activities in OS and the teacher had Moodle registration in a transparent way. This made it possible for us to:

- Design and set up an island in OS that could be accessed via Moodle from Sloodle.
- Make an initial assessment of whether students would be able to learn skills by using the 3D OS space.
- Associate a learning pattern to the final results obtained and recorded in Moodle.
- Define a strategy for curriculum integration for self-management skills work and team work in OS useful for teachers.

2.2.2 The method: Project-Based Learning (PBL)

In coherence with our work philosophy, we felt that the PBL method was especially suitable for organizing the didactic sequence to deliver the students in the simulation. The joint construction of a project that must be presented to an assessment committee is an extremely powerful way of developing generic skills. There are many reasons why PBL is a very good option for preparing students for work: it increases motivation, it connects theory and practice, it builds knowledge jointly, it obliges them to share their own capabilities with others, and it establishes connections between different disciplines, etc.

Proulx (2004) defines seven features that are consistent with our idea of work and which we used as a basis for our decisions:

- A systematic process
- Acquisition and transfer of learning
- The three major moments: anticipation, planning, construction
- Individual or pairwork
- Supervision by a teacher
- An observable activity
- A final product that can be evaluated

These features, and the following statement by Grant (2002), are the base of our didactic proposal following a PBL structure: *"Project-based learning is centered on the learner and affords learners the opportunity for in-depth investigations of worthy topics. The learners are more autonomous as they construct personally-meaningful artifacts that are representations of their learning"*.

2.3 The educational proposal

To explain the educational proposal, we organize the information in three steps: the process, the teacher and the student. These three points of view have some common elements.

The aim of the teaching project is to construct a particular product (School Olympic Games or Tourist Trade Show), but we shall focus on the process independently of the specific content of the product.

2.3.1 The process

The process is described according to the different moments of decision making:

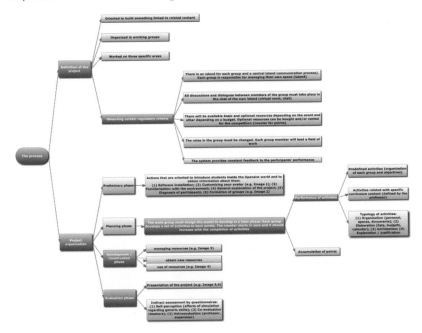

2.3.2 The teacher

This section describes the decisions that are the responsibility of the teacher during the process:

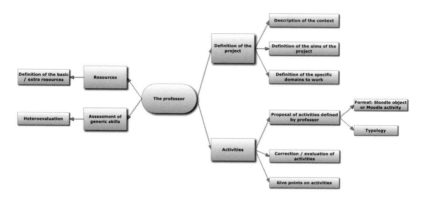

2.3.3 The student

Finally we present the sequence that the student has to follow in order to carry out the project successfully.

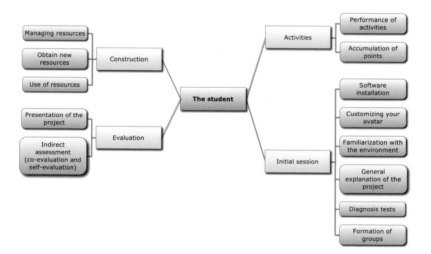

Image 1: Editing appearance

Image 2: Island map

Image 3: Empty group island

Image 4: Building their island   Image 5: Project presentation   Image 6: Final island

Figure 2. Scenes from the educational proposal

3. CONCLUSIONS

Although this work describes the skeleton of the training process by which university students are trained using simulations in 3D environments, the findings should be used to provide continuity in both pedagogy and technology.

Before any analysis is made, it must be understood that pedagogy needs to be applied before technology. Working with advanced technologies requires a considerable amount of planning and design; every decision must be made with a subsequent step in mind. This work of anticipation is one of the main characteristics of this kind of process. The strategy mus be centered on the students' tasks and the learning outcomes they must acquire.

Teamwork is also very necessary when designing this kind of learning scenario. Designers have a wide range of different profiles: experts in graphic design, experts in computer management and systems, experts in pedagogy, experts in specific content (subject). The fact that they all have to put into practice such skills as expertise, patience, trust in others, planning, commitment, etc. constitutes a learning process in itself.

It is also shown that teachers and students need to be assigned different roles. Once again, the student is the center of the process but the teacher is responsible. In this regard, the evaluation process plays a special role. This kind of technological environment facilitates the assessment process because all events are recorded. This process must be planned and anticipated so that the most relevant information is collected to regulate the process and make good decisions regarding learning outputs.

Regarding technology, it constitutes a real challenge to observe other virtual worlds using the same or similar didactic sequence. In this sense, tools like Unity 3D provide a good opportunity to follow this idea. Unity 3D is a game development tool with a visually very rich browser based client. It allows developing for web, mobile, or console device. But, Unity doesn't support the Sloodle module at this moment; this is a problem but it becomes a challenge at the same time to search options in this regard.

This paper describes a process that involves one of the elements that is the basis of its content: learning by doing. The whole design process is an experience that is now a rough diamond that requires analysis. The exploitation of the data resulting from this experience will be the next step in the Simul@ Project.

We have designed a process based on the principles of active learning using PBL methodology and it is now time to analyse the dynamics generated. And there is also the need to share our findings with the scientific community to extend our knowledge on these issues.

REFERENCES

Bonwell, C. C., & Eison, J. A. (1991). *Active Learning: Creating Excitement in the Classroom. 1991 ASHE-ERIC Higher Education Reports*. ERIC Clearinghouse on Higher Education, The George Washington University: Washington, DC.

Castronova E. (2005). *Synthetic Worlds: the Business and the Culture of Online Games*. University of Chicago Press: Chicago.

Chang, Y. C., Peng, H. Y., & Chao, H. C. (2010). Examining the effects of learning motivation and of course design in an instructional simulation game. *Interactive learning environments, 18*(4), 319-339.

Chickering, A.W., & Gamson, Z.F. (1991). Applying the Seven Principles for Good Practice in Undergraduate Education. *New Directions for Teaching and Learning. 47.*

de Freitas, S. (2006). *Learning in Immersive Worlds*. London: JISC.

Engeström, Y. & Ghron T.T. (2000): *Conceptualizing transfer: from standard notions to developmental perspectives.(internal document).*

Grant, M. M. (2002). Getting a grip on project-based learning: Theory, cases and recommendations. *Meridian: A Middle School Computer Technologies, 5*(1), 83.

Gredler, M. (2004). Games and simulations and their relationships to learning. In D. Jonassen (Ed.), *Handbook of research on educational communications and technology* (pp. 813 - 828). Mahwah, NJ: Erlbaum.

Greeno, J. G., Smith, D. R. & Moore, J. L. (1993). Transfer of situated learning. In D. K. Detterman & R. J. Sternberg (Eds.), *Transfer on trial: Intelligence, cognition, and instruction* (pp. 99 – 167). Westport, CT,US: Ablex Publishing.

Henderson, L. (2005). Video games: A significant cognitive artifact of contemporary youth culture. In: *Proceedings of DiGRA 2005 conference. Changing views e Worlds in play.* http://www.diagra.org/dl/db/06276.11341.pdf.

Johnson, L. F. & Levine, A. H. (2008). Virtual worlds: Inherently immersive, highly social learning spaces. *Theory Into Practice, 47*(2), 161-170.

Kluge, S., & Riley, L. (2008). Teaching in Virtual Worlds: Opportunities and challenges. *Issues in Informing Science and Information Yechnology, 5,* 127-135.

Koster, R. (2006). Declaring the rights of players. In J.M. Balkin and B.S. Noveck (Eds.), *The state of play: Law, games, and virtual worlds.* (pp 55–67). New York: New York University Press.

Lave J.; Wenger, E. (1991). *Situated learning. Legitimate peripheral participation*. UK: Cambridge University Press.

Meyers, C. & Jones, T.B. (1993*). Promoting Active Learning: Strategies for the College Classroom*, San Francisco, CA: Jossey-BassPublishers.

Minocha, S., & Reeves, A. J. (2010). Design of learning spaces in 3D virtual worlds: an empirical investigation of Second Life. *Learning, Media and Technology, 35*(2), 111-137.

Olson, C. K., Kutner, L. A., Warner, D. E., Almerigi, J. B., Baer, L., Nicholi, A. M., & Beresin, E. V. (2007). Factors correlated with violent video game use by adolescent boys and girls. *Journal of Adolescent Health, 41*(1), 77-83.

Peters, V., Vissers, G., & Heijne, G. (1998). The validity of games. *Simulation & Gaming, 29*(1), 20-30.

Pivec, M., Dziabenko, O., & Schinnerl, I. (2003, July). Aspects of game-based learning. In *Proceedings of I-Know , 3,* 216-225.

Poonruksa, S. (2007). The Integration of Student-Centered Approach for Field Trip in Mental Health and Psychiatric Nursing Practicum: Case Studies among Third Year Nursing Students of Assumption University of Thailand. *AU Journal of Technology. 10(4)*, 225-231.

Prensky, M. (2001). *Digital game-based learning*. New York: McGraw-Hill.

Prince, M. (2004). Does Active Learning Work? A Review of the Research. *Journal of Engineering Education, 93(3)*, 223-231.

Proulx, Jean, (2004). *Apprentissage par projet*, Sante-Foy: Presses de l'Université du Québec

Savery, J. and Duffy, T. M. (1996). Problem-Based learning: An instructional model and its constructivist framework. In B. G. Wilson (Ed.), *Constructivist learning environments: Case studies in instructional design* (pp. 135 - 148). Englewood Cliffs, NJ: Educational Technology Publications. Spiro, R. J., Feltovich.

Slunt, K. M., Giancarlo, L. C. (2004). Student-centered learning: A comparison of two different methods of instruction. *Journal of Chemical Education, 81*, 985-988.

Spector, J.M. (2001). An Overview of Progress and Problems in Educational Technology. *Interactive Educational Multimedia, 3 (October 2001)*, 2737.

Thomassen, Aukje & Rive, Pete (2010). How to enable knowledge exchange in Second Life in design education?, *Learning, Media and Technology, Vol 35 (2)*, 155-169.

Virvou, M., Katsionis, G., & Manos, K. (2005). Combining software games with education: evaluation of its educational effectiveness. *Educational Technology & Society, 8(2)*, 54-65.

Acknowledgements: This research is funded by national R&D plan of the Ministry of Science and Innovation of Spain, SIMUL@: "Evaluation of a Simulation Technological Environments for the Learning of Transversal Competences at University", with reference EDU2008-01479.

AUTHORS

Jose Maria Cela-Ranilla. *Department of Pedagogy. Rovira i Virgili University. Tarragona, Spain. Email: josemaria.cela@urv.cat*

Vanessa Esteve-González. *Department of Pedagogy. Rovira i Virgili University. Tarragona, Spain. Email: vanessa.esteve@urv.cat*

CHAPTER 4:

EXPERIENCES AND GOOD PRACTICES

Vincent TY Ng
David K Herold

4.1

TEACHING AND LEARNING IN VIRTUAL WORLDS – THE POLYU EXPERIENCE

1. BACKGROUND AND MOTIVATION

In the early 90s, The Hong Kong Polytechnic University (PolyU) pioneered elearning as a tool to support student learning. Initially, materials with simple graphics were put online and students could read or download the notes through the Internet. Later on, a second generation of elearning would support interactive multimedia with online materials and assessment. Recently, a new trend is worldwide is emerging which uses serious games and simulations within educational institutions as well as the effective training of professionals. In this third generation of elearning, highly interactive technologies, such as online visualization, virtual worlds and simulations, have been employed to support a constructivist elearning model for students (Connolly and Standfield, 2006; Connolly, McLellan, Stansfield, Ramsay and Sutherland, 2004).

The younger students, such as PolyU students, are digital natives. Many digital natives exhibit a cognitive preference for certain media. They prefer video, audio and interactive media. The traditional classroom lecture may not be able to fully utilize the new media. Difficulties have been encountered when having large number of students in a class or students are not regularly attending classes. Students feel they do not have sufficient individual mentoring. It is believed that virtual worlds have the desirable qualities for helping these problems by supporting situated learning or cognitive apprenticeship (Prensky, 2003). By creating virtual worlds, through various embedded activities, we can bring ways of doing, ways of being, and ways of analysing to our students (Shaffer, Squire, Halverson and Gee, 2005).

During Fall 2007, the School of Hotel and Tourism Management (SHTM) together with School of Design (SD) in PolyU designed a virtual campus to support the School's student orientation programme. This provided Year 1 students with an alternative way to become familiarized with their new study environment and understand how to become effective and successful students at PolyU. A Virtual PolyU Campus was built on the Second Life platform as shown in Figure 1. The virtual orientation programme aimed to cultivate new learning experiences for students and to support education activities. Over 400 full-time Year 1 HD, BSc and MSc hotel and tourism students were invited to join the orientation programme. Academic staff and Year

2 and 3 students took the roles of "teacher" and "student mentors". During term 2, January – March 2008, the project was expanded to provide for tutorials within Second Life for the General Education course APSS285 "Media and Everyday Life" and 80 students were taught in 6 weekly tutorials using a space within the virtual PolyU Campus created with the support of a team from EDC. In addition, 4 SHTM subjects (with around 300 students in total) used Second Life for a range of teaching and learning activities in Semester 2.

Figure 1. PolyU Campus

Today's educators face new challenges not experienced by teachers in the past. They are dealing with students who are part of the 'Net Generation' (Oblinger, 2003), brought up in a 3-D world of virtual communication, visual complexity and online identities. They want and expect more engaging, empowering and interactive learning experiences in their student life than universities are often able to give them. Prensky writes of the differences between 'Digital Natives', the generation that grew up with video games and computers, and 'Digital Immigrants', people who have started using computers as adults (Prensky, 2001). The digital natives are used to instant gratification, hyperlinked information, and the need for rapid reflexes, and yet they are being taught by digital immigrants, who are used to learning from books and communicating by phone. Higher education is led by digital immigrants, using the same teaching methods used for many centuries, the didactic lecture. However the world has changed, and universities have been painfully slow in utilizing and harnessing the power of technology to enhance and stimulate student learning – the use of PowerPoint and email are probably the most widely used technologies in academia today.

Students today are in touch with technology and innovation in their everyday lives through digital media, smart phones and their online networks. Young people are community-focused, they belong to virtual communities to discuss shared interests (communities of interest), to develop social relations (community of relationships), and to explore new identities (communities of fantasy) (Hagel and Armstrong, 1997). According to Zemsky and Massey (2008), students want to use technology in order to be entertained through music, games and movies, to be connected to one another and to present themselves and their work. Our institutions are playing catch up, and not doing it very successfully. Yet, despite this situation, there are signs of change, with learning taking place in some academic departments which demonstrate student-centred and innovative teaching through e-Learning and "Serious Games" (Annetta et al., 2006)

Virtual worlds are being increasingly used by education. Platforms such as Second Life make it relatively fast and cost-effective to design and set up a virtual environment for teaching and learning compared to a few years ago. Virtual worlds are the next generation of e-learning and something PolyU should explore seriously now. While PolyU is the first university in Hong Kong to explore the possibilities of Second Life, a large community of educational institutions worldwide has already established itself in Second Life and is using this platform to develop new teaching and learning solutions. Institutions with Second Life presence include the universities of Harvard and Stanford in the USA, Edinburgh and Nottingham University in the UK, the universities of Hamburg and Aachen in Germany, and many others.

2. DESIGN AND METHODOLOGY

In line with the blended learning approach, the Core-SL project has been started in 2009 to build an interactive and efficient hybrid learning environment with technology support for conducting teaching & learning activities within an interactive learning atmosphere to encourage students to become active learners outside the classroom.

The initial development of Core-SL is consisted of four functional spaces: Teaching & Learning, Assessment, Design and Resources. Within the Teaching and Learning space, interactive and experiential teaching and learning solutions will be developed that increase independent learning by students while maximising peer group and student-teacher interaction opportunities. This will include the design of learning spaces, e.g. lecturing, seminar, or tutorial areas, as well as the creation of spaces for student interaction, the display of student works, etc.

In the Assessment space, a new form of interactive and online assessment and student feedback will be produced and validated for future large-scale deployment. It is to provide easy-to-use solutions for teaching staff, the library, and other interested parties to assess students according to university standards, as well as to gather student feedback on teaching, online and offline learning provisions, etc.

The Resources space will set up structures for highly accessible and interactive delivery of information while also developing safe-guards to protect intellectual property rights. The space would support the development of general learning activities of students and staff. Start-up packages, e.g. guided tours, introductory walk-throughs, etc. will be collated to improve user-friendliness and accessibility of online learning. One initiative is to design a virtual library and resource centre that aims to provide guidance of The Pao Yue-kong Library as well as accesses to its electronic resources. The virtual centre would include corners, shelves and areas for the provision of course materials, displays of interest to the PolyU community, etc. The space can also be used for the public around the world to know more about the achievements and activities in PolyU.

The Design space acts as a knowledge sharing hub among staff and students. It is established as a place for idea exchanges and mutual support. The Design space can be further divided into 2 areas: staff and students. These areas are aimed to provide a platform to cultivate good practices, new tools, teaching and learning approaches, and knowledge sharing.

With the four functional spaces, an integrated virtual 3D environment is developed which forms a generic teaching and learning platform providing, but not limited to, (i) a series of standard teaching tools usable for holding teaching & learning activity for different academic departments; (ii) a role play simulation as demonstration of teaching and learning possibility in Second Life; and (iii) a series of standard assessment tools usable for assessing students' knowledge acquired, ability and cognitive development for different academic departments.

For the Department of Computing, we have the Intelligent Company for Interview Training set up. In the virtual company, students have role-play interaction with AI robots to collect requirement specification for system design and development for in a database subject (Figure 2).

Figure 2. Interviews to collect requirements for a software project

In another computing subject, students are divided into groups with scheduled timeslots. They were required to visit the PolyU virtual campus to attend tutorial class or complete their presentations to tutor through voice chat. Virtual tutorials had been conducted for Master level part-time students in the virtual theater with Powerpoint presentations (Figure 3).

Figure 3. Group Interaction and Powerpoint Presentation

For the case of the SHTMK, students were asked to do presentations on their virtual guestroom setup (Figure 4). In a customer relationship management subject, in order to well prepare the students for their placement and career, the school simulated different types of hotels in the virtual campus. Providing the space, student can play different roles and practice their customer handling skill to solve cases designed by the teaching staff.

Figure 4. Virtual Guest Rooms Set Up

Taken the "international" nature of the platform, students in the Department of Applied Social Science (APSS) can explore around the world and study different cultures. They can also meet with people of different nationalities so as to have first person interaction with them to get accurate information. A discussion area has been built in our virtual campus for providing space to teacher-students and student-student interactions (Figure 5).

Figure 5. Cultural & Media Study with Discussion Zone

An interesting use of CoreSL is from the Institute of Textiles and Clothing. They have constructed the Bioengineering Laboratory (Figure 6) which includes Information section, Lecture room, fabric and garment laboratory, scenario chamber and assessment zone. The laboratory provided students with space to have outside class to study on fabric and garment features which cannot be covered in class, as well as an assessment zone for them to test and evaluate themselves.

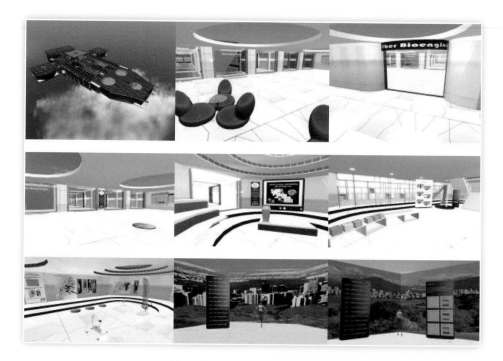

Figure 6. Bioengineering Laboratory

Another impressive use of CoreSL is from the School of Nursing. A hospital simulated environment has been built for students to have procedural training. This is a safe environment where students can try utilizing their taught skill on practical cases. From changing hospital uniform to completing the procedure on wearing PPE and intubation, all students' behavior will be monitored. Every student can have an evaluation report on their performance by the end of each practice, and teachers can also have a log of students' behaviors as a reference to their teaching and research purpose.

Figure 7. Procedural Training on Personal Protective Equipment and Intubation

3. REVIEWS AND EVALUATION

In the past few years, CoreSL has served over 3000 students from over 25 different subjects organized by the 10 participated departments. We have organized over 50 workshops for teachers and students, helping them to learn and adapt to the new learning platform. In the library workshop, there were 40 participants. Among them, 84% of the participants expressed an interest in further involvement in our project and around 30% of them stated that the workshop provided would be advantageous for their work as well as their personal development.

Student Reviews

In Computing, students were expected to have enough background knowledge to adapt to Second Life using an instruction booklet, and therefore no introductory workshop was held for them. The result in a survey as shown in Figure 8 proved this assumption wrong. The students were not successful in their first attempts to follow the guide without an instructor. This demonstrated the significant of workshops for a successful introduction of Second Life to beginners.

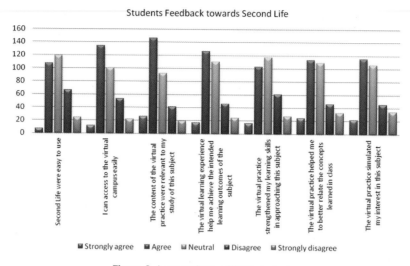

Figure 8. A survey for the COMP students.

In general, we have around 50% of participated students express their enjoyment on virtual learning while most of the teachers are rather positive towards their virtual teaching experience. A student handbook was published for students as a step-by-step introductory guide. This was very successful as most of the students managed to sign up for, to enter the Second Life, and to reach our campus island by referring to the guide book on their own. Figure 9 shows the APSS students' impression after they used Second Life in their learning, we can see that most students feel interested in this "interesting" platform for simulation / game based learning activities. This can reflected, in certain degree, how this platform can potentially motivate students' learning attitude on top of traditional learning method.

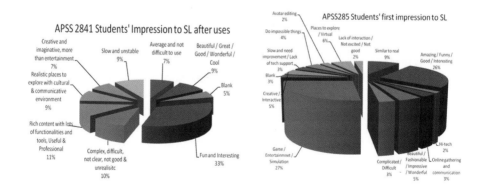

Figure 9. Two surveys done for APSS Students

We have conducted a collective feedback from our students who participated in Second Life learning. From the results shown in Figure 10, we can see that students are having positive attitude and impression towards the new mode of learning. They did agreed that this interactive and interesting new platform can be provide a fun and interactive learning environment in their learning process, even thought the learning curve is a bit too long corresponding to complexity of their in-world activity. There are over 50% of them even tends to satisfied with their learning experience on this new platform.

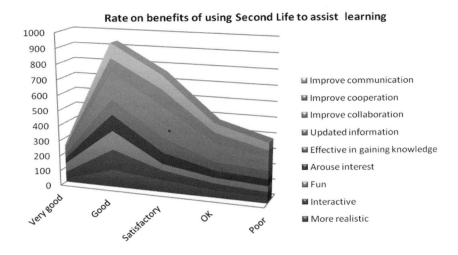

Figure 10. Students Views of CoreSL

Teacher Reviews

Apart from the feedbacks of students, our majority of participated teaching staff, over 90%, agreed that the virtual campus did help their students' learning in certain degree. In addition, academic staff also agree that the CoreSL project has brought us the following advantages:

- We are breaking the physical boundaries of learning, and have invited overseas educators to give lectures in our virtual lecture theater for the benefit of our students.
- We have introduced easy and effective ways to allow students to work collaboratively in realizing 3D designs, so as to allow them to practice their acquired skills in a simulated, but realistic environment.
- We are connecting our students to the world and people in other countries. In several of the courses held in Second Life, students have interacted with people from the USA, Canada, Europe, Australia, and Japan which has served to broaden their perspectives and enriched their learning experience.

In a PolyU teaching review on CoreSL, teachers are generally agreed with the beneficial of adapting to our new teaching and learning platform and rather positive towards its potential on its contribution of effective teaching & learning, though there are still spaces to advance the quality of our virtual campus. We have around 80% of participated teaching staff found technical barrier when they first learning about Second Life, this is a significant number. Since most of the participated department and servicing sections are not in technology domain, they met various challenges when employing in their teaching.

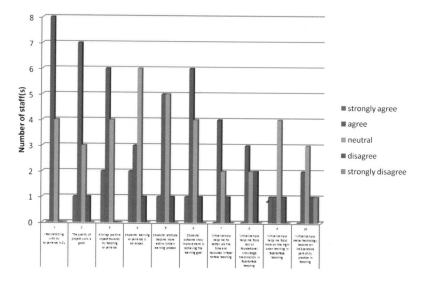

Figure 11. Teacher Survey

4. CHALLENGES AND CONCLUSION

At the early to middle project development stage, the network speed in PolyU, especially during peak hours was slow, which has repeatedly led to the poor and unacceptably slow performance of the Second Life software. This has discouraged many users and had an impact on the uptake of Second Life in teaching and learning. However, the situation has been improved and provided a satisfying environment for University-use of Second Life now.

In addition, Second Life makes high demands on the quality of hardware, e.g. graphics cards, which are not met by the low-cost machines available in some departments. As a result, some of the teaching staff and students have encountered problems entering Second Life. We finally adapted a third-party developed viewer which have less demand on computation power, called Kirstens S16, instead of the official Second Life viewer to ensure our staff can have a smooth use of Second Life in their offices, and we have managed to include the Kirstens Viewer as an official software installed in student computing laboratories which provide enough support to students using Second Life in PolyU to solve the equipment hinder.

Virtual learning environments are new and not widely known or accepted in Hong Kong, Second Life has been a new and unfamiliar platform for many Hong Kong students which required a comparatively long learning curve. Students demonstrated low levels of acceptance for the introduction of unknown, new learning technologies, and required additional motivation before they even attempted to make use of Second Life, and continuous encouragement to keep entering the virtual environment.

With the growth of participating departments, larger diversified teaching and learning activities have been arranged for different professional aspects. With various levels of success and failure, we notice the impact on activity design verse their Second Life uptake time. Since it cannot be denied that the learning curve for adapting Second Life is a bit long compare to students' packed curriculum. Usually, students spent more time for adapting the platform rather than to learn through the virtual activities. This is the issue raised after the network accessing speed solved.

With all the challenges which we faced, the overall students' feedback did show that we are going in a right direction of developing a fun and interactive learning environment which they did have an obvious increase in interest of learning through this platform.

REFERENCES

Annetta, L. A., Murray, M. R., Laird, S. G., Bohr, S. C., & Park, J. C. (2006). Serious games: Incorporating video games in the classroom. *Educause Quarterly, 29*(3), 16-22.

Connolly, T. M., McLellan, E., Stansfield, M. H., Ramsay J. & Sutherland J. (2004). Applying computer games concepts to teaching database analysis and design. In Q.Mehdi & N.Gough (Eds), *International Conference on Computer Games, AI, Design and Education*, Reading, UK, 8–10 November.

Connolly, T., & Stansfield, M. (2006). Using Games-Based eLearning Technologiesin Overcoming Difficulties in Teaching Information Systems.*Journal of Information Technology Education: Research*, 5(1), 459-476.

Hagel, H & Armstrong, A. (1997) *Net Gain: Expanding Markets through Virtual Communities.* Boston, Mass. Business School Press

Oblinger, D. (2003). Boomers, Gen-Xers, and Millennials: Understanding the 'New Students,' *EDUCAUSE Review*, 38 (4), 37–47.

Prensky, M. (2001). Digital natives, digital immigrants part 1. *On the horizon,9*(5), 1-6.

Prensky, M. (2003). Digital game-based learning. Computers in Entertainment (CIE), 1(1), 21-21.

Williamson, D., Squire, K., Halverson, R., & Gee, J. P. (2005). Video games and the future of learning. *Phi Delta Kappan*, 87(2), 104-111.

Zemsky, R & Massey, W.E. (2004) Why the E-Learning Boom went Bust, *Chronicle of Higher Education*, Vol. 50, 9 July. Retrieved from http://chronicle.com/article/Why-the-E-Learning-Boom-Went/29259

AUTHORS

Vincent TY Ng. *Department of Computing, The Hong Kong Polytechnic University. Email: cstyng@inet. polyu.edu.hk*

David K Herold. *Department of Applied Social Sciences, The Hong Kong Polytechnic University. Email: ssherold@polyu.edu.hk*

Noemí Rabassa-Figueras
Miquel Àngel Bové Sans
Dolors Setó Pamies
Misericordia Domingo Vernis

4.2

THE PROCESS OF ACTIVE LEARNING AND 3D SIMULATIONS IN TECHNOLOGICAL ENVIRONMENTS ON ECONOMICS AND BUSINESS COURSES

1. IMPLEMENTING ACTIVE LEARNING STRATEGIES IN ACADEMIA

The process of adapting to the European Higher Education Area (EHEA) involves considerable changes to university teaching methods and an opportunity to improve teaching quality. Making students a part of their own training process is the most innovative teaching aim. Nevertheless, lectures are still undoubtedly the most widespread method in university teaching and highly suitable if the objective is to transmit information. The results of a several empirical studies show that in comparison with other disciplines, economics has been slow to adopt teaching methodologies other than the traditional lecture (Becker and Watts, 1996). Even those teachers who have carried out experiments to increase active student participation in learning processes point out that lectures are still the prevailing teaching methodology (Benzinger and Christ, 1997). The lack of student involvement in classroom lectures has been the object of much criticism. Partly in response to these criticisms, economics teachers have started to consider other methodologies for teaching economic concepts. A good example of this are the experiences described in the books Teaching Economics to Undergraduates: Alternatives to Chalk and Talk (Becker and Watts, 1998), and Teaching Economics: More Alternatives to Chalk and Talk (Becker, et. al., 2006).

The transmission of ideas and concepts through traditional classes (chalk and talk) is a passive method that disregards any effort students might make to actively involve themselves in the learning process and is of no use for the acquisition of competences if it is the only type of activity that students carry out during their university education. However, lectures have survived many generations of criticism because, despite their limitations, they are an efficient way of transmitting the content of a subject. The new paradigm of the teaching-learning process that is being put forward with the construction of the EEES, though, means that both teachers and students must get involved in new ways of teaching and learning. In this context, formulating competences is fundamental if the expected learning outcomes are to be achieved.

Specific and general competences should enable students to learn to think and generate their own ideas and reasoning in such a way that learning is more genuine. This new system requires new methodologies based on active student learning. These new instruments search for the most appropriate way of involving students in their own learning process. The aim is to include students in their own education, to encourage students to reflect about their deductions and to see how students can obtain results and draw conclusions that were traditionally obtained and drawn by teachers.

The fundamental objective of active learning methodologies is not only that students memorize content but that they acquire the professional competences that the degree course is expected to provide. They should be able to cope with new challenges on their own initiative and not merely limit themselves to applying what they memorized, which they gradually forget as time goes by. Active learning encourages a critical spirit and invites students to regard themselves as the constructor of their own knowledge and the central element of everything that is done in the classroom. Interaction with other students is encouraged through work groups, debates or presentations in class. In this way, the students actively discover and understand the topics studied for themselves, they construct their professional competences and improve their communicative skills.

Both teachers and students benefit from these active methodologies. On the one hand, students learn to assess the extent of their learning and their ability to cope with new problems and concepts. And on the other, teachers feel themselves to play a more relevant role in the process of generating and monitoring the students' education. The teaching and learning process must make the most of the resources available to teachers. The wide range of ways in which teaching methodologies and educational resources can be used should focus on searching for the best strategy by which students can acquire the expected knowledge and competences.

Therefore, active methodologies can be used to diversify the strategies that can be applied in teaching and learning processes. These alternatives to the traditional lecture have gradually gained importance in the planning and distribution of time allotted to the various activities that students carry out during their university education. And it is here that simulation games can play an important role.

2. TECHNOLOGICAL INNOVATION AT THE SERVICE OF TEACHING IN ECONOMICS AND BUSINESS COURSES

Innovations in the field of ICT have led to the creation of new communication environments that have made it possible to develop new teaching and learning experiences by allowing activities that were unimaginable until very recently (Ferro et. al. 2009). The incorporation of ICT into university teaching has provided new opportunities for improving the quality of student learning, although in themselves they are not sufficient to improve the educational process. Canós et al. (2009) point out that ICT requires teachers and students to develop new competences if the innovations are to be successful. And they also require teachers to have new competences in the preparation of information and in relating to the students. Likewise, students need to have the ability and the attitude to undertake a process of autonomous learning, and to maintain a fluid relationship with their teachers.

Ferro et al. (2009) point out the following advantages of using the information and communication technologies in university teaching:

- Space-time barriers are removed from teaching and learning activities.

- Communication between teachers and students is improved.
- Teaching can be personalised, adapted to the characteristics of the students.
- Students can interact with information. After searching for information on the Internet, they can analyse and reformulate what they have found.
- Students' motivation and interest improve
- The development of new teaching methodologies improves educational efficiency.

Canós and Ramón (2007), however, pointed out that the new technologies also have some drawbacks:
- Students and teachers depend on technology to interact with and use the material.
- There is a risk of students being cut off from the teacher and classmates because of the depersonalisation of relationships in the educational process
- Materials and activities require more effort and time to prepare,
- Some teachers opposed to change may reject the new ways of organizing education.

University faculties and schools, then, are acquiring computer supplies and equipment that are to be largely used for teaching purposes. However, finding the tools and programs that are appropriate for the educational process is a task for teachers.

3. SIMULATION GAMES IN ECONOMICS AND BUSINESS STUDIES

Business games have increased quite considerably in recent years and they have a long and varied history. Faria et al (2009) made a detailed review of the history, uses and changes that have taken place over time in business games, particularly since the advent of the new technologies. The first use of a business game in a business management seminar can be traced back to 1956. The game *Top Management Decision Simulation* was developed by the American Management Association (Hodgetts, 1970) although it was not until 1957 that there is any reference to a simulation game being used in a university course. The game *Top Management Decision* was used in a course on commercial policy at the University of Washington (Watson, 1981).

From then on, business games developed rapidly. The *Business Games Handbook* published in 1969 (Graham and Gray, 1969) listed more than 190 business simulation games. Later, *The Guide to Simulation/Games for Education and Training* (Horn and Cleaves, 1980) identified more than 228 business simulation games. In 2004 an e-mail survey of university lecturers from business schools in North America, which generated 1,085 responses, confirmed that 36.6% were current users of business simulators in their teaching activities (Faria and Wellington, 2004).

In the reviews on teaching applications of business simulation games it is important to analyse the role that technology has had and the different types of game if their evolution is to be understood. At the beginning, business simulation games were quite simple: few variables were taken into account in the decision-making process, only a small number of participants could take part, the number or products or brands was limited, and participant feedback almost non-existent.

As we mentioned above, the increasing availability of computer equipment in universities and business schools and ever-improving technology have been key factors in the incorporation of this tool into education. At present, simulation games are hosted in platforms, which makes it possible to increase their complexity quite considerably. Some versions are more economic or even free, and can be installed in students' personal computers, which increases connectivity and speed of use. And it is also of particular importance that the problems of securely storing the data, which provides evidence of the learning process, have been greatly reduced.

4. TYPES OF BUSINESS GAME SIMULATION

As far as planning teaching is concerned, in the traditional curricula of formal courses, the syllabuses of the subjects are divided into lists of topics and it is assumed that the students will understand the complexity involved once they have studied them all. On the other hand, in simulated environments complexity can be introduced into the technological environment in such a way that students have to face up to complex activities and situations, which they have to resolve (Lehti and Lehtinen, 2005).

If the use of simulations games in teaching is to be fully understood, it is important to know the general features of the different types of game in existence. To this end, we would like to make particular mention of Wolfe's classification (1993) of business simulation games:

- *Top Management Games*. In these games the participants take on the role of the company's chief executive officer and accept responsibility for taking strategic decisions for the whole company
- *Functional Games*. In these games the participants take on the role of director of a functional area of the company (for example, marketing, production or accounts) and accept responsibility for more concrete, operational decisions.
- *Concept Simulation Games*. In these games the participants assume the responsibility for decisions in small functional areas (for example, specific decisions about publicity, sales management, personnel, etc.)

It is only to be expected that different game types will have different teaching uses depending on the aims and the competences that need to be acquired.

Depending on type, games can be central to a course or subject or merely be used as a support tool in combination with other methodologies. After analyzing 1,115 articles published over a forty-year period in the journal *Simulation & Gaming*, Faria et al. (2009) identified 304 articles in which business simulation games are used as an education and learning tool, and they highlight the following nine main reasons for use mentioned by teachers:

- The **experience** gained through business games. The opinions expressed by teachers and students suggest that participatory pedagogical tools make teaching experiences more memorable.
- The **strategy aspects** of business games. The games clearly incorporate strategic decisions. The complexity of the decisions has been increased by the technical advances of the programs themselves.
- The **decision-making** experience gained through business games. Nowadays games include a considerable number of variables, all of which are inter-related. This enables students to develop their decision-making competence. The main contribution of business games is that they clarify academic knowledge and make it possible for students to experiment with decision making and see the economic and business effects that their decisions have in different scenarios.

- The **learning and objectives** provided by business games. The use of business games and the results obtained by students while they play provide evidence of the learning process itself
- The **teamwork** experience provided through business games. Most simulation games involve teams, and teamwork is always more gratifying if all the members adapt to the role they have been assigned.
- The **student motivation** provided by business games. The use of business games provides feedback that is not provided by other pedagogical tools. For example, in case studies, students have a passive role in which they can learn from the strategies that a particular case shows, but they are unlikely to see the results of their decisions.
- The **application of theoretical concepts** in a practical way. Business games make it possible to apply theoretical concepts and if students do not apply the concepts as they should, they can rethink and thus consolidate their theoretical knowledge.
- **Active learning** by students during games. On other occasions we have discussed how important active learning is in the learning process. Business games are tools that allow active learning to take place.
- The **integration of ideas** provided by business games. Numerous variables interact in economic and business environments, and there are a wide variety of different scenarios, all of which can be portrayed in business games.

Of these nine reasons, the first five have constantly been repeating ever since business games first emerged. We should point out that one of our interests is to promote those tools that make active learning possible and, in the light of the results, it is clear that active learning is one of the main reasons why simulation games are used. We are convinced that including interactive virtual reality in simulation games will not substantially change the reasons for use but it will certainly make all areas more realistic.

It is very important to understand the main reasons why simulation games are used in teaching, but it is even more important to understand the real benefits that are expected from the use of these games in economics and business studies. Considerable emphasis has been put on the importance of anchoring learning through authentic activities and simulations by the prevailing education theories (Bransford et. al. 2000). Simulations, then, can be used to anchor learning through authentic activities, which help students to cope with complex situations and encourage collaborative work (Lehti and Lehtinen, 2005).

The possible benefits of using games and simulations in teaching and learning processes, as Siewiorek et. al. (2012) have pointed out, have been discussed in numerous studies which emphasise their advantages (Aldrich, 2004; Kafai, 2006; Keys and Biggs, 1990; Prensky, 2001; Wolfe and Crookall, 1998; Woods, 2004). Simulations and simulation games have been widely used in studies in the field of business (Burgess, 1995; Dickinson and Faria, 1996; Faria, 1990; Faria et. al. 2009). The literature provides interesting results that show that games and simulations are highly appropriate to university education with a professional focus. Simulations and games enable students to come into contact with complex situations that are typical of real-life processes.

Another important advantage of simulations is that they can be used as platforms for collaborative learning and the acquisition of negotiating skills (Susskind and Corburn, 2000). In many cases, games and simulations allow students to share experiences and use them as a basis for more detailed discussion of problems and cases that need to be solved (Lehtinen, 2002). Having the chance to respond to real –or at least realistic– problems in controlled learning situations is also very important for training in leadership. Simulated environments can be used so that students can carry out activities that are very similar to the sort of activities they will have to carry out in professional contexts but protecting them from any serious consequences that their mistakes might have (Garris et. al., 2002). Therefore, the players can take risks, explore and try out new things. In a learning context, these experiences can be linked to theoretical models, making them easier to understand and interpret. Students need conceptual instruments to understand the situations they are faced with and their own behaviour in these situations. In this regard, Siewiorek et. al. (2012) point out that simulated games are an interesting way of learning leadership topics. However, as well as carrying out the simulation, it is important to have time to reflect and analyse the content that is to be taught because otherwise the learning outcomes will not be achieved.

Despite all these positive points, some features of simulations and games hinder their application in education. The main barriers to learning with simulations are the following: the availability of resources and the time required for preparation, the lack of fit between the simulation and the course syllabus, technical problems and the lack of information on simulations (Faria and Wellington, 2004). It should also be borne in mind that students do not always perceive the expected connection between the simulated cases and real-life situations and, if they perceive that the simulation is not realistic, they may lose interest and motivation when taking part (Adobor and Daneshfar, 2006).

5. FROM ASSIGNING THE BUSINESS ROLE TO DESIGNING THE AVATAR

Having discussed the historical evolution of simulation games and the main reasons teachers have for using them, we move on to discuss the new options provided by interactive virtual business games. The technological evolution that is available to teachers has led to a change in paradigm in the way in which business simulation games are being developed. The intelligent agents or virtual characters are now the protagonists of simulation games. Students can have the real sensation that they are in the place where the events are unfolding. What is more, as Gerhard et al. point out (2004), avatars are the embodiment of users in collaborative virtual environments.

As has been discussed with reference to the experiences of applying virtual simulation (chapter 3), the design and personalization of avatars is fundamental if students are to play a specific role in the game, and it is this process that they considered to significantly mark the beginning of the game.

The development of artificial intelligence and its application to avatars, which can even be made to transmit emotions, has provided a wide range of new teaching options. These new options give as much importance to the evolution of the process throughout the game as to the final results obtained. It is particularly interesting to point out the results obtained by Vogel et al. (2006), who used three-dimensional images in education. Their study showed that the use of virtual reality programs can be a useful aid for helping students to understand complex ideas.

Virtual simulation games in economics and business, in which reality is constructed by avatars, provide a wide variety of teaching options particularly as far as developing entrepreneurship, and economic and business management and planning is concerned. In our opinion, in the field of business one of the most important competences is teamwork as companies are made up of human capital. In most professional situations we are required to work as part of a team and we have to adapt. Working on the composition of virtual teams, with the characterizations of the avatars that are to take part in the game, can be fundamental to the learning process.

6. CONCLUSIONS AND FUTURE REFLECTIONS

The incorporation of virtual simulation undoubtedly involves a change in the role of teachers and students. Teachers are no longer mere lecturers who provide notes that students must memorize if they wish to pass exams; they are now tutor-trainers who guide learning processes. Students must learn how to learn and not only listen; they must be able to work effectively as members of a group; they must know how to search for information that is relevant to the decisions that have to be taken and think critically about issues so that headway can be made and the objectives of the simulation reached.

However, the methodological changes being made to the teaching process mean that both teachers and students have to invest more time. Teachers have to do more work before contact with students when preparing the various activities, and they have to spend more time on monitoring the learning process and motivating students. Teachers must also draw up appropriate and detailed plans of the activities that are to be carried out as part of the subject, so that students can plan their time and fulfill the aims of the course.

These processes of designing and implementing new teaching methodologies need to be accompanied by a system that provides proof of learning so that the results of this sort of application can be assessed. We believe that these mechanisms of assessment are essential if we are to understand whether the methodological changes have the desired effect of improving educational systems and student learning, and if we are to detect which aspects are not working as we had predicted so that improved mechanisms can be designed. Likewise, systems need to be developed for assessing the learning process generated by the use of these tools. Since competences are only acquired gradually, graded scales of competence acquisition are required.

The inclusion of interactive virtual games in economics and business courses should help the student's learning process. However, we must take care that the complexity of games does not hinder the learning process: that is to say, that the technical complexity of games does not demotivate students and force them to drop out.

As Porter et al (2004) point out, in the field of economics at this point in time we have enough information to design simulation programs. However, if these simulation programs are to be used correctly they must contain supplementary material and clear instructions about how they are to be integrated into courses to guarantee successful use. Further study should also be carried out on the effectiveness and the validity of simulation games in the learning process. Although they are expected to be effective and valid, as yet there is little evidence in the literature that this is the case. Stainton et al. (2010) state that simulations must be designed with great care, and must take into account such essential criteria as complexity, the realism of the representation, the depth of the content and the method of application.

To date, business virtual simulation games have been used as tools for teaching a whole subject or part of one. Experiences and projects in which virtual simulation is the centre of the process and not only a tool may provide more evidence on the learning potentiality they have.

We believe that in economics and business studies it is very important to continue using interactive virtual games, and that work should be done on developing international university experiences to create global economy scenarios in which interactivity among students makes it possible for them to develop specific and general competences and also intercultural ones. Technological advances, then, must be used correctly by teachers and always focused on students and their learning process.

REFERENCES

Adobor, H., Daneshfar, A. (2006). Management simulations: determining their effectiveness. *Journal of Management Development, 25* (2), 151-169.

Aldrich, C. (2004). *Simulations and the future of learning.* San Francisco: John Wiley.

Becker, W. E., Watts, M. (1996). Chalk and Talk: A national survey on teaching undergraduates economics. *American Economic Review,* 86 (May), 448-53.

Becker, W. E., Watts, M. (1998). *Teaching Economics to Undergraduates: Alternatives to Chalk and Talk.* Cheltenham. UK: Edward Elgar.

Becker, W. E., Watts, M., Becker, S. (2006). *Teaching Economics. More Alternatives to Chalk and Talk.* Cheltenham. UK: Edward Elgar.

Benzinger, C., Christ, P. (1997). A summary of teaching methods among economics faculty. *Journal of Economic Education,* 28 (spring), 182-88.

Bové, M. À., Angla, J., Domingo, M., Martín, M., Rabassa, N., Setó, D. (2012). Experiències d'innovació docent en els ensenyaments d'Economia i Empresa, a les universitats catalanes. *Congreso Internacional de Docencia Universitaria e Innovación,* Barcelona (CIDUI).

Bransford, J.D., Brown, A.L., Cocking, R.R. (2000). *How people learn: Brain, mind, experience and school.* Washington, D.C. National Academy Press.

Burgess, T.F. (1995). Business gaming: and historical analysis and future perspectives. In D. Saunders (Ed.), *The simulation and gaming workbook. Games and Simulations for Business* (pp. 64-75). Vol. 3. London: Kogan Page.

Canós, L., Ramón, F. (2007). Una experiencia sobre la interacción entre la formación universitaria y el uso de nuevas tecnologías. *Jornadas de la Red Estatal de Docencia Universitaria (REDU).* Valencia.

Canós, L.; Canós, M.J., Liern, V. (2009). El uso de las nuevas tecnologías aplicadas a la educación superior. *XVII Jornadas ASEPUMA.* Burgos.

Dickinson, J.R., Faria, A.J. (1996). A random-strategy criterion for validity of simulation game participation. In D. Saunders, F. Percival and M. Vartiainen (Eds.), *The simulation and gaming workbook. Games and Simulation to Enhace Quality Learning,* vol. 4. London: Kogan Page.

Faria, A. J., Hutchinson, D., Wellington, W. J., Gold, S. (2009). Developments in business gaming: A review of the past 40 years. *Simulation and Gaming, 40*(4), 464-487.

Faria, A. J., Wellington, W. J. (2004). A survey of simulation game users, former-users, and never-users. *Simulation & Gaming, 35,* 178-207.

Faria, A.J. (1990). Business simulation games after thirty years: current usage levels in the United States. In J.W. Gentry (Ed.), *Guide to business gaming and experiential learning* (pp. 36-47). London: Nichols/GP.

Faria, A.J., Wellington, W.J. (2004). A survey of simulation game users, former users and never users. *Simulation & Gaming, 35* (2), 178-207.

Ferro, C., Martínez, A.I., Otero, M.C. (2009). Ventajas del uso de las TICs en el proceso de enseñanza-aprendizaje desde la óptica de los docentes universitarios españoles. EDUTEC. Revista Electrónica de Tecnología Educativa, no. 29. 11-11.

Garris, R., Ahlers, R., Driskell, J.E. (2002). Games, motivation and learning: a research and practice. *Simulation & Gaming, 35* (2), 178-207.

Gerhard, M., Moore,D., Hobbs, D. (2004). Embodiment and copresence in collaborative inter-faces. *Human-Computer Studies*, 61(4), 453–480.

Gisbert, M., et al. (1997). El docente y los entornos virtuales de enseñanza-aprendizaje. In Cebrián et al.: *Recursos tecnológicos para los procesos de enseñanza y aprendizaje* (126-132). Málaga: ICE / Universidad de Málaga.

Graham, R. G., Gray, C. F. (1969). *Business games handbook.* New York: American Manage-ment Association.

Hodgetts, R. (1970). Management gaming for didactic purposes: A new look. *Simulation & Gaming, 1*, 55-66.

Horn, R. E., Cleaves, A. (1980). *The guide to simulations/games for education and training.* Beverly Hills, CA: Sage.

Kafai, Y.B. (2006). Playing and making games for learning: instructionist and constructionist perspectives for games studies. *Games and Culture*, 1, 36-40.

Keys, J.B., Biggs, W.B. (1990). A review of business games. In J.W. Gentry (Ed.), *Guide to busi-ness gaming and experiential learning* (pp. 48-73). East Brunswick, NJ: Hichols/GP.

Lehti, S., Lehtinen, E. (2005). Computer-supported problem-based learning in the research methodology domain. *Scandinavian Journal of Educational Research, 49,* 297-323.

Lehtinen, E. (2002) Developing models for distributed problem-based learning: theoretical and methodological reflection. *Distance Education, 23* (1), 109-117.

Porter, T. S., Riley, T. M., Ruffer, R. L. (2004). A review of the use of simulations in teaching economics. *Social Science Computer Review, 22*(4), 426-443.

Prensky, M. (2001). *Digital game-based learning.* New York: McGraw-Hill Companies.

Siewiorek, A., Saarinen, E., Lainema, T., Lehtinen, E. (2012). Learning leadership in a simulated business environment. *Computer & Education, 58*, 121-135.

Stainton, A. J., Johnson, J. E., Borodzicz, E. P. (2010). Educational validity of business gaming simulation: A research methodology framework. *Simulation and Gaming, 41*(5), 705-723.

Susskind, L.E., Corburn, J. (2000). Using simulations to teach negotiation: pedagogical theory and practice. In M. Wheeler (Ed.), *Teaching negotiations: Ideas and innovations* (pp. 285-310). Cambridge, MA: PON Books.

Vogel, J., Greenwood-Ericksen, A., Cannon-Bowers, J., Bowers, C. (2006). Using virtual reality with and without gaming attributes for academic achievement. *Journal of Research on Technology in Education*, 39(1), 105-118.

Watson, H. J. (1981). *Computer simulation in business.* New York: John Wiley.

Wolfe, J. (1993). A history of business teaching games in English-speaking and post-social-ist countries: The origination and diffusion of a management education and development technology. *Simulation & Gaming, 24*, 446-463.

Wolfe, J., Crookall, D. (1998). Developing a scientific knowledge of simulation and gaming. *Simulation & Gaming*, 29 (1), 7-19.

Woods, S. (2004). Loading the dice: the challenge of serious video games. *Games Studies*, 4 (1).

AUTHORS

Noemí Rabassa Figueras. *Department of Business Management. Rovira i Virgili University. Tarragona, Spain. Email: noemi.rabassa@urv.cat*

Miquel Àngel Bové Sans. *Department of Economics. Rovira i Virgili University. Tarragona, Spain. Email: miquelangel.bove@urv.cat*

Dolors Setó Pàmies. *Department of Business Management. Rovira i Virgili University. Tarragona, Spain. Email: dolors.seto@urv.cat*

Misericòrdia Domingo Vernis. *Department of Economics. Rovira i Virgili University. Tarragona, Spain. Email: coia.domingo@urv.cat*

Gema Bello-Orgaz

David Camacho

4.3
EXPLOITING VIRTUAL WORLDS AND 3D SIMULATION ENVIRONMENTS FOR HIGHER EDUCATION

1. INTRODUCTION

The concept of metaverse (Stephenson, 1992) can be described as a collective on-line shared space, created by joining some virtually enhanced physical reality with a physically persistent virtual space (Castonova, 2005). It has been defined as a digital or electronic representation of the real world where people can interact freely using the metaphor of their real lives in a world that is not limited by physics, age or other real world characteristics. In recent years, such new software applications as virtual worlds (VWs) and augmented reality have been developed.

Virtual worlds provide a 3D environment that can be used as a fictional virtual world in which people with different interests and skills can interact, share or cooperate in a wide range of activities (Sinrod, 2007, Talbot, 2008). Users can interact in the VW with other users or with the elements (objects) in the world through avatars that represent them. Their ease of use, collaborative facilities and the attractiveness of their 3D features, which give users a new and highly immersive sensation, have made VWs interesting tools for a wide range of different fields. In our specific case, VWs are a good environment in which to carry out educational, training, and collaborative tasks (Berns, Gonzalez-Pardo and Camacho, 2011; 2013).

This paper presents an innovative educational platform, Virt-UAM (Virtual Worlds at the Universidad Autónoma de Madrid), which makes it possible to design and implement virtual spaces in which a set of avatars can be intensively monitored using a set of tools managed by the platform administrator or a particular avatar (i.e. the teacher in an educational domain). The data obtained from the monitoring tools can be analysed using information theory-based techniques. In this way we can understand the avatars behaviour during their stay in the world and try to improve it in the future (Gonzalez-Pardo, de Borja Rodriguez, Pulido and Camacho, 2010; Bello-Orgaz, R-Moreno,; Camacho, and Barrero, 2012).

Two language courses and an introductory language programming course have been designed to analyze how VWs can improve both the motivation and learning of university students and teacher effectiveness. These courses were designed to stimulate learners with opportunities for real and meaningful interaction through task-based and goal-oriented activities as well as cooperative learning. Using the Virt-UAM platform, the students could take a leading role in the learning environment and work with other students and teachers to create knowledge that can be shared between them. Finally, this knowledge was applied in a practical workshop that was held as part of the International Seminar for Simulation-based Environments (Simul@) in November 2011.

2. RELATED WORK

VW technologies have been traditionally applied in a wide variety of domains ranging from business (Sinrod, 2007; Talbot, 2008) to massively-multiplayer online games (Castonova, 2005), which is the most popular application at present. In recent years videogames and virtual worlds (VWs) have attracted the attention of many people from very different fields and have become quite popular (de Freitas, 2007; Bellotti, Berta, Gloria and Zappi, 2008; Bellotti, Berta, de Gloria and Zappi, 2008). However, VWs have already been recognized by many educational institutions (universities and high schools) as having considerable potential for teaching and learning purposes (Nardi, Ly and Harris, 2007; The New Media Consortium, 2007). These environments have been used to improve educational techniques (Berns, Gonzalez-Pardo and Camacho 2011; 2013) because they allow teachers and students to use innovative learning strategies: practical training, group work, discussions, field practice, simulations, and visualization of concepts. Our interest in VWs was initially motivated by the challenge of making courses more attractive for university students.

Currently, a considerable number of VW platforms are available that can be used to design and implement virtual spaces. Some of the most popular ones are Active Worlds, Second Life (SL), OpenCobalt and OpenSim. Second Life has been applied to several learning and educational processes (Jarmon, Traphagan, Mayrath, and Trivedi, 2009; Lamb, and Johnson, 2009; Trotter, 2008; Waters, 2009). For example, it has been used by psychology instructors as a space to meet students and create labs, buildings and objects that can be used to learn content and skills (Baker, Wentz, and Woods, 2009). Cunha, Raposo and Fuks, (2008) use Second Life as an environment for collaborative learning and the generation of new educational content, and De Lucia et al. (de Lucia, Francese, Passero, and Tortora, 2008) used Second Life to create an environment and a location for collaborative learning in which objects were modeled and programmed to support the synchronous role-based collaborative activities required by the jigsaw learning technique in a 3D virtual meeting setting. In the specific context of teaching technical subjects, medical and health librarians and educators have explored the pedagogical potential of Second Life (Boulos, Hetherington, and Wheeler, 2007). Another approach (Bourke, 2009) analyzes how multiple remote participants can engage with 3D geometry within a virtual environment.

Several other initiatives are using virtual worlds for technical education. Park et al. [26] compare instructor-led with simulation-based environments for engineering students, and measure two variables: achievement and interest. They conclude that both environments produce similar results. Slator et al. (Slator, Hill and Del Val, 2004) present a virtual world with no teachers (called ProgrammingLand MOOseum). In this world, computer science students explore rooms populated with interactive objects. These objects are designed to facilitate the learning experience. Nelson and Ketelhut (Nelson and Ketelhut, 2008) use an individualized guidance system (IGS) for students in a virtual world (called River City) with no real teachers.

The IGS prompts students with questions and hints, and collects data about simple student activities such as clicking on pictures or reading charts.

3. VIRTUAM PLATFORM

OpenSim is an open source multi-platform that can be used as a multiuser 3D application server. It makes it possible to create VWs which can be accessed through a variety of clients (for example, RealXtend or HippoViewer) and on multiple protocols. It is also an open source project which allows developers to extend the base functionality by means of pluggable software modules. In order to use OpenSim as an e-Learning and virtual lab platform, we designed a VW environment named VirtUAM (Virtual Words at the UAM) built on a grid over OpenSim simulator. VirtUAM consists of four basic components:

1. **A grid of computers hosting the virtual spaces** (islands, buildings or any other virtual spaces that can be requested by users) that allows all the VWs generated to be executed and managed. In these virtual spaces, lectures, laboratory activities, or working activities, can be placed, and the educational objects created by teachers and students stored. If the number of objects within the VW increases then several computers are needed to avoid performance problems.

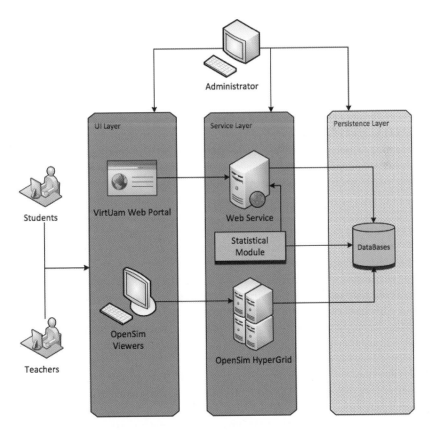

Figure 1. Software architecture of the VirtUAM platform

2. **A web portal** to provide users access to public information and data about the courses (technical guides, construction and programming tutorials, etc.). There are three different types of user roles in this web portal: administrator, teachers and students. Teachers and administrators can use the web portal for administration tasks. For instance, teachers can create courses, include new students on their courses, and obtain statistics on student behaviour and performance. Administrators can manage teachers' accounts, analyze the system performance and access the logs stored in the database system. Students, on the other hand, can only change their own information and access the documentation related to the courses.

3. **A back-end** service built on different database servers which contain all the required data: technical and user guides, user information (group, teacher and student profiles), data mining information (such as logs, chat conversations, tracking movements, documents and objects developed by users, or student and educator interactions in the VW). This large amount of information can be used by both teachers and administrators to analyse data of student behavior.

4. **A statistical module** that receives the data stored from interactions in the VW. Once these data are appropriately mapped, they are processed using data mining techniques to retrieve patterns from them.

The main characteristics of OpenSim make this platform seem the most appropriate for our educational purposes. The reasons for this decision can be summarized as follows:

- OpenSim is **open-source software**, which makes it possible for teachers and administrators to modify and adapt the program, in line with their teaching goals and student needs.
- A specific **programming language**, called LSL (Linden Scripting Language), can be used to add functionality to virtual objects.
- **Information about avatar behaviour** such as interaction with the objects in the world or chat records can be easily retrieved from external VW applications. In this way all this information about the avatar or the student can be analysed.
- The platform can be accessed only by registered users. Usually, VW platforms such as ActiveWorlds or SL are public virtual places but OpenSim is **not a public virtual place** and administrators can configure the VW to restrict the access to limited users. This means that other external non-authorized users cannot visit the VW-learning environment and perhaps interfere in the course tasks.
- The **virtual space** that can be built by users, and the number of prims created in this platform, are both **unlimited**. Users can build their own virtual space with an almost unlimited number of objects with which to interact. However, there can be problems with the system performance when the number of prims and programs running in the VW grows too quickly. This can be managed using the grid-based configuration of the platform.

In this platform, the educators have the control of the avatars connected, their actions, and which kind of task they can do. The platform provides for three kinds of users:

- **Administrators**. These users control the access of any avatar and virtual world within the platform, create new objects, program and extend the base functionality by generating new software modules.

- **Teachers**. They can control their student groups through the stored logs and manage the educational materials. The VirtUAM platform extends the OpenSim functionality by allowing teachers to use (and eventually create) in-world objects with a given functionality. These new objects can also be modified and extended by other teachers, evolving according to the users' (teachers') needs, and so on.
- **Students**. They can access the educational material uploaded through the web portal by the educators, and solve the tasks proposed through the virtual world.

At present students are controlled by means of a peer-to-peer process in which the system administrator provides a set of predefined avatars (including names and passwords) to the educators in charge. Therefore, the teachers can control student access to the platform and monitor their behavior in the VW.

4. COURSES DEVELOPED USING VIRTUAM

Several educational-based courses have been developed using the VirtUAM platform. Two of them were designed to teach languages (German and French), and one to program concepts through a programming language called Linden Scripting Language (LSL), which it is provided by the OpenSim platform. This language syntax is similar to Visual Basic or Java and provides behavior to the virtual world objects, making them sensitive to such events as being touched.

In the first two game-like language courses, the students move with their avatar through different rooms or levels, in each of which they face a new challenge. The aim is to improve their listening and reading skills through several activities (teaching basic vocabulary by means of photos in combination with audio recordings, quiz-like activities designed to test the listening skills acquired, etc.). The addition of a scoring system aims to encourage students to improve their language skills and increase their motivation before they proceed to the next level.

Figure 2. Training room for basic German vocabulary

Finally, the platform has been used in several seminars and introductory courses the main goal of which was to introduce basic programming concepts through the use of VWs. A secondary goal was to evaluate the impact of the platform on student motivation and learning. Therefore, the courses were designed to make them more interesting for students and, at the same time, to minimize the effort required to learn a programming language. Students report that the framework helped to enhance two basic aspects of the learning process:

1. They are more motivated because the results have an immediate 3D visualization.
2. They engage in **collaborative and cooperative work** by free interaction with other avatars. The 3D world is an attractive environment in which students can chat on a public channel (that anyone can hear in a 20 meters radio), and ask questions in public as in a traditional learning environment or in a one-on-one private chat channel.

The programming course was structured in several sessions as Table 1 shows:

Session	Duration	Description
1	1.5 h	Definition of VWs or metaverses and description of Opensim platform (sims, terrain properties, avatar customization, prims or objects, message system and navigation).
2	2 h	Design and building with objects (prims) in the VM: basic use of building tools, prim creation and combination to design complex objects and advanced attributes (rotation, position, texture, flexibility, light, etc.).
3	2 h	Free session to customize avatars and start to design a project. All students are responsible for creating their own environment in the VM using the functionalities of the building tool.
4	2 h	Introduction to the programming language LSL. Description of the language's syntax, how to create scripts to perform basic operations and how to compile and debug a program.
5	2 h	Basic data types and variables in LSL and control flow structures (conditional statements and the three different loop structures available in LSL) for managing the execution control of the script instructions.
6	2 h	Free session in which the students develop and test scripts (programs) belonging to their designed objects.
7	4 h	Free session to finalize the project.

Table 1. Programming language course on the VirtUam platform

Each session involved ten students and two teachers who provide students with some individual support. During the sessions students were connected to an island divided into regions (one region per student). Once the students had become familiar with the VW dynamic, they were free to customize their avatars and to build their own VW in their own regions. Designing their regions of the island gives the students the opportunity to reinforce the knowledge acquired in all of the sessions.

As Table 1 shows, the first session describes how to customize avatars and interact within the 3D VW (see Figure 4).

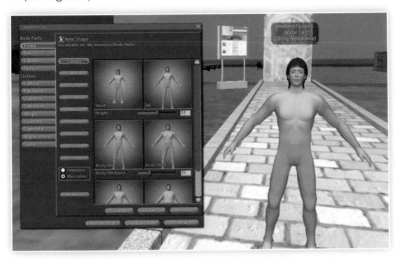

Figure 4. Customizing the avatar in the VW

Students are shown how to design and build objects (prims) in the VM in the second session. Then, in a free session, students can customize their avatars and start to build their own environment in the VM. Figure 5 shows a complex example of Japanese building designed using basic objects.

Figure 5. Designing and building complex objects using basic forms (prims)

Finally, sessions 4, 5 and 6 describe the basis of the LSL programming language. First, the data types allowed in LSL are described and then the essential control structures in any programming language: the conditional and loop structures. Figure 6 shows an example of a script (program) in LSL. It represents a piece of code that is executed when an avatar interacts with the object. In this example the program sends a message (Touched) to the public channel when the "touch" event occurs.

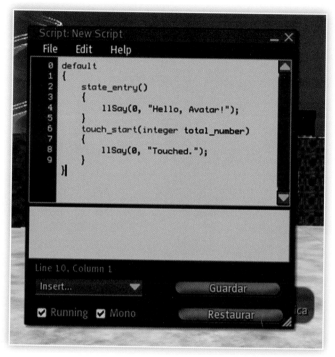

Figure 6. Associating a particular script to an object

5. PRACTICAL DEVELOPMENT OF VW SPACES AT THE SIMUL@ SEMINAR

One of the goals of our workshop was to decrease the traditional duration (but maintain the basis of our teaching schedule) of our VW courses, by reducing the fundamentals of VW design and development to a two-hour workshop. In this course, some of the material described in the section above was actively used to improve the learning capacity of the assistants by allowing better and faster interaction with a real VW scenario. The schedule of this short introductory course to VW is shown in Table 2.

Session	Duration (min)	Brief description
1	45	Definition of VWs or metaverses and description of Opensim platform (sims, terrain properties, avatar customization, prims or objects, message system and navigation).

2	15	Introduction to main differences between Second Life and Open-Sim, some basics on avatars and user facilities in the VW. Users can interact with their avatar and the surroundings (other avatars and objects previously deployed from other courses).
3	45	Design and building with objects (prims) in the VM: basic use of building tools, prim creation and combination to design complex objects and advanced attributes (rotation, position, texture, flexibility, light, etc.).
4	15	Introduction to basics of the programming language LSL. Description of the language's syntax, and the essential concepts of event and state.

Table 2. Virtual worlds introduction course on the VirtUam platform at Simul@ International Seminar.

Although a complete and interactive VW space cannot be designed in only two hours, the following conclusions were drawn from this short course:

- During first 45-minute session, the assistants became aware of the main differences between open platforms (i.e. Opensim) and commercial platforms (i.e. SecondLife) and their main implications for the educational problem (for instance, development expenses, the property of the data, controlling avatars' access to the world, etc.).
- In the first and second session, participants accessed a predefined VW space to interact with their avatar (that's to say, customize it), and communicate, navigate and interact in the world.
- In the third and fourth sessions, participants designed and developed objects in the VW to better understand how the technology works and what kind of virtual spaces can be easily developed.
- Finally, some software examples (in the form of basic programs or scripts) were briefly described and explained to the assistants showing (from a very general point of view) how objects and avatars can interact in a VW.

Our main conclusion from this experience is that a short course on this kind of technology is feasible. Although long-term dedication is required if this kind of environment is to be completely developed (and particular effort must be put into the design), introducing this kind of technology in education is no more difficult than other technologies that are currently being used in virtual learning and internet-based courses. A short course on VW can show potential users what the main features and pitfalls of these 3D technologies are, and therefore where resources should be applied (design, programming, teaching resources, etc.).

ACKNOWLEDGMENTS

This work has been partly supported by: Spanish Ministry of Science and Education under project TIN2010-19872, and by the company Jobssy.com under project FUAM-076913.

REFERENCES

ActiveWorlds. (2012) *ActiveWorlds*. Retrived from http://www.activeworlds.com/(November 2012)

Baker, S.; Wentz, R and Woods, M. (2009) Using Virtual Worlds in Education: Second Life as an Educational Tool. *Teaching of Psychology, 36*, 59-64.

Bello-Orgaz, G.; R-Moreno, M.; Camacho, D. & Barrero, D. (2012, April). Clustering avatars behaviours from virtual worlds interactions. In *Proceedings of the 4th International Workshop on Web Intelligence & Communities (p. 4). ACM.*

Bellotti, F.; Berta, R.; De Gloria, A. & Zappi, V. (2008, September). Exploring gaming mechanisms to enhance knowledge acquisition in virtual worlds. In*Proceedings of the 3rd international conference on Digital Interactive Media in Entertainment and Arts* (pp. 77-84). ACM.

Berns, A.; Gonzalez-Pardo, A. and Camacho, D. (2011, October). Designing videogames for foreign language learning. In *4th International Conference ICT for Language Learning, Florence (Italy).*

Berns, A.; Gonzalez-Pardo, A. and Camacho, D. (2013). Game-like language learning in 3-D virtual environments. *Computers & Education, 60*(1), 210-220.

Boulos, M. N. K.; Hetherington, L. and Wheeler, S. (2007). Second Life: an overview of the potential of 3D virtual worlds in medical and health education. *Health Information & Libraries Journal, 24*(4), 233-245.

Bourke, P. (2009). Evaluating Second Life for the collaborative exploration of 3D fractals. *Computers & Graphics, 33*(1), 113-117.

Castonova, E. (2005) *Synthetic Worlds: The Business and Culture of Online Games*. University of Chicago.

Cunha, M.; Raposo, A. and Fuks, H. (2008, April). Educational technology for collaborative virtual environments. In *Computer Supported Cooperative Work in Design, 2008. CSCWD 2008. 12th International Conference on* (pp. 716-720). IEEE.

De Freitas, N. (2007). *Learning in Immersive Worlds. A Review of Game-Based Learning*. London: JISC.

De Lucia, A.; Francese, R.; Passero, I. and Tortora, G. (2008, July). Supporting Jigsaw-based collaborative learning in Second Life. In *Advanced Learning Technologies, 2008. ICALT'08. Eighth IEEE International Conference on* (pp. 806-808). IEEE.

González-Pardo, A.; Rodríguez Ortíz, F.; Pulido, E. and Fernández, D. (2010, October). Using virtual worlds for behaviour clustering-based analysis. In *Proceedings of the 2010 ACM workshop on Surreal media and virtual cloning (p. 9-14). ACM.*

Jarmon, L; Traphagan, T.; Mayrath, M. and Trivedi, A. (2009). Virtual world teaching, experiential learning, and assessment: An interdisciplinary communication course in Second Life. *Computers & Education, 53*(1), 169-182.

Lamb, A., and Johnson, L. (2009). The potential, the pitfalls, and the promise of multi-user virtual environments: Getting a second life. *Teacher Librarian, 36*(4), 68-72.

Nardi, B.; Ly, S. and Harris, J. (2007, January). Nardi, B. A., Ly, S., & Harris, J. (2007, January). Learning conversations in World of Warcraft. In *System Sciences, 2007. HICSS 2007. 40th Annual Hawaii International Conference on* (p. 79-79). IEEE.

Nelson, B. C. and Ketelhut, D. J. (2008). Exploring embedded guidance and self-efficacy in educational multi-user virtual environments. *International Journal of Computer-Supported Collaborative Learning, 3*(4), 413-427.

OpenCobalt. (2012) *OpenCobalt*. Retrived from http://www.opencobalt.org/ (November 2012)

OpenSimulator. (2012) *OpenSimulator*. Retrived from http://opensimulator.org (November 2012)

Park, Y. B.; Lee, Y.; Lee, J.; Kang, J. and Wang, B. (2008). Effects of 3D-simulation-based instruction on students' achievement and interests in a manufacturing engineering class. *International Journal of Engineering Education*, *24*(4), 843-849.

Ritzema, T., & Harris, B. (2008). The use of Second Life for distance education. *Journal of Computing Sciences in Colleges*, *23*(6), 110-116.

SecondLife. (2012) *SecondLife*. Retrived from http://secondlife.com/ (November 2012)

Sinrod, E.J. (2007) *Virtual world litigation for real*. Available on line at http://news.cnet.com/ Virtual-world-litigation-for-real/2010-1047_3-6190583.html.

Slator, B. M.; Hill, C. and Del Val, D. (2004). Teaching computer science with virtual worlds. *Education, IEEE Transactions on*, *47*(2), 269-275.

Stephenson, N. (1992). *Snow Crash*. Bantam Books.

Talbot, D. (2008). The fleecing of the avatars. *Technology Review -Manchester NH-*, 111(1), 58.

The New Media Consortium. (2007). *The Horizon Report*. Technical Report: Nathan Abbott Way, Stanford.

Trotter, A. (2008). Educators Get a "Second Life". *Education Week*, *27*(42), 1-17.

Waters, J. (2009). A 'second life' for educators. *THE Journal, 36(1),* 29-34.

AUTHORS

Gema Bello-Orgaz. *Escuela Politécnica Superior of the Universidad Autónoma de Madrid.*
Email: gema.bello@uam.es

David Camacho. *Escuela Politécnica Superior of the Universidad Autónoma de Madrid.*
Email: david.camacho@uam.es

Esther Monterroso

Jose Ignacio Baile

Sandra Pérez

4.4

INNOVATIVE EDUCATIONAL EXPERIENCES IN THE UNIVERSITY TEACHING OF LAW AND PSYCHOLOGY USING VIRTUAL ENVIRONMENTS

1. INTRODUCTION

It cannot be denied that our education system is being revolutionised by the incorporation of the new technologies into our learning environments. We are currently immersed in a period of constant change in which students are no longer merely passive participants in their own teaching-learning process; they now have an active role because of the increasingly greater importance of on-line tools. These new technologies applied to education encourage student-centred learning.

One of the tools used in these new learning contexts are metaverses or virtual worlds. According to Pan et al. (2006), in distance learning the fundamental difference between 2D environments, which focus mainly on the exchange of content, and 3D environments is that the latter have the significant advantage that they induce a strong feeling of presence. We believe that the presence of the student increases both significant learning and motivation.

In this context, in June 2003 Linden Lab developed Second Life (SL), a computer application that functions as a client program: that is to say, it is installed in the user's computer and it connects to the Second Life servers when it is executed, thus facilitating user access. Its website (http://www.secondlife.com) advertises itself as "Your World! Your Imagination!" and enables users to create their own world by building a variety of environments and creating their own self in the form of an avatar that can move and communicate in this virtual medium.

One of the essential features of virtual worlds is that users can interact with one another in real time, which gives rise to the possibility of virtual learning environments that use role-playing techniques. The use of these tools is an innovation in learning environments because it allows students to take control of the process, facilitates experiential learning and makes it possible for students practise the skills and competencies they have acquired during their study of the subject. The teacher shifts from being a content facilitator to a mediator of the learning process who guides the student. In this regard, "Second Life provides a perfect arena for education to cease focusing on content and to become a 'utility' that focuses on students and their interests, and which enables them to learn 'by doing' while permanently on-line." (Checa, 2012: 147).

In an attempt to adapt their degree courses to the innovative teaching methodologies required by the European Higher Education Area (EHEA), the Distance University of Madrid (UDIMA) has made a commitment to the new technological-teaching potential of the Web 2.0. Teaching by means of these 3D environments is still only incipient, although it has already been satisfactorily implemented in international institutions. In Spain, our university has exported this system as a complementary activity, which involves simulating a trial in the virtual environment.

One of the tools that the University has made available to students is our own virtual space −an island− within Second Life, which they use during the teaching-learning process of various degree courses. The island is designed to be a space for interaction, communication and simulation of several learning activities, which takes advantage of the benefits that virtual worlds bring to distance education.

Thus, a variety of activities can be provided by this tool −from practising languages to carrying out simulations of meetings− but undoubtedly two of the most novel activities that can be found in UDIMA's virtual world are the ones that we describe below.

The lecturers Monterroso and Baile have been the driving forces behind the development of innovative educational experiences in a Second Life courtroom and psychology clinic, respectively, where students can acquire the competencies required by their degree courses in the virtual world and subsequently apply them in real life. The aim of these activities is to enhance the acquisition and transmission of knowledge, and to allow the practical learning of Law and Psychology through role plays in which students act out different characters.

The first teaching activity simulates a trial, and combines content from the degree course in Law, Civil Law and Judicial Law with role playing that involves the agents of the judicial system (plaintiffs, defendants and judges).

In the second activity, the students of the degree in Psychology, and more specifically those studying the subject Psychological Intervention and Treatment, simulate the first session in a process of psychological intervention. One of the students represents the therapist and the other the patient, and the activity helps them to develop therapeutic and diagnostic skills.

2. EXPERIENCE IN THE FIELD OF LAW: SIMULATION OF A VIRTUAL TRIAL
2.1. Introduction

Trial simulation is an attractive idea for the degree in Law because students can experiment with a variety of different identities: lawyers, public prosecutors, judges or court secretaries. To do so we used the stage of a 3D courtroom in Second Life.

This virtual environment enables our distance learning students to interact directly and take part in drawing up an argument that they have to defend in court versus another group of students who act as the opposing party and a third group who act as judges.

Thus, an efficient tool is constructed to carry out an educational strategy that is much more participatory and appropriate to the acquisition of the competencies specific to the degree in Law. In fact, by means of this experience we have attempted to cover the general and specific competencies from the academic and theoretical point of view (knowing and understanding), the professional and practical point of view (knowing how to act), and the disciplinary and ethical point of view (knowing how to be) (Monterroso and Escutia, 2011).

In fact, the current state of this technology has opened up a range of possibilities in teaching methodology by which learning can be improved and these competencies can be developed. At the same time, university students work more autonomously to construct their knowledge.

2.2. Description of the experiment.

Our experiment consisted of creating a practical activity for students of Law in the Second Life courtroom. First, in a virtual law classroom a practical case provided by the lecturer was solved. Subsequently, in the 3D courtroom, the students took on the roles of lawyer for the prosecution, lawyer for the defence (accompanied by their respective lawyers) and judges. Figure 1 shows the scenario in which our students worked.

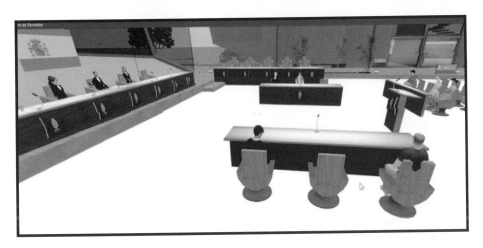

Figure 1. Courtroom on UDIMA's Second Life island

The first thing students had to do when they entered the courtroom was to sit in the place allocated to the person whose role they had adopted, and ensure that they were wearing the perceptive gown. Figure 2 shows a student putting on the perceptive gown before occupying her position.

Throughout the activity, attempts were made to faithfully reflect a real trial, in which students were required to develop the competencies that will be essential for them in future professional practice. Therefore, depending on whether they were playing the role of lawyer for the prosecution, lawyer for the defence or judge, the avatars had to respect the trial instructions provided by the lecturer. Not only did they have to find a legal basis for their arguments, they also had to respect the time allocated to them and use the appropriate legal vocabulary. For example, the lawyers had to use the expression "with leave of the court" before speaking or making a suggestion or request to the judge. For their part, the judges had to draw up the order of the parts of the trial and, among other things, give the parties permission to speak, call the witnesses and supervise the questioning.

Figure 2. Avatar putting on a gown on UDIMA's Second Life island

This experiment involved active learning, designed and applied on the basis of a practical experience, and taking advantage of and effectively developing the students' qualities and abilities. What is more, the lecturers were able to assess the students' rhetoric and the solidity of their legal arguments.

2.3. Contributions to university education

In the legal Framework, the simulation of trials is a highly attractive experience that allows students to immerse themselves in a courtroom and act out the various identities of the judi-cial agents that they will have to in real life. Students can develop competencies that will be essential for their future professional activity and, in particular, many of the specific competen-cies that will be highly valued by their future employers such as: (1) the ability to analyse and synthesise the legal problems raised; (2) the ability to communicate orally (legal oratory and rhetoric); (3) the ability to draft legal texts, 4) the ability to present a convincing argument and defend one's own theses while refuting others; (5) the ethical commitment that must always govern the deontological norms of the profession; and (6) the ability to solve problems by apply-ing knowledge to practice in the context of a simulated immersion that reflects reality as closely as possible (Monterroso & Escutia, 2011).

2.4. Conclusions/bibliography

The considerable flexibility and personalisation made possible by improvements in access to digital networks enable students to acquire their competencies and knowledge through a more autonomous learning process led by students themselves.

Virtual environments have been used to culminate a learning process for law students. As well as enhancing the acquisition and transmission of knowledge, they have been used to create practical learning experiences in the field of law through role playing. The simulation of trials, then, is presented as an innovative educational experience in which students enter a virtual environment and act out the various identities of the legal agents involved as if they were in the real world.

3. EXPERIENCE IN THE FIELD OF PSYCHOLOGY: SIMULATION OF A CLINICAL INTERVIEW

3.1. Introduction

According to the Spanish and European regulations currently in force, university courses in psychology require an appropriate combination of theoretical and practical teaching.

In such subjects as Psychological Intervention and Treatment or Psychology Health Clinic, practical experience is particularly important because the procedural competencies that students have to acquire are priority.

Providing practical training is a considerable challenge for lecturers at distance universities because they are not in direct contact with the students and therefore cannot organise the classical empirical activities that can be organised in face-to-face classes. Therefore, virtual environments make it possible to carry out activities of a practical nature and simulate face-to-face situations with similar or greater learning opportunities. The potential of the virtual environments for science has already been highlighted (Sims 2007), as has their applicability to the field of psychology.

This section describes UDIMA's unit of clinical psychology in Second Life and the results of a practical experiment carried out with students in 2011.

The unit of clinical psychology is a section of UDIMA's island in Second Life that has four areas: a traditional psychological consultation room/office, a group therapy room, an area for phobic stimuli and a plane cabin for treating fear of flying. Figure 3 shows the entrance to section for psychological consultation. Students can simulate such psychological interventions as assessments, diagnoses and the application of psychological intervention techniques. The system of virtual reality makes it possible to deal with practical situations and dynamics that even in real face-to-face practicals would not be readily accessible to students (for example, flight simulation or touching such phobic stimuli as spiders.

Figure 3. Psychological consultation room on UDIMA's Second Life island

3.2. Description of the experiment

The activity carried out in the clinical psychology unit consisted of simulating an intervention and diagnosis session in which all of the students took on one of two different roles: the psychologist or the patient. In particular, the objective was to carry out an initial assessment interview in a possible case of depression in an elderly patient. The student's avatar that represented the patient was created with an elderly appearance; the student's avatar that represented the psychologist wore a a white coat.

Both students prepared their respective roles —elderly patient with possible depression and psychologist specialising in assessing elderly patients— using the theoretical content that had been studied throughout the degree course and, in particular, the content of the subject Psychological Intervention and Treatment, of which this practical experience was a part.

On the day of the practical session, the two participating students went to the clinical psychology unit to carry out the clinical interview in the presence of the lecturer of the subject and two other invited lecturers who took notes.

After the practical session had finished, the lecturer of the subject made a technical assessment of the intervention by the student who was playing the psychologist and explained how a psychological intervention of this sort could be improved. Figure 4 shows both of the students represented by their avatars as a psychologist and an elderly patient.

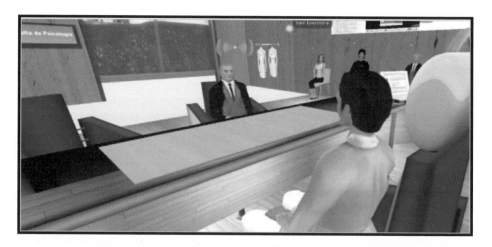

Figure 4. Avatars of the two students playing a psychologist and an elderly patient

3.3. Contributions to university education

The experiment described above enabled students, through their avatars, to engage in simulating habitual roles in contexts of psychological intervention. Oral interaction in real time, the display of emotions and the behaviour of the avatars enabled students to develop skills and competencies resembling those of a face-to-face interview in a psychological consultation.

This practical experience in a virtual environment had the following advantages: it was held at a time that was convenient for all participants, the students did not have to travel to get there, the interview was recorded for subsequent analysis, it contributed to the achievement of the educational goals, and students were more motivated because they had the opportunity to use a novel environment.

3.4. Conclusions

The simulation of clinical psychology practicals in virtual environments enables students to acquire competencies in clinical diagnosis, apply their knowledge on disorders and therapies in a situation that resembles real life, and acquire such general competencies as handling their emotions and dealing with patients. Activating emotional competencies depends more on the responses of the patient and are difficult to acquire in the analysis of clinical cases on the basis of written texts.

What is more, virtual environments make it possible to carry out practicals in clinical psychology that are extremely difficult to do face to face in groups of students who are so geographically dispersed as distance university students usually are.

These environments also make it possible to simulate roles (elderly patients, children, handicapped people, etc.), cope with phobias, organise group sessions, etc. that are more difficult in face-to-face situations.

For all these reasons, we must conclude that virtual environments such as Second Life are a good teaching tool for psychology students in the clinical and health areas.

REFERENCES

[1] PAN, Z., CHEOK, A., YANG, H., ZHU, J., & SHI, J. (2006). "Virtual reality and mixed reality for virtual learning environments". *Computers & Graphics,* Vol. 30, pp. 20–28.

[2] ANTONACCI, D. and MODARESS, N (2005). "Second Life: The Educational Possibilities of Massively Multiplayer Virtual Worlds (MMVW)", *Educause* [on-line article], available at http://connect.educause.edu/Library/Abstract/SecondLifeTheEducationalP/43821?-time=1228223370.

[3] AREITIO, G. and AREITIO, A. (2002). "Nuevas formas de trabajo para el docente frente a los nuevos modelos de enseñanza universitaria". *Scripta Nova,* Universidad de Barcelona, Vol. VI, no. 119, pp. 138 and ss. [on-line article], available at http://www.ub.es/geocrit/sn/sn119138.htm).

[4] CHECA, F. (2012) "El uso de metaversos en el mundo educativo: gestionando conocimiento en Second Life". Revista de Docencia Universitaria, vol. 8, no. 2, 147-149.

[5] DE MIGUEL DIAZ, M. (Coord.) (2006) *Metodologías de enseñanza y aprendizaje para el desarrollo de competencias. Orientaciones para el profesorado universitario ante el Espacio Europeo de Educación Superior.* Madrid: Alianza.

[6] ESCUDERO and MONTERROSO (2010): "Udima. INNOVALab.: Simulación de un juicio en el Campus virtual de Second Life", *RELADA*, Vol 4, No 2 [on-line article], available at http://serviciosgate.upm.es/ojs/index.php/relada/article/viewFile/102/98

[7] GONZÁLEZ MARTÍN C. (2007): "Campus Virtual para las titulaciones en modalidad presencial, semipresencial y/o distancia", in A. LANDETA (coord.): *Buenas Prácticas de E-Learning.* Madrid: Anced.

[8] LEZCANO, L. (2010). E- Learning y Second Life. En Landeta (Ed.). *Nuevas tendencias de e-learning y actividades didácticas innovadoras.* Madrid: CEF.

[9]   MONTERROSO CASADO, E (2009). "Los entornos virtuales de aprendizaje: una aplicación práctica". In Palomino R. and Rodríguez-Arana J (Dir.): *Enseñar Derecho en el siglo XXI* (pp. 317-329). Pamplona: Aranzadi

[10] MONTERROSO CASADO, E. and ESCUTIA ROMERO, R. (2011). "Educación inmersiva: enseñanza práctico del Derecho en 3D." *Revista ICONO 14, Revista de Comunicación y Nuevas Tecnologías,* year 9, vol 2, 2011, pp. 1-17.

[11] MONTERROSO CASADO, E. and ESCUTIA ROMERO, R. (2011). "Enseñanza práctica en 3D: juicio virtual", *@tic. revista d'innovació educativa* (nº 6), January-June 2011, pp. 8-16.

[12] MONTERROSO CASADO, E. and ESCUTIA ROMERO, R. (2011). "Práctica Jurídica en mundos virtuales". In CERRILLO and DELGADO: *Las TIC al servicio de la docencia del Derecho en el marco del EESS.* Barcelona: Huygens Editorial.

[13] GONZÁLEZ MARTÍN C. (2007): Campus Virtual para las titulaciones en modalidad presencial, semipresencial y/o distancia", in A. LANDETA (coord.): *Buenas Prácticas de E-Learning.* Madrid: Anced.

[14] SIMS, W. (2007). "The Scientific Research Potential of Virtual Worlds". *Science, 317,* 472-476.

[15] http://www.publico.es/16271/practicas-de-psicologia-en-un-mundo-virtual (retrieved on 2-11-2012).

AUTHORS

Esther Monterroso. *Madrid Open University, Spain. Email: esther.monterroso@udima.es*

Jose Ignacio Baile. *Madrid Open University, Spain. Email: joseignacio.baile@udima.es*

Sandra Perez. *Madrid Open University, Spain. Email: sandra.perez@udima.es*

4.5

EVEA3D: USE OF 3D VIRTUAL WORLDS IN SECONDARY EDUCATION

1. INTRODUCTION

The ever-increasing progress made by the information and communications technologies (ICT) has led to their being adopted in a wide range of human activities, among which are primary, secondary and tertiary educational environments, which need "...to constantly adapt to changes in society, but never cease to transmit the acquisitions, the fundaments and the fruit of human experience" (Jaques Delors).

Computer education has advanced in parallel with computer technology over the years. The system known as PLATO (Programmed Logic for Automatic Teaching) was one of the first automated education systems and was initially developed at the University of Illinois. In the mid 1970s, it was first commercialized by Control Data Corporation. Subsequently, an author language called TUTOR was added, which made it possible to provide several lessons simultaneously and was designed for business clients. The evolved version of the software can now be found at PLATO Learning.

Over time PLATO has evolved from having an exclusively military application to being introduced into universities thanks to the creation of simulators and entertainment games. One example of the games available is Panther, a war game used for military training with tanks.

Technological advances that have improved graphic systems, touch screens and peripherals such as virtual headphones (controlled by movements of the head), haptic devices,[1] on-screen keyboards, joysticks and gamepads make it easier to design training systems that rely on graphics and simulations. These technologies make it possible to interact with the virtual world and give users the feeling that they are fully immersed in the computer-generated artificial situations.

The decrease in the cost of hardware, the increase in the computational power of graphic processors and the reduced prices of peripheral devices have all given a considerable boost to

---

1. Gloves that transmit sensation through touch. They are known as Data Gloves.

the creation and design of non-immersive virtual worlds because they are less expensive and increasingly resemble the reality that they wish to make virtual.

According to the e-Isea report (2008) virtual reality has already found consolidated applications in medicine and defence, and important opportunities in entertainment and business promotion. And significant opportunities are expected in education, communications and industry.

Modern-day society uses information as a raw material. The capacity to transform it is the base of production and education is the driving force behind the society (Mominó, Sigalés and Meneses, 2008) to which our students −the so-called digital native generation− belong. This new generation is characterized by its use of means of communication in which quality images, sound and the multimedia play a leading role.

This changing and ever-evolving technology makes it increasingly possible to construct graphic environments that are intuitive to use. According to the Gartner Group's Hype Cycle[2] for the year 2012, a study of the emerging technologies, 3D virtual worlds will still have to wait five or ten years for hardware and software to improve and production and sales costs to come down before they can be applied in education.

Students: *Competencies*

The introduction to the Organic Law on Education of 2006 (LOE) points out the need to train citizens in the basic competencies that stimulate them not only to carry on learning but also to do it for themselves.

As far as the digital competence is concerned, the objective of the period of compulsory secondary education in Spain is the following: "To develop basic skills in the use of information sources so that students can apply their critical sense to acquire new knowledge. To acquire basic training in the field of technologies, and particularly the information and communication technologies." (RD 1631/2006, December 29).

The competencies that have a direct effect on the use of virtual worlds are: language competence, learn to learn, the competence directly associated to the subject matter and digital competence. This latter competence is associated with the following abilities, knowledge and attitudes.

Some of the abilities associated with the digital competence are searching, finding and processing information, and using it critically and systematically. Students also need to understand the wide range of creative and innovative options that being digitally competent will give them, and the need to be critical and reflexive towards the information available.

STUDENTS: *Characteristics*

The students who are the targets of 3D virtual world technology have, among others, the following characteristics (VI Informe España 2010):
- Highly interactive and with diversified attention.
- Considerable visual intelligence.
- Videos, two- and three-dimensional simulations, access to databases and games are some of the sources of information and knowledge that students must be able to process, select and include in their learning sets.
- Highly interactive and unreflective.
- Diversified attention and lack of ability to concentrate.

---

2. http://www.infoq.com/news/2012/08/Gartner-Hype-Cycle-2012.

VIRTUAL REALITY (RV): *3D virtual worlds*

The coining of the term "virtual reality" has traditionally been attributed to Jaron Lanier[3] although several authors have used other terms such as cyberspace, artificial reality or virtual worlds.

The e-lsea report (2008) provides a long list of possible definitions of virtual reality one of which is the following: "Virtual reality is the man-machine interface that enables users to submerge themselves in a computer-generated 3D graphic simulation (virtual world), navigate through it and interact with it in real time from a user-centred perspective."

In general the various definitions of virtual reality include references to:

– The use of computers.
– The creation of a virtual world.
– The manipulation of objects that exist in the virtual world (interaction).
– The sensation of immersion both with and without the aid of peripherals.

Users of a virtual world communicate synchronously. This makes it possible for users to interact and take part in collaborative processes, and it provides solutions in real time. The drawback of synchronous communication is that it requires users to be online at the same time and this may present some problems because they may be in different time zones or their timetables may be incompatible.

This difficulty can be overcome by using a LMS that is compatible with the virtual world to equip the system with an asynchronous connection. In our case, we use the virtual world Second Life and the LMS Moodle. The inclusion of a forum and a Moodle-linked blog allows the information to be processed asynchronously.

All users who take part in the virtual world are known as avatars, human graphic representations that are associated with particular users and which identify[4] them in the virtual world.

Second Life, the virtual world selected, facilitates synchronous communication by two chat options: text and voice. The voice chat option helps to improve communication between the users of the virtual world thanks to the richness of nuances that can be transmitted by the voice. And to reinforce communication the avatar can be given a wide range of gestures that can be used to accompany our discourse when necessary.

2. PEDAGOGICAL THEORIES

The first experiences in computer-aided teaching and learning (CAT/L) were based on the behaviourist theories of Pavlov and Skinner. With the passage of time, the generalized use of the computer and easier access to the Internet, new media and methods have been applied to teaching and learning processes.

Pedagogical theories: *Net learning*

One of the models that uses computers and networks in learning is Harasim's model, which is designed for an environment of information networks. These networks facilitate work between teaching and learning communities and there is a high degree of social and cogni-

3. Jaron Lanier, founder of VPL Research
4. http://es.wikipedia.org/wiki/Avatar_%28Internet%29 [Last accessed on 28 November 2012]

tive interaction, which reinforces collaborative learning for the joint construction of knowledge (Harasim, 2000). Harasim describes four features that are necessary if communication is to take place between all the elements of the network. Communication must be

- in groups,
- independent of the location at which it takes place,
- asynchronous,
- based on multimedia.

In this networked communication of knowledge, the participants pursue information and the ways of understanding and applying this information. Information is obtained by accessing other users connected to the network or files on the Internet. It is transformed into knowledge when those who receive the information interact in an attempt to learn how to use it. In these environments, teachers become assistants, guides and companions of the students who, in turn, become an active part of the learning process. The rate of learning depends on the individual and the student is the centre of the process.

PEDAGOGICAL THEORIES: *Connectivist theory*

Since the emergence of computers, the increase in the amount of information available has led to a reappraisal of how we learn. In recent years the amount of information has doubled and it is now doubling every 18 months.

The persistence of information decreases as a function of the rate of growth and the amount of information that is circulating on the Internet. This information can be accessed by the means provided to us by technology. The persistence of information is measured as the half life of knowledge, defined as "the time that passes between the moment we acquire the knowledge and the moment at which it becomes obsolete."

Such a changing environment as the information on Internet requires companies to implement training programmes that can respond to these changes. Of course, these programmes should also be used to train teaching staff and in the formal education of students.

Connectivism is presented by Siemens (2007) as "the use of networks to describe knowledge and learning", where knowledge is distributed and interconnected. In this theory, the starting point of learning is the individual who feeds the network, which goes on to feed organizations. These organisations then feed the networks, which finally feed back to the individual.

3. SELECTION OF THE EVEA3D ENVIRONMENT

The use of graphics in virtual worlds requires the availability of RAM memory, a fast graphic system and a powerful processer and other hardware components. There must also be an audio system so that users can communicate with one another. For the system requirements recommended for Second Life see http://secondlife.com/support/system-requirements/?lang=es-ES. The graphic cards that are not on the recommended list may work but you cannot know until you try them out. Therefore, it is better to stick to the ones on the list.

Selection of the virtual world

To select the virtual world (Second Life), we used the data in the Meta-Mole virtual world database, which describes 25 parameters considered to be the most important technological features of a virtual world. This search engine was created by dLab (Institute of Digital Innovation, Teesside, UK) to compare the features of the various virtual worlds on the market today.

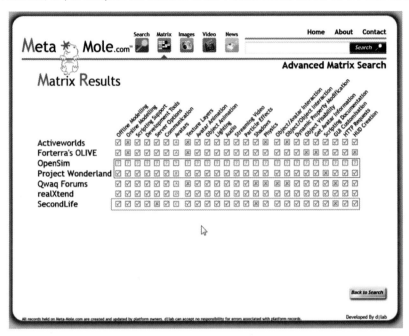

We selected the virtual world Second Life because it was the tool that adapted most to our needs: it has a voice chat service, its own programming language and can link to 2.0 tools.

The final platform is made up of the following complementary resources:

[1] Moodle to manage the content, monitor student activity and carry out evaluations.
[2] Scratch as the programming language that can integrate with LSL (Second Life's own language).
[3] MySQL as the database management system.

The EVEA3D platform selected using the established criteria consists of:

Virtual world:	Second Life.[5]
Educational platform:	Moodle.[6]
Database:	MySQL.[7]
Programming environment:	Scratch.[8]
Mashup	Sloodle.[9]

---

5. Second Life: a program that enables users to navigate through a virtual world while creating and handling 3D objects.
6. Moodle: a program generated by the virtual platform that manages the educational content. It is the associated LMS.
7. MySQL: a database in which the data from the platform, the courses done and the movements of the avatar are stored.
6. Scratch: Object-oriented programming language. A constructivist programming language developed at MIT, on the basis of the ideas of Papert
9. Sloodle: a mashup between Moodle and Second Life (beta phase).

The database can be accessed using Second Life's own programming language (**LSL L**anguage **S**econd **L**ife). These tools provide a wide range of options for collaborative work and learning

4. COMPETENCES

The basic competencies that we hope to cover are the following:

Linguistic communication

Such language skills as listening and reading are required to respond to the instructions to problems and express opinions about the news items that are selected in the reading room and then analysed and discussed, thus developing their logical skills and relational skills with other users of the virtual world.

Mathematical communication

Interpretation of instructions and transformation of algebraic expressions to word phrases
Solving mathematical puzzles scattered throughout the virtual world, which help to reach objectives
This area links to other more general competencies such as social competence, language competence and learning to learn

Digital competence and information processing

By compiling information, classifying, ordering and drafting reports with the data obtained.
Computers and audiovisual media are highly attractive to the users of virtual worlds because they help to awaken their interest in activities.

Learning to learn

This competence is developed by verbalising the instructions in conjunction with their graphic representation.
The interpretation of instructions and their presentation to users can promote competence.

Knowledge and interaction with the physical world

This competence is developed by students handling objects in the virtual world that behave more simply than in the real world so they can learn how to relate to the world that surrounds them.

Autonomy and personal initiative

This competence is developed by students taking part in a variety of spaces in the virtual world. Students develop and improve this competence by taking part in such spaces in the virtual world as the reading area, and the meeting and debating room, which can be found in the space for work or problem and puzzle solving.

5. WORK SPACE

The aim of this study is to create a virtual space that can be displayed in the form of open or closed sites, or environments that cannot be constructed in the real world. Closed sites simulate spaces such as one or more classrooms, while open spaces remove physical barriers and make it possible to modify the work environment.

The work space is designed so that it can be easily used by teaching staff and students, and modified to adapt to the needs of each teacher and the characteristics of each subject. The teaching staff can begin to use the virtual world with their own resources, of which they already have a good command, and subsequently move on to creating or using new objects.

The methodologies used include learning by means of storing and retrieving the information compiled by each user and the information shared and generated by other users of the same virtual world. We can also access other virtual spaces that supplement the information in this one. The link with Moodle makes it easier to develop procedures that evaluate knowledge.

A total of six main work spaces have been defined for reading, holding meetings, collaboration, information, socialisation, and practice and evaluation.

WORK SPACE: Reading room

This area allows students to develop their language competence, and their personal autonomy and initiative. It is designed so that a variety of media can be chosen and the news used as a way of improving reading comprehension in several languages by contrasting opinions on the news selected.

Making presentations covers the aspect of oral comprehension. This area enables students to have access not only to news but also to radio programmes, journals and videos. The newspapers and journals that students wish to consult can be changed at any moment simply by indicating the change in a box specially designed for this purpose.

The teacher and the student propose which newspaper and which article are to be discussed. The teacher can change a newspaper for a video, a TV connection for Internet or a simulation that illustrates a news item and explain it subsequently.

WORK SPACE: Meeting room

In this room, students, their parents or legal guardians, and the teaching staff can access a variety of media by which they can access several virtual worlds in Second Life, websites or newspapers, and organise a chat session to help students to socialise and communicate. This room is particularly helpful when the voice chat option is used in instrumental subjects. The synchronism is fundamental.

The minimum components required are a digital virtual whiteboard, access to websites, and places with similar features that exist in Second Life. Since it is a space that is often used for communication and relaxation, games should also be made available. In fact, there is no need for a separate space to be assigned; an area that already exists −for example, the simulation of a beach− can be adapted for the purpose.

The room should be used in a relaxed and respectful fashion so that students can voice their concerns and suggest reasoned and well-argued improvements.

WORK SPACE: Collaboration area

The collaboration area is particularly suitable for working on language, mathematical, social and cultural competences. We can choose the collaboration tools we use from the ones provided by Google, and add a digital virtual whiteboard and map manipulation tools such as Google Earth.

This space aims to encourage collaborative and group work within the virtual classroom. Although the students are not physically close together, they can find this proximity in the virtual world. It is possible to get in touch with other centres of the community and even centres from other communities and other cultures.

As soon as students have accessed the virtual space, they can consult the information areas, carry out searches outsider their virtual space and, finally, consult an 'expert'.

The students themselves animate this area with their contributions and the comments they make about the issues raised.

WORK SPACE: Information area

Information areas have various features that contain static and dynamic information, which can be used at any time, even during personal evaluation exercises. Various types of information are available throughout the virtual world and can be accessed at any time.

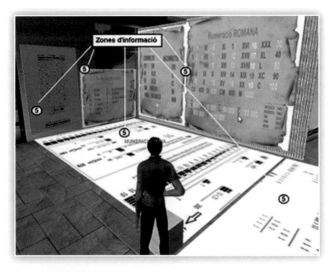

They are of the following five types:

Knowledge sphere. An extensive library that increases the number of items as a result of the contributions made by teachers or students.

Notepad help. Specific to the virtual space in which we are working at the moment. It can link to websites or other regions of Second Life.

Information boards. They are part of the scenery of the virtual space. They are always visible and they contain limited information, which can only be found if the students solve some sort of word puzzle, thus awakening their interest.

Links to websites. The information they provide is often linked to an object in the virtual space.

Hidden clues. These elements are often hidden by other elements thus challenging students to establish individual or collective strategies to find them.

WORK SPACE: *Socialization area*

There are no restrictions on access to this area, which can be used by students to talk to each other, read magazines or newspapers, play games, watch videos or use other multimedia objects. There are spaces for interaction with the physical environment, a space for making presentations and the option of viewing two videos that complement each other. One section of this area can be used for the teletransporter that takes users to other regions of Second Life. The main competencies that are developed here are social and language competencies.

WORK SPACE: *Practice and evaluation area*

This is the area that links up to Moodle. The exercises are posted on Moodle and are selected by each student individually or as a group. In all cases students can do the evaluation and the results can be accessed by students, parents and teachers because they are stored in Moodle. The work space is configured so that users can access all the related Help topics.

The competencies covered are language, learning to learn and mathematics.

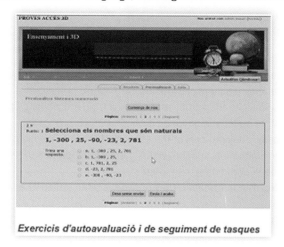

Exercicis d'autoavaluació i de seguiment de tasques

REFERENCES

Fundación Encuentro (2010). *INFORME ESPAÑA 2010. Una interpretación de su realidad social*. Madrid: Fundación Encuentro.

Harasim, L.: Hiltz, Starr R.: Turoff, M.: Teles,L.:(2000) *Redes de aprendizaje: Guía para la enseñanza y el aprendizaje en red*. Editorial Gedisa (1ª edición 1995),

Marquès, P. (2001). Impacto de las TIC en la Educación: Funciones y limitaciones. Retrieved from http://www.peremarques.net/siyedu.htm.

Mominó, J,M.Sigalés,C. Meneses,J. (2008) *La escuela en la sociedad red. Internet en la educación Primaria y Secundaria* (1 ed.) Barcelona: Ariel

Second Life Wiki (n.d.). Retrieved from http://wiki.secondlife.com/wiki/LSL_Portal

Siemens, G. (2004). Conectivismo. Una teoría de aprendizaje para la era digital; Retrieved from: http://edublogki.wikispaces.com/file/view/Conectivismo.pdf

e-ISEA (2008). *INTERNET 3D, Análisis prospectivo de las potenciales aplicaciones asociadas a los Mundos Virtuales*. Retrieved from: http://www.iseamcc.net/eISEA/Vigilancia_tecnologica/informe_3.pdf

e-ISEA (2009). *3D-Learning, Análisis prospectivo de las potencialidades de la Realidad Virtual en los procesos de enseñanza-aprendizaje.* Retrieved from http://www.iseamcc.net/eISEA/Vigilancia_tecnologica/informe_5.pdf

Spain. Royal Decree 1631/2006, of 29 December, which establishes the minimum requirements of Spanish Secondary Education. *(BOE nº 5 of 5 January 2007)*

AUTHORS

Enrique Llácer Gimeno. *SES Bages Sud, Spain. Email: ellacer@xtec.cat*